About the Book and Editors

The people of Afghanistan stand at a crossroads, with resistance to the Soviet occupation entering its eighth year. The question of survival must be weighed against the difficult political choices of fighting or reaching an accommodation with the Soviet-backed Kabul regime. The vast majority choose to continue the struggle--aided in part by covert arms shipments--and to search for a uniquely Afghan nationalism despite rumors of an impending USSR-U.S. deal whereby, in return for Soviet troop withdrawal and cessation of arms aid to the Mujahideen, Afghanistan and Pakistan would become neutral Muslim nations.

Drawing on Afghan cultural and historical background, this collection of original essays provides fresh insights into the nature of the Afghan conflict, the country's threatened national infrastructure, the continuing decimation of its citizens, and the prospects for their survival. Showing that popular resistance is not limited to the Mujahideen, or freedom fighters, but encompasses the Afghan people as a whole, the contributors examine the impact of the world's largest refugee population on the shape of the future Afghanistan. Based on their extensive firsthand experience in the region, the contributors provide an interdisciplinary analysis of a country, a people, and a war still too little known to the outside world.

Grant M. Farr is professor and head of the Department of Sociology, Portland State University, Oregon. **John G. Merriam** is associate professor in the Department of Political Science, Bowling Green State University, Ohio.

Afghan Resistance

The Politics of Survival

edited by
Grant M. Farr
and John G. Merriam

Westview Press / Boulder and London

Westview Special Studies in International Relations

Published in 1987 in the United States of America by Westview Press, Inc.; Frederick A. Praeger, Publisher; 5500 Central Avenue, Boulder, Colorado 80301

Library of Congress Cataloging-in-Publication Data
    Afghan resistance.
    (Westview special studies in international relations)
    Bibliography: p.
    1. Afghanistan--History--Soviet occupation, 1979-
2. Refugees--Afghanistan. 3. Refugees--Pakistan.
I. Farr, Grant M. II. Merriam, John G.
DS371.2.A338 1987   958'.1044   86-9124
ISBN 0-8133-7232-1

Composition for this book originated with conversion of the editors' word-processor disks. This book was produced without formal editing by the publisher.

Printed and bound in the United States of America.

The paper used in this publication meets the requirements of the American National Standard for Permanence of Paper for Printed Library Materials Z39.48-1984.

6   5   4   3   2   1

Contents

Foreword

Toward the end of 1979, nearly two years after the coup which brought the communists to power in Afghanistan, but before the Soviets invaded, the Afghans' opposition to their communist government had become quite strong, and fighting had begun in certain parts of the country. The main factors which aroused this opposition were 1) the nature of the government's ideology--i.e., communism and specifically Sovietism; 2) the political subordination of the Afghan government to the Soviet Union; and 3) most important, the instances of torture, killing, incarcerations, and other severe or unjust measures that were effected by the new Afghan communist government in Kabul.

However, at this stage the confrontation was one between those who opposed and those who favored a communist Afghan government. It was a struggle between Afghans of differing persuasions. Moreover, the armed struggle was not generalized, for many Afghans remained passive and had not actively taken sides one way or the other. In short, Afghanistan was engaged in a civil war of limited scope.

The invasion by the Soviets in late December, 1979, brought a basic change in both the extent and the nature of the confrontation. Faced with a massive foreign force occupying the country, Afghans could not remain uncommitted. Although a small minority took sides with the Russians, the vast majority actively joined with the forces against them. Quantitatively, then, the struggle was no longer waged by a relatively small number of groups and local leaders but became a war in which the absolute majority of the Afghan people began to participate in one way or another. The conflict had become a national uprising. In addition, the essential nature of the confrontation had changed. That is, qualitatively, the struggle was no longer a war between opposing internal forces. The civil war had been transformed into a war of resistance by the Afghans against a foreign occupation. The struggle had become a war of liberation.

The difference between those two stages of the war in Afghanistan is real and important. It is unfortunate that foreign observers have not always recognized the distinction. Perhaps even more unfortunately, the Peshawar-based leaders of the Afghan resistance organizations have not adapted their strategies and tactics to reflect the fact that the present struggle is a war of liberation. Whether an effective resistance survives in the long term depends to a great extent upon whether it does adapt to that reality.

In a war of liberation against an occupying foreign force, a key element in effective resistance is coordination among the various political and military forces resisting the invader. Under such circumstances, all of the national forces must operate jointly in a common national program for a common national goal, namely to regain the independence of their country. Unfortunately, the various Afghan resistance organizations continue to operate separately on party-specific goals.

If an effective Afghan resistance is to continue, coordination of action for a common goal is critical. However, it has proved virtually impossible for the different resistance organizations to establish any sort of workable leadership hierarchy to allow for *political* unity.(1)

It is, then, essential that the Afghan resistance seek an alternative which allows *military* activities to be conducted from a single center. The most promising such alternative mechanism is perhaps a military council of advisors, including both selected guerrilla commanders and military experts from outside, acceptable to all resistance groups. In addition to coordinating military operations, such a military council can implement more effective military training programs for guerrilla troops and work for a more equitable distribution of weapons among guerrilla forces. However, to be workable, such a council has to function as an advisory body to all the resistance groups and must demonstrate, in practice, that its sole purpose is to improve the military operations of all groups.

Another major condition for the survival of effective resistance in any war of liberation is the existence of a means or a mechanism for promoting the cause internationally. In the Afghan instance, the critical need for such a mechanism can be met by the creation of a small, permanent body, whose primary goals are to generate greater international awareness and support of the Afghan resistance and to exert diplomatic pressure on the Soviets. Expanded international support and diplomatic pressure, when combined with the continued pressure exerted by the armed resistance, of course constitutes the best hope for nudging the Soviets toward consideration of a negotiated withdrawal.

At the outset, the body or group so essential for generating international support can function effectively with as few as three to five Afghans as staff members, if several conditions are met. First, the members of this body must have a good reputation in the Afghan community, or at least in a limited portion of it, even if they are not particularly well-known in the whole community. Second, because good reputation and good intentions are simply not sufficient, considerable political acumen and skill are indispensible. In addition, and very important, the members of such a body have to be able to devote themselves exclusively to this goal of generating support for the Afghan cause--a condition which has prevented such a group from emerging to date. At the same time, even though any such body would need to be a permanent, professional entity with full-time members, it is essential that it avoid giving any suggestion that it seeks any political identity of its own. To be able to function, it should not be identified with particular Afghan resistance political groups, but should act for them all. Under the present circumstances, where the Afghans are fighting a war against a super-power and where there is a bloodbath in the country, seeking out international support and increasing pressure on the Soviets is too important and too difficult to be accomplished on an amateur, part-time basis or from a narrow political stance.

In the last analysis, then, the long-term survival of the Afghans and their resistance as a whole depends upon whether some such mechanisms evolve for ensuring military coordination of action and for generating internationally based support.

Afghan Resistance: The Politics of Survival offers a timely examination of the Afghan situation today. Some of the chapters provide valuable insights into the complex question of survival, most often survival in some specific domain, examining various aspects of how and why a people and their quest for liberation survive or do not survive. Other chapters, while they do not relate directly to the question of survival, provide insight into the larger question of the nature of Afghan life today.

The authors of the various chapters are sincere, dedicated observers of the Afghan situation. Diverse in their orientations, the contributors present quite distinctive views, each from his or her own vantage point, often with rich, first-hand involvement or research. Such an eclectic collection affords the reader the opportunity to see the issues from a variety of standpoints, making this set of articles a fresh, somewhat atypical, contribution to the literature on the Afghan situation.

Habibullah Tegey
Margery E. Tegey

NOTE

1. The full support of the Pakistani government for the resistance movement is taken for granted. Without that support, the Afghan resistance cannot survive. In fact, if the war becomes greatly prolonged, Pakistan will have to allow her own tribal Pushtuns to become involved in the resistance alongside their "Afghan brothers" or else risk having the Russians use those Pushtuns against the government of Pakistan. In short, not only the survival of the resistance but the integrity of Pakistan herself depends on the support of the resistance against the Soviets in Afghanistan.

Introduction

Grant M. Farr and John G. Merriam

It has been over seven years since the Soviet invasion of Afghanistan. While Afghanistan has been largely forgotten by the world press, it has come under study by several groups of people, including the Western intelligence community, various humanitarian groups, right wing anticommunist groups, those interested in guerrilla warfare, and a handful of scholars who study this area of the world. This work is from the latter group.

Despite some books, a few hundred articles, panel papers, workshops, and conferences on the general topic, we remain perplexed and inadequately informed about the way in which events in Afghanistan unfold. We do not yet understand the Afghans or Afghanistan. And, just when we seem to be getting a handle on the Afghan situation, it changes, presenting harsh, new, almost incomprehensible challenges.

The "Afghan situation" actually encompasses several distinct aspects that, while related, are separate realities. What all aspects of the Afghan situation have in common is that they are direct or indirect consequences of the April 1978 communist coup and the subsequent Soviet invasion in late December, 1979, and include the war of liberation, the jihad or holy war, the war's effect on the Afghan people, the large refugee cross border migration with its major consequences for Pakistan, the formation of exile Afghan political parties in Pakistan, and, finally, the international political process affected by the invasion.

This book is principally about the Soviet penetration and invasion, its causes and consequences, but does not purport to be a complete or exhaustive account of recent Afghan events. Rather, it provides a more focused set of studies on various key aspects of the Afghan crisis--aspects we feel are important to our understanding of what is happening in Afghanistan and to the Afghan refugees, most of whom are in Pakistan. All of the authors whose works are in this book have spent time in Afghanistan, Pakistan, or both, with the refugees and the Mujahideen or holy warriors. Needless to say, all are experts on this tragic and destabilizing situation.

If the Afghans have one thing to teach the rest of the world it is how to resist against great odds and to survive. Survival is a theme that runs through this entire work. Facing great odds in a harsh terrain and often fighting with inadequate arms, the Afghan resistance not only has survived but has somehow grown stronger. The Soviet army has been unable to subdue these guerrilla fighters. Similarly, the Afghan refugees in Pakistan have survived, managing to keep their culture intact in the difficult political climate of the crowded refugee camps.

Much of the reason for this astonishing survival capacity lies in the basic characteristics of Afghan social structure and culture. In this beautiful, mountainous country which Afghans know and love, harshness, poverty, and deprivation are all too well known. Paradoxically, Afghan cultural traits enable survival because the social structure, while strongly traditional, is at the same time surprisingly resilient, not rigid and intractable. Ironically, the historical penchant for small, autonomous or semi-autonomous units has made Afghans less targetable by the Soviet-Democratic Republic of Afghanistan (DRA) forces bent on penetration or military attack.

Afghans are a proud people who are willing to fight for what they believe in and to die if necessary, but this pronounced cultural characteristic has its negative side, too. The Afghans do not easily take advice from others and hate to admit they are wrong. Most observers agree they badly need training in military tactics and in handling ordnance, but their deep-seated pride often keeps them from accepting crucial advice. Sometimes they become trapped in their own cultural myths of manhood and bravery. While they are greatly admired in the West for these traits, we and they should remember that the Afghans are very human. They too become weary and tired, and even scared. To admit to such conditions is not to admit defeat. Nevertheless, close observers of the Afghan people under Soviet siege find a growing resiliency and capacity for adaptation among refugees and Mujahideen alike with important developmental consequences for social structure and military effectiveness.

The general historical outline of the events in Afghanistan is known, although many of the specifics regarding the Soviet invasion and the preceding events are still to be learned. In April, 1978, a rather small group of Marxists took power in Afghanistan and deposed Muhammad Daoud Khan, the last of the Durrani rulers. These Marxists were part of the Peoples Democratic Party of Afghanistan (PDPA), which renamed Afghanistan the Democratic Republic of Afghanistan. These Marxists who deposed Daoud constituted a temporarily reunited PDPA in which the Khalq (People's Party or Masses) undoubtedly had the upper hand.

The people of Afghanistan took a wait-and-see attitude toward the new government in the first few months after the PDPA came to power, for they had seen governments come and go before, and the leadership change seldom affected their daily lives. However, with the sweeping systemic change that the 1978 "Saur" Revolution entailed, such was not to be the case this time. ["Saur" refers to the month in the Afghan calendar, April by Western reckoning, in which the coup occurred]. The communists planned nothing less than social, political, and needless to say, economic, transformation. Quickly alienating the majority of the citizens of Afghanistan were reforms involving the deeply held conventions on bride-price, legal age of marriage and women's education, land reform, and literacy. When these reforms failed to take hold, the communists turned to coercion and then brutal repression. Tens of thousands were jailed and killed, resulting in mass rebellion. Within a year of taking power the government was near collapse.

In late December 1979, the Soviets invaded Afghanistan, installing Babrak Karmal as the new DRA leader. Babrak represented the rival PDPA branch, Parcham (banner or flag, derived from the name of the party's newspaper), that had historically been closer to the Soviets. Many of the Khalqi leaders were jailed or killed, starting with the President Hafizullah Amin. The Soviet invasion, which eventually brought in about 120,000 troops, has resulted in the insurgent war now being fought in Afghanistan, and the large refugee migration to Pakistan, Iran, and elsewhere.

This dismal picture of Afghanistan under Soviet occupation remained largely unchanged until this last year. The conflict now appears to be at a new, important crossroads in its development, for this past year has brought a number of important events that are changing the complexion of the struggle. While it is still too early to tell what the results will be, these events largely have had a negative impact on the ability of the Afghans to continue to fight and somehow survive. In making these remarks, however, it is necessary to note that even the contributors to this book who are close observers have at times underestimated the Afghan people's capacity to carry on.

Reports from Afghanistan during 1985 and 1986 indicate the fighting is not going well for the Mujahideen, although there is some debate in the intelligence community over this conclusion.(1) The Spring and Summer of 1986 appeared to go particularly badly in comparison to successes earlier in the war. Two reasons surface for this downturn in the guerrillas' fighting effectiveness, broadly speaking.

The first and foremost reason has to do with improved Soviet fighting capabilities. The Soviets have evolved better tactics and strategies, including the use of special forces (the *spetznaz*, whose effectiveness contrasts with the frequently poor performance of regular Soviet-DRA forces), the deployment of these forces near the Pakistan-Afghanistan border in an attempt to seal off guerrilla supply lines, and the development in general of better counterinsurgency techniques.

In addition, the Kabul government seems to be making some political gains at the local or village level, consolidating its strength in some parts of the country, particularly the North. Afghans in some areas are growing weary of the war, cooperating less with the Mujahideen and more with the Kabul government. Also, the Soviet attempts to depopulate large areas of Afghanistan, especially those areas near the Pakistani border, have been largely successful, making fighting difficult for the Mujahideen where there is no civilian cover.

The second major reason for the apparent decline in the fortunes of the Afghan freedom fighters is their own frequently inadequate tactics and strategies, inappropriate weapons (particularly when attempting to deal with heliborne assaults), and poor leadership and training. The leadership's internecine squabbling both in and out of Afghanistan continues, although examples of cooperation at the field level among heretofore rival groups and the Peshawar-based alliance can be seen. Many of the Mujahideen's guerrilla tactics that were successful earlier in the war have been rendered largely ineffective because of the previously mentioned Soviet and counterinsurgency actions. While the Afghan guerrillas have made progress in some areas of the fighting, they have not in others, and are now paying the price. Not having control of the air gives the advantage to the much feared Mi-24 "Hind" helicopter gunships. While the mountainous terrain favors guerrilla operations, in a few rare instances recently, the Mujahideen have directly confronted Soviet-DRA troops and have lost heavily in the process.

On the political front the alliance of the seven political exile groups in Peshawar took place on May 16, 1985. The new alliance, called the Islamic Unity of Afghan Mujahideen, has lasted longer than most observers thought it would. Greater unity in the struggle for Afghanistan is badly needed for several reasons, although there are those who argue that disunity is a more desirable form of organization, given the nature of the guerrilla war, the mountainous topography, and the historically independent nature of the Afghans.

This new alliance represents both of Peshawar's moderate groups: the "traditionalists" and the Islamist groups, usually called the "fundamentalists." To deal with the problem of how and in what proportion to share power, the new alliance has a rotating spokesman, with each of the leaders of the seven political parties assuming the role of spokesman for a period of three months.

If the new alliance has had any success, it is in the world political arena. Gulbuddin Hekmatyar, a fundamentalist leader, led a delegation to the United Nations during the UN's 40th anniversary, and demanded the Afghan UN seat. Sayyid Ahmad Gailani, a moderate leader, led a delegation to the Islamic Conference in Rabat, Morocco, where he was spokesman for the Unity. More recently, another guerrilla leader, Burhanuddin Rabbani, traveled, also with a delegation, to the U.S. and met with President Reagan to dramatize the Afghan cause to the President and the American people.

In other areas, however, the Unity has done less well. Each group, for example, continues to control its own finances and ordnance. Despite statements to the contrary, guerrilla operations in Afghanistan have not been brought under unified command, with the result that lives and precious ammunition are being wasted on bloodletting among fellow Afghans.

A more basic problem with the insurgency leadership is that no one, neither the Peshawar groups nor the Kabul government, speaks for the vast majority of the people of Afghanistan. In reality, many Afghans, including both non-Pushtun ethnic and religious minorities, are not represented in Peshawar. Some of those excluded groups are now turning to other countries for support, primarily to Iran or to the Soviet-backed regime in Kabul itself.

Other recent changes in the Afghan situation include the resignation on May 4, 1986, of Babrak Karmal, who had been the leader of Afghanistan since late December, 1979, at the time of the Soviet invasion. His place at the head of the party was taken by Dr. Najibullah, or Najib as he is simply called. Najib represents the new leadership cohort in the PDPA. Trained as a medical doctor, Najib most recently had successfully run the Afghan secret police (the KHAD, an acronym for *Khedamat-e Ettelat-e-Dawlati*, literally but euphemistically the Government Information Service). This notorious organization had been one of the few "success" stories of the Kabul government, with more numerous and effective employees than the Afghan military. Its high level though ruthless performance certainly has helped Najib's rise to power.

Important to the KHAD's success and probably Najib's assumption of the key leadership post was its not entirely unsuccessful campaign to develop rural support for the Kabul government. It developed this support by two means: the first was a *Loya Jirgah* (national council) to attempt to bestow legitimacy on the Kabul government through the traditional means of a tribal gathering. Held in the Spring of 1985 the *Loya Jirgah* has been branded a farce as there was very little real participation from the tribes or rural areas, and most Afghans in attendance were in the government's pay. The great majority of the Afghan people rejected this *Loya Jirgah*, but it did take place and probably had some impact, no matter how limited.

The Afghan police's second attempt to win rural support has been to form village militias where the villagers are given arms and ammunition to keep the Mujahideen out of their area. The resistance largely has assumed that most

Afghans are against the government and thus support their cause. The development of these village militias has caused concern among the resistance commanders. The importance of the village militias is more significant in their potential than in their reality, and there are many stories of these village militias turning their newly gained guns on the very government officials who had given them arms. However, even the limited success of these village militias could strike a symbolic blow against resistance morale. Growing indications are that part of the north of Afghanistan has been brought under Kabul government control by this method.

The larger issue of what the change in the Kabul government ultimately means for the outcome of the conflict is still not answered and probably will not be for some time. However, what it does indicate is that Soviets are in Afghanistan for the long term. The leadership shift probably does not presage positive forward movement in the ongoing peace talks. While Dr. Najib is still somewhat of an unknown quantity, he is reputed to be capable, ruthless, and well connected to the Soviets. His greatest disadvantage may be that he has no independent political following among the Afghan people, as did Babrak. Pro-Babrak PDPA member demonstrations were reported shortly after Najib came to power. The change in the Kabul leadership cannot and should not be interpreted as a sign of Soviet-DRA weakness. To argue that the Soviets have installed Najib to secure their hold and make possible their phased withdrawal is specious reasoning and wishful thinking.

While there has been some change in the refugee situation in the past year, it cannot compare with the dramatic shift in Kabul. It is now thirteen years since the coup which ousted King Zahir Shah and saw Daoud declare a Republic with himself as President. The event marked the first trickle of refugees fleeing from Afghanistan into Pakistan. Over six years ago the Soviet invasion turned that trickle into a flood. The government of Pakistan now estimates that there are 2.7 million Afghan refugees registered in Pakistan. Another half million are thought to be unregistered. Refugees were reported to be registered in 312 camps in three provinces: 240 in the NorthWest Frontier Province, 61 in Baluchistan, and 11 in the Punjab. The most recent figures indicate that number has swollen to 358.

Iran claims another 1.5 million in its country, although

technically not all are refugees. Nevertheless, Afghan refugees total something over 4 million, nearly half of all the refugees in the world. One quarter of the people of Afghanistan has now fled. In addition, perhaps a million internal refugees have sought the dubious safety of the capital city of Kabul. The Afghan refugees coming to Pakistan are largely Pushtun, the ethnic-linguistic groups that also dominate the NorthWest Frontier Province (NWFP) of Pakistan and that part of Afghanistan closest to the Pakistani border, where some of the heaviest fighting has taken place. As the scope of the fighting has broadened, however, many members of other ethnic groups have fled to Pakistan.

The Afghan refugee situation in Pakistan has been handled quite well by the government of Pakistan and the various agencies involved, especially the United Nations High Commissioner for Refugees (UNHCR), given the size and complexity of the problem. In the final analysis, Pakistan, with its own share of problems, deserves a great deal of praise.

A number of potential problems, however, do face the Afghan refugees in Pakistan. For one thing, there is growing unrest among the Pakistani population regarding this massive refugee incursion. In Peshawar, for example, a citizen's group has been formed to protest against the policy of permitting refugees free movement. In the areas of Pakistan where the refugees are concentrated, municipal utilities are crowded, buses full, and the parks overflowing. These conditions are found in almost all areas of Pakistan, even areas such as Karachi, which is some distance from the major refugee concentrations.

While the government of Pakistan has tried to keep the refugees out of the Pakistani economy, the Afghans are inexorably beginning to make significant inroads into the local economies of the host country. More and more Afghan shops compete with Pakistani shops for business, and Afghan laborers compete with their Pakistani counterparts for scarce jobs. Also, Afghan trucks and light vehicles have now preempted a large portion of the trucking business in Pakistan. The job problem promises to become worse as more Pakistanis are compelled to return from once lucrative jobs in the Gulf.

Afghan participation in the Pakistani economy is a double edged sword. On the one hand, the more the Afghans work, the less dependent they are on the largess of the government of Pakistan and on the world refugee relief agencies for subsistence support. Refugees employed in meaningful jobs also are much less apt to suffer from depression and the psychological problems associated with camp life. On the other hand, the more the refugees are employed in the local economies of Pakistan, the less likely they will return once the war somehow ends. Afghans with secure jobs will not want to leave those positions for the insecurity of a post-war Afghanistan.

In addition, the Afghan refugees are growing impatient with their own leaders in Peshawar. While these refugees live in tents or mud huts, their leaders live in comfortable houses. As a result of these glaring lifestyle contrasts in the camps, a cultural tradition is evolving that portrays the difficulties and ironies of camp life through songs, skits, and poems. While mostly humorous, the lyrics do contain sharp barbs for those whom the refugees dislike or mistrust. The songs attack most often the local Pakistani refugee camp officials and the Afghan political leaders in Peshawar. Many of the songs also depict the sadness for their lost homeland and Mujahideen bravery.

Physically, the Pakistan refugee camp situation is satis-factory, in stark contrast to recent scenes in Ethiopia or the Sudan, but psychologically the problems are growing. Camp life is weary and dreary for most Afghans. Since many men bring their families to Pakistan, but return to Afghanistan to farm or fight, the camps have a high propor-tion of women (many of them widows), old men, and children, producing conditions markedly different from traditional village life.

The camps alter Afghan culture in other ways. Conflicts arise as a new generation of children grows up too fast and threatens its elders. The psychological stress is great as the once proud Afghans find themselves, on top of everything else, on the receiving end of welfare.

For the Pakistani authorities the refugees are a cause of growing concern since the longer they stay in Pakistan, the less the chance of their returning to Afghanistan after the war. Pakistani refugee officials now believe that not much more than half will return when the conflict somehow ends. On the one hand, it may be pointed out that Pakistan is a country made up of refugees from the time of partition and from the war with Bangladesh. On the other hand, Pakistan does want the Afghans eventually to go home, and as the war drags on interminably they are fearful that the Afghans will not ever leave. With the growing turmoil in Pakistani internal politics, the Afghan refugee issue will no doubt continue to be controversial and one that politicians of whatever stripe must take into account.

Finally, the peace talks in Geneva have reached a critical stage. Called the "proximity talks" because the two sides do not talk directly to each other, the talks have gotten much further than most expected. Of the four accords originally to be negotiated, three have been resolved and the fourth is now on the table.

The first accord called for non interference in Afghanistan's affairs, the second for international guarantees of a final peace settlement, the third for voluntary return of the Afghan refugees to Afghanistan, and the fourth calls for a withdrawal of Soviet forces from Afghanistan. The timetable for such a withdrawal remains the most critical and intractable issue. The DRA is proposing, formally at least, that the Soviets withdraw over a four- or five-year period, while Pakistan has proposed a much shorter timetable that would have the Soviets withdraw in a matter of months. Recent Soviet token withdrawals, announced with much fanfare, are illusory. The gulf between the two sides on this crucial issue may be too great to bridge. Certainly, American and other covert arms suppliers to the Afghan Mujahideen will not agree to an immediate cessation of shipments as a precondition to Soviet-phased withdrawal, as this would enable the Soviet-DRA troops to devastate resistance forces prior to pullout.

These and other events indicate change in the Afghan situation. Yet we fail to understand why they are occurring, and unanswered questions remain. Why do not the Afghans cooperate more in the leadership of the insurgent war when it would seem clearly to be to their benefit? Or, why don't they use classic guerrilla tactics that would maximize their effectiveness as small groups operating under the protection afforded by the mountainous terrain? They lack effective countermeasures to deal with Soviet-DRA control of the air and anything but the most primitive communications among independent groups that might well coordinate operations. What are the reasons: lack of supply, inadequate training, unwillingness to use new, unfamiliar equipment?

Perhaps the answer to these questions is found, in part,

in the nature and character of Afghan society. Made up of both tribal and quasi-feudal ethnic groups, the Afghans behave in a way that is consistent with their social structure. The Soviet challenge and the embrace by Kabul regimes at least since 1978 of what are viewed as alien Marxist dogma have reinforced that traditional commitment to steadfast resistance.

Since the refugees are largely Pushtun, and Peshawar is in the tribal belt of Pakistan, we assume that the Afghans are all tribally organized. Most Afghans and in fact many Pushtuns are not in fact tribally demarcated but rather live in settled villages in a quasi-feudal system sometimes called the *arbab* system. The two systems of social structure are quite dissimilar and account in part for the differences in their behavior and reactions to the war.

In dealing with these diverse issues, the chapters of this book examine several features of the present Afghan situation. The first chapter, by David Edwards, is "Origins Of The Anti-Soviet Jihad." Dr. Edwards here examines the events in the early period of the communist rule of Afghanistan, 1978-1979, under the rule of the Khalqi governments of Nur Muhammad Taraki and Hafizullah Amin. His purpose is to trace the motivations behind the reforms undertaken by those governments and to explain the dramatic and nearly unanimous rebellion of the Afghan people against these reforms.

Both Taraki and Amin were mindful of the history of Afghanistan and the fate of Amanullah Khan, the ruler of Afghanistan who was ousted in 1929 for his reformist policies. Consequently, they early on denied that they were Marxists and instead argued that their reforms were in the Islamic and Afghan tradition. The rejected reforms were in three areas: women's rights, literacy, and land reform. All were designed, Dr. Edwards shows, to develop a political proletariat in Afghanistan among the women and the small landowners from which to build a base for social change.

These attempts at reform had quite the opposite effect, however. Rather than building support for the new Marxist government, they led to a nearly unanimous popular uprising that brought the government down quickly and precipitated the Soviet invasion.

Edwards then turns to examine the other side: why in the eyes of the common Afghans did these reforms fail and why was their response rebellion? By examining in detail the narrative of one of the rural religious leaders involved in the early rebellion, he finds two kinds of complaints about the Khalqi government and their reforms. The people objected to specifics of the reforms, that is, individual parts of the reform that the local Afghans felt betrayed them. Also, they responded to the ideological nature of the reforms which they regarded as anti-Islamic and anti-Afghan. The Afghan people quickly smelled detested foreign influence in these reforms.

The issues treated in this first chapter are important and raise further issues. How could the early government of Taraki, or any future government, have introduced these specific reforms or any other reforms without having them lead to mass rebellion? Is it the nature of traditional cultures like that of Afghanistan that they will oppose such reforms from the center, no matter what? Or is it the case that the Taraki government was doomed from the start, given its narrow ideological base and the restricted class background of its followers? To phrase the problem differently, it is no surprise that an ideologically based party made up almost exclusively of the urbanized technocratic elite with its very small support base could fail to effect sweeping reforms in a traditional country, especially reforms touching very sensitive cultural and religious issues.

Another important topic that David Edwards suggests is the question of the leadership of the rebellion. Local political leadership in Afghanistan traditionally has not been in the hands of the Islamic clergy, the mullahs. However, in the Afghan war of liberation this clergy has emerged in most parts of the country to become the rebellion leaders.

The issue of leadership leads to the second chapter, by Sultan Aziz, entitled "Leadership Dilemmas: Challenges and Responses." He contends that leadership among the Afghans has been historically fragmented, and that the lack of unity or the inability of the Afghan resistance to rally around a central figure is a natural outgrowth of Afghan social structure. Nevertheless, he detects a dynamism and a capacity for change within these traditional, seemingly intractable societal forms that indicate a strong capacity for survival.

Political leadership is flexible and in the last few years of Zahir Shah's monarchy in the late 1960s and early 1970s the people of Afghanistan did begin to coalesce around a national leader. The collapse of that national government has meant the return of the Afghans to a more traditional form of political structure, one that is appropriate for the current situation.

Rather than viewing the present disunity among the resistance groups as a problem, we should see that it is an eminently Afghan solution to a complex struggle for survival. Sultan Aziz especially cautions against using a simplistic Western model to understand the intricacies of Afghan leadership.

His thought-provoking chapter leads to several further questions. While the Afghan leadership patterns reflect the character and structure of Afghan society, they also reflect external pressure from foreign agencies and governments. Clearly the leadership structure of the Kabul government mirrors Soviet intentions. Similarly, the political structure of the exiled political groups in Peshawar reflects the intentions and desires of the several governments supporting the Afghan cause, especially the U.S.A., Pakistan, and Saudi Arabia. While the influence of these three countries may not be as obvious nor as strong in Peshawar as the Soviet influence in Kabul, clearly the wishes of these nations are reflected by both the type of political groups that are given official status in Pakistan and by the degree of their cooperation.

"Arms to the Resistance: The Means to Survival," by Dr. John G. Merriam, comprises the third chapter, which deals with covert arms shipments to the Mujahideen. His chapter discusses the type, amount, and source of arms the resistance forces receive insofar as such information can be derived from sources in the public domain.

He especially looks at the initial role of Egypt in supplying CIA-funded arms. Egyptian arms were important early in the fighting if only because Egypt had Soviet-made or copies of Soviet arms which the resistance (and for different reasons the CIA) preferred because they matched the weapons and ammunition available. More important today are the supplier roles of the People's Republic of China, certain Gulf States, Great Britain, and invariably the CIA.

Ordnance is a key problem in any war, and the Afghan war is no different. Weapons supplies were problematic in the earlier part of the war, and reports from Afghanistan indicated that many of the guerrilla warriors were using pre-World War I rifles. This use of antiquated rifles appears largely not to be the case now. The problems with the

increasingly sophisticated and complex arms now seem to be
the type of arms, the training to use them, and of course,
sufficient maintenance to keep them operational. Reports
from Afghanistan often tell of the misuse of arms and the
wasting of ammunition, not to mention the needless loss of
the guerrillas' lives. Nevertheless, there are signs of better
Mujahideen cooperation, improved training, and a greater
sense of professionalism as evidenced by the writings of
Muhammad es-Haq in Jamiat-i-Islami publications, for example, though much needs to be done.

The arms problem, in any case, is a complicated one and
relates to more than just adequate supplies. Afghans fight
the war in the ways consistent with their social structure
and conceptions of manhood. Because they believe that
they are naturally good fighters, they often eschew training
and at times engage in tactics that are dangerous and
unnecessary. Their choice of weapons seems to be dictated
less by the realities of guerrilla war and more by the notions
of prestige and manhood. For foreign powers, arms shipments are more than just a matter of difficult logistics;
they should also be viewed as expressions of concrete policy
commitments.

The AK-47 assault rifle has become the standard weapon
for the Mujahideen, but it is not the best weapon given the
nature of the Afghan guerrilla war. Its effective range is
short and, being semiautomatic, it tends to waste ammunition.
The AK-47 has nevertheless become a symbol of manhood
and prestige.(2)

Reports from the front now indicate that arms are not
so much of a problem as is keeping open supply lines into
Afghanistan. Since arms have been coming into the NWFP
faster than they can be sent into Afghanistan, insurgent
commanders have been building large stockpiles just across
the Afghan border, awaiting shipment further into Afghanistan, but just out of reach of the Pakistan government.
Without protection these arms caches become targets for
Soviet or DRA forces, as the recent experience in Zhawar
demonstrated. The Soviet attempt to disrupt supply lines
into Afghanistan is having an effect, and the field commanders
now find getting arms into the interior is more difficult and
dangerous. At the same time, getting Soviet weapons from
U.S.S.R.-DRA troops is more problematic.

The fourth, fifth, and sixth chapters deal in various ways

with the Afghan refugees now in Pakistan. The fourth contribution is Kathleen Howard-Merriam's "Afghan Refugee Women and the Struggle For Liberation." For many years the role of women in Islam has been largely ignored or forgotten. Happily, this omission is being corrected thanks to the excellent work of scholars like Dr. Howard-Merriam.

Camp life is never easy, but it is especially stressful for the women. The physical conditions of the camps make life difficult for the women since in Islamic society women should not be seen by strangers. By their very nature, camps are areas where people crowd together, making privacy difficult. A greater problem is the changing role of the women in the Afghan camp families. Since many men are off in the war fighting and dying, the women in the camps must often be the sole family supporters, playing a dual role as they are called upon by sheer necessity to keep up the morale and maintain the family structure. A third, most important role to play is that of motherhood.

In the camps, the birth rate appears to be higher than in Afghanistan, thus reflecting the disruption of camp life but perhaps also underscoring the certainty that a people concerned with survival must replace lost lives. If the survival of children is threatened by harsh conditions, it is better to have more to increase the chances of enough living beyond their first year, it is reasoned.

The role of the women in the camps touches on the larger issues of camp life. A number of problems arises in any camp situation, and the Afghan camps in Pakistan are no exception. A specific problem is the generational conflict as young men better adapted to the new situation in the camps challenge their more traditional elders for leadership. These generational tensions have been handled relatively well among the Pushtuns, who have a more flexible and democratic social structure, but less well with such other ethnic groups as the Hazaras with their more rigid, hierarchical structure. Growing psychological stresses in the camps result from forced, prolonged inactivity. The women's role in helping to deal with this stress is important.

"The New Middle Class As Refugees and Insurgents," the fifth chapter, written by Grant M. Farr, traces the development of the new middle class in Afghanistan and of modern university education up to the Soviet invasion. This new middle class is composed of the modern, educated professionals and bureaucratic elite who have worked primarily for the government or for government-funded organizations such as Kabul University.

As an emerging elite possessing modern education, this class began to find itself estranged from the common Afghan. Educated in a country of overwhelming illiteracy, leading a modern lifestyle in a very traditional country, and being urban in a land that is largely rural, this group found itself cut off from tribal or rural ties. From this class the Marxist and also the fundamentalist leaders have emerged.

The Marxist coup has placed the majority of this class in a most difficult situation, for the Marxists soon turned on them after coming to power. Many were jailed or killed while others fled to Pakistan, only to find themselves as refugees suspect among their own people. Many found themselves in a quandary as they had lost their traditional ties and had no resources on which they could rely. Most from this class do not or will not live in the camps. Some either choose not to participate or are not welcome in the political parties. Others remain under suspicion in Peshawar, and a few have been killed or kidnapped while in exile. Thus, most choose to seek asylum in the U.S. or Western Europe.

Several important issues come out of Dr. Farr's discussion. One might ask who is at fault here. Should the new middle class make more of an effort to be involved in the fight for their country rather than to seek comfortable exile in the West? Many in Peshawar think so and accuse them of not being willing to make sacrifices for their people and country.

Or should the political leadership in Peshawar be more open to including members of this group in their rank? Many of the new Afghan middle class have skills that would be of great use to the resistance. Some of this class already work for these groups.

This chapter also brings up the larger role of the secular intellectuals in revolutionary times. By their nature, intellectuals are people of thoughts and ideas, and not of action. Perhaps insurgent wars require doers, not thinkers. Intellectuals, almost by definition, are taught to be critical, to question, to look for inconsistencies. These traits do not sit well in guerrilla wars where believers who are willing to die for that belief are needed.

Professor Farr's study also points out that not all Afghan refugees are rural peasants. Many are highly educated and skilled, and come from an urban setting with needs different from the bulk of the refugees. They understandably seek education for their children and find themselves unable to live in the refugee camps established primarily for the peasants. The situation of the educated, then, is tragic as many of them would love to fight for their country but the circumstances do not allow it.

The sixth chapter, by Dr. Kerry M. Connor, is entitled "Rationales for the Movement of Afghan Refugees to Peshawar, Pakistan." Dr. Connor interviewed 771 Afghan refugee families in Peshawar. Most of those whom she interviewed were Pushtun. She sought to find out why they became refugees, and how these flight motives were associated with their dates of departure as well as personal attributes such as who they were and what they were doing in Peshawar.

She concludes that the refugees came out of Afghanistan for a variety of reasons. Some refugees, for example, fled from the bombing and fighting, some wanted to avoid conscription into the Afghan military, and others wanted to fight with the Peshawar-based resistance.

Her conclusions are particularly interesting. Most of the refugees did not flee *en masse*, as the decision to leave Afghanistan was calculated and in most cases carefully considered. Many waited for several years before conditions became intolerable. Also, as in Farr's chapter, she found the urban/rural differences important since the urban Afghans suffered more acutely the effects of the communist oppression.

Although Kerry Connor's research does not address the issue of repatriation directly, her findings do shed light on the issue in suggesting that the refugees will remain in Pakistan or return to Afghanistan when it is in their best interest to do so. As basic as this conclusion may sound, it is significant inasmuch as many have suggested the refugees will either return or not do so because of emotional and patriotic concerns. Dr. Connor's work suggests otherwise.

The seventh and last chapter, by Ralph Magnus, is "Afghanistan: Humanitarian Response to an Inhuman Strategy," detailing the inhumane tactics employed by the Soviets to crush the Afghans, and the Western humanitarian response or the lack of it. The Soviet military strategy seems to be to bomb Afghanistan flat. Dr. Magnus states that an essential strategy of the Soviet effort to subjugate Afghanistan is to subject the 85 percent of the population living in the rural areas to a deliberate process of "rubbleization."

A not insignificant amount of aid has been provided to the Afghan refugees and the guerrilla fighters, it is true. Unfortunately, the Western world has not responded by helping those who have experienced the Soviet brutality most severely, the Afghans still in Afghanistan. The first response to this tragedy was to begin providing medical help. The Afghan doctors in exile in Pakistan formed a group called the Society of Afghan Doctors, an organization attempting to aid the sick and the wounded being brought to Pakistan for treatment and to set up clinics in Afghanistan itself. However, political problems and internal squabbling have diminished this group's effectiveness.

Foreign agencies, including the Swedish committee and the French groups, *Medicins sans Frontieres*, *Aide Medicale Internationale*, and *Medicins du Monde*, also have provided medical help for the Afghans inside the country by establishing clinics primarily to deal with the wounded, both guerrillas and civilians.   In addition, other private groups like American Aid for Afghans got help into Afghanistan sometimes in the form of medical personnel. However, the U.S. government did respond until 1985 by establishing special funds for humanitarian purposes inside Afghanistan.   Other important needs exist besides the medical, including food and clothing.   Dr. Magnus's chapter points to a common problem found in situations such as the Afghan crisis. Governments and other agencies tend to focus on the war and the fighting rather than on civilian conditions.   Clearly, whether the war in Afghanistan is won or lost, the civilians will bear the brunt.

These chapters, then, focus on different aspects of the Afghan crisis.   Each author brings a different but complimentary perspective to the understanding of the Afghan tragedy, although the one common theme to this work is that of survival. While each assessment is based on empirical research, this book is not written by detached intellectuals. All of us deeply care about Afghans, Afghanistan, and its freedom. This is a work of love and caring for a people we deeply admire and respect. When we criticize, we do so in the spirit of trying to help. As intellectuals we are trained to be objective, but we cannot always be objective when it comes to the issue of Afghanistan.

NOTES

1.   For a rather optimistic, recent assessment elsewhere of the Afghan war, see Craig M. Karp, "The War In Afghanistan," *Foreign Affairs*, Summer 1986, Vol. 64, No. 5, pp. 1026-1047.   For more pessimistic, apparently pro-Marxist reports of the fighting, see Jonathan Steel, "Moscow's Kabul Campaign," and Joe Stork, "The CIA In Afghanistan," in *MERIP* [*Middle East Report*], July-August, 1986, no. 141.

2.   See, for example, Edward Clinton Ezell, *The AK47 Story: Evolution Of The Kalashnikov Weapons*.

1

Origins of the Anti-Soviet Jihad

David Busby Edwards

The vigorous and successful resistance of the Afghan people to the Soviet-backed regime in Kabul did not begin with the December 1979 invasion. Rather, it assumed significant proportions following the April 1978 Marxist coup. Some would date the beginnings of resistance even earlier when Muhammad Daoud, first as prime minister (1953-1963) and later as president (1973-1978), opened the door to Soviet penetration of a heretofore neutral state. Yet, reasons for the resistance cannot be found in any mono-causal explanation. They are far more complex.

What will be the outcome of this interminable conflict? It is enough to say that the resistance is "successful" simply because it has not lost the struggle even though it has yet to win it. A conflict assessment appears elsewhere in this book, but what follows here provides an in-depth analysis of the Marxist precursors of Babrak Karmal, and now Najibullah, the present Afghan leader whose leadership is vehemently denied by the great majority of a people strongly conscious of its recent tumultuous history.

Resistance to the introduction of the Marxist-Leninist ideology prior to the December 1979 invasion may be accurately termed a civil conflict which turned into a war of liberation only with the arrival of the Soviet troops, but the ideology as well as the forces from across the border have been considered equally foreign by the great majority of the Afghan people.

The Editors

HISTORY OF THE COUP

On the morning of April 27, 1978, a small group of officers in the Afghan army and air force initiated a coup d'etat against the government and person of President Muhammad Daoud. By evening, the President along with most of his family had been killed, and the people of Afghanistan listened over their radios to the announcement that power was in the hands of a Revolutionary Council composed primarily of military officers. Although not announced at the time, all of these officers were secret members of the People's Democratic Party of Afghanistan (PDPA), the principal Marxist political group in the country. By early May, the orientation of the new government became clearer as the members of the cabinet were announced. Instead of the junior military officers whose names were first broadcast, veteran leftist politicians--Nur Muhammad Taraki, Chairman of the Revolutionary Council and Prime Minister; Babrak Karmal, Vice-Chairman of the Revolutionary Council and Deputy Prime Minister; and Hafizullah Amin, Deputy Prime Minister and Minister of Foreign Affairs--held the three top leadership positions.(1)

To foreign observers, the events of April 27 represented one more Third World coup d'etat, bringing with it another unstable regime that would have to be factored into geo-political equations. The real significance of the change of leaders in Kabul had little to do with Afghanistan and much to do with Soviet-American relations. For Afghans, however, the coup d'etat--grandly proclaimed as "the Glorious Saur Revolution" after the month in the Afghan calendar when the coup d'etat took place--represented the end of the political domination of the Durrani Pushtun tribe which had supplied the rulers of Afghanistan since the founding of the 'Kingdom of Caubul' by Ahmad Shah Durrani in the late eighteenth century.(2)

In 1978, Durrani rule came to an end, and power was assumed by a political party whose roots were ideological rather than tribal. Despite its claims to represent the best interests of the masses, the PDPA was a small party without any significant popular backing. The membership of the organization in 1978 has been estimated at about 5,000, and these were primarily, if not almost exclusively, residents of Kabul and members of what in Afghanistan passed for a "technocratic elite": government bureaucrats, military officers, and students (Halliday 1980). Although many of these early party members were born in the rural areas, it remained to be seen if they were still in touch with the wellsprings of their native social and religious traditions. As one observer noted in 1980:

> Whilst the PDPA's triumph and the Soviet willingness to assist provided a very real opportunity for Afghanistan, there was also danger that the urban-based party would, while expropriating the landowners, fail to win the mass of poor peasants by a bureaucratic imposition of reforms. There was also the risk that the potential for transforming Afghan society would be distorted by the imposition of political models . . . drawn from the USSR (Halliday 1980).

The initial policy articulated by the PDPA appeared to demonstrate a recognition of the tenuous position of an ideologically-oriented party with strong foreign roots in a deeply conservative society whose chief source of pride was their success in vanquishing would-be foreign rulers. Thus, the Marxist principles and Soviet connections of the PDPA were denied at first: "In our program which was devised 13 years ago . . . Marxism and Leninism do not enter, but nonetheless it is a very progressive and democratic program" (*Kabul Times* May 13, 1978). Instead, the official line emphasized more general notions which were intended to neutralize opposition before it could arise:

> The leading of Afghanistan from backwardness toward social, economic and cultural progress, under the leadership of the People's Democratic Party of Afghanistan (PDPA), the party of the working class and other toilers of the country, will be based on the intention of the broad masses of people, deep respect and the strict observance of the national, historical, cultural and religious traditions of our people, with the resolute following of the principles of the sacred religion of Islam, respect for the universal declaration of human rights, based on the policy of peaceful coexistence, friendship and cooperation with all the people of the region and the world.(3)

This relatively neutral policy stance was accompanied by a concerted effort by the PDPA to appeal to the tribal and nationalistic sentiments of ethnic Pushtuns, presumably because they represent approximately half of the total population of the country and because of their history of rebellion against rulers too closely aligned with foreign powers or too progressive in their orientation. Being a Ghilzai Pushtun himself, Taraki seemed ready at first to appease the forces of tribal autonomy and, within a fortnight of taking power, initiated a series of well-publicized *jirgahs* (tribal assemblies) in which he met with groups of tribal elders, most of whom were members of the traditionally rebellious eastern border tribes.

In meeting with these tribal leaders in his first few weeks in office, Taraki took a stance which appeared to represent a conciliatory approach to the role of tribalism in the nation-state. In actuality, Taraki's *jirgahs* were an example of the cautious 'realpolitik' of a leader fully cognizant of the autonomous heritage of the Pushtun tribes and their instinctive wariness toward whichever group ruled in Kabul. Alluding to the downfall of the progressive government of King Amanullah in 1929 and the takeover by the Tajik, Bach-e Saqao, Taraki warned his "brother tribes" to "be aware and consider the bitter experience of the Amani movement . . . the state is yours. It is not your master. It is your servant."(4) For their part, the tribes appeared mollified by the early pro-Pushtun orientation of the new regime and its assertions that "We are sons of Muslims and respect principles of Holy Islam" (*Kabul Times* June 13, 1978).

However, within three months, the non-ideological line that characterized the initial Khalqi statements was replaced by a more confident policy emphasizing the rapid transformation of Afghan society along Marxist lines. On July 17, the first step in the reform program was announced through the publication of the new government's Sixth Decree. This decree, which attacked the considerable problem of rural debt, altered the legal obligations of debtors and attempted to eliminate the crushing burden of excessive interest rates that had placed many small landholders into permanent debt. For example, further interest payments on mortgages taken out more than four years earlier were cancelled; a sliding rate ensured that all payments on more recent mortgages would cease after a maximum of five years. Finally, in the case of landless peasants, all outstanding debts were nullified.(5)

The second major reform was embodied in Decree No. 7 and announced by the PDPA on October 18, 1978. The stated objective of this decree was to ensure "the equal rights of women" and the elimination of "the unjust patriarchal feudalistic relations between husband and wife." According to the PDPA, the root causes of female exploitation were economic in nature, and the primary thrust of the reform was therefore the destruction of the economic underpinnings of the marriage relationship. Decree No. 7 therefore outlawed the practice of giving bride-price (*walwar*) and other gifts by the groom and his family to the father of the bride (Articles 1 and 2).(6) In addition, the amount of a woman's dowry was limited to Afs. 300 (in 1979, Afs. 44 = U.S. $1), which, it was claimed, was equivalent to the 10 Dirhams allowed for dowry by Islamic *shariat* law (Article 3). The other, non-economic aspect of this decree, contained in Articles 4 and 5, outlawed forced marriages and the traditional practice of remarrying widows to close patrilineal kin (Article 4, Sections 1 and 2); abolished child marriages by fixing a minimum age of marriage for males (18) and females (16) (Article 5); and attacked other abuses of the marriage institution whereby more powerful individuals were able to gain women through subterfuge and coercion (Article 4, Section 3) (*Kabul Times* October 18, 1978).

Another dimension of the PDPA plan to reconstruct Afghan society involved its various programs designed to eliminate sexual discrimination. In its early espousal of women's rights, the PDPA seemed determined to strike at the heart of traditional values and relationships concerning women. Although the reasons why they chose to attack this particularly sensitive area so soon after coming to power are unclear, one factor would appear to be the desire of the regime to create what Massell has referred to in the Central Asian context as "a surrogate proletariat" among women whom, it might be assumed, could then be counted on to support the regime responsible for their liberation (Massell 1974).

Despite public assertions that the PDPA intended to dramatically alter the situation for women in Afghanistan, the reality was that major social transformations were not envisioned, and, following the purge by Taraki and Hafizullah Amin of the predominantly non-Pushtun Parcham wing of the party in July 1978, social reforms aimed at assisting women were largely abandoned, in part because Anahita

Ratibzad, the principal advocate of women's rights, was among the Parchamis expelled from the government. The Ministry of Social Affairs, which Anahita had headed, was dissolved "since [it] was not needed right now," and women's issues were handed over to the Ministry of Education (N. Dupree 1984a). Concerning this policy change, Nancy Dupree writes that:

> Women prominent in the DOAW no longer made public appearances. No woman was appointed to subsequent cabinets or to any other substantive positions. Mrs. Taraki and Mrs. Amin only rarely appeared at functions. Neither functioned in the forefront of the political scene, and both primarily fulfilled ceremonial roles. Following patterns set by past regimes, they graciously received flowers and opened exhibitions of needlework (1984a, 317).

While the actions of the regime on women's rights essentially continued the efforts of previous governments, the professions of the PDPA were much more radical. Despite the absence of concrete programs to alleviate women's inequality, Taraki continued to rail against the patriarchal conditions in the countryside that kept women enslaved and declared that "without the participation of the toiling women no great movement relating to the toiling classes has achieved victory, because women form half of the society." These sentiments were backed up by numerous demonstrations and rallies in which women "gather[ed] in the streets to participate in 'grand marches,' shouting 'Hurrah, hurrah,' and slogans condemning 'the reactionary plotters,' and supporting the 'Glorious Saur Revolution' while they waved huge posters of 'our Great Leader,' Taraki. Frequently, these grand marches ended in 'volunteer clean-up' sessions, and the people of Kabul were treated for the first time to the sight of girls wielding brooms, sweeping the streets in public in the company of men" (N. Dupree 1984a, 317).

One of the few initiatives directly affecting women was the program to expand literacy. The objective of the literacy program was to provide basic skills in reading and writing to all citizens--men and women alike--within a year. However unrealistic the time frame might have been, the literacy campaign itself was not unprecedented as similar, though less comprehensive, efforts had been made by Amanullah in the 1920s and by King Zahir Shah and President Muhammad Daoud in the late 1960s and early 1970s. Generally confined to the cities and large towns, participation remained voluntary. Individuals were given the choice of whether or not they wanted their wives, sisters, and daughters to attend school, and most chose to keep them at home, although it was not unusual for pre-pubescent girls in rural areas to attend a mosque *madrassah* for a few years to obtain a rudimentary grounding in Islam.

The two principal innovations in the PDPA literacy campaign over past attempts to bring education to women were the element of coercion, whereby women and girls, as well as old people, were forced to attend classes and the explicitly political message conveyed in these classes:

> Khalq spokesmen adapted Lenin's dogma that 'An illiterate person stands outside politics; he must first learn his ABC's. Without that there can be no politics'; they 'Afghanized' it by claiming that 'An illiterate woman cannot carry on the struggle, cannot handle properly the family affairs, and cannot rear properly sound and heathly children.' . . . While these were worthy objectives, in practice the literacy classes were merely political meetings in disguise. Instead of beginning with A, B, or C, Lesson No. 1 began with 'jim,' 'dal,' 'kha,' and 'alif' for Jamhuriyat-i Demokratik-i Khalqi Afghanistan--the Dari (Afghan Persian) equivalent of PDPA. Marxist ideology dominated the curriculum. Practical, non-formal, functional teaching materials which had been developed a few years previously were shelved (N. Dupree 1984a, 320-321).

For the PDPA, literacy clearly was conceived to be a necessary precursor to popular acceptance of their regime. The majority of party members, particularly those coming from rural areas, were fully aware of the importance of literacy for breaking the grip of traditional cultural influences and creating a new ideological constituency. In the books used by the PDPA in their literacy classes, the association between literacy and ideology is evident in the symbolic images employed to convey Marxist propaganda while teaching basic reading skills. As Olivier Roy has noted:

The text rewards urban and Westernized behavior (this
tendency was already at work under the old regime).
A caricatural page presents the people marching (three
intellectuals in suits and ties carrying a banner against
a background of the crowd in traditional garb). Behavior
having to do with the land and the peasantry is
attributed to the grandparents. The father, in contrast,
is a worker in a modern plant. "The" book is no longer
the Qur'an but the textbook. One entire page presents
the tank as the symbol of people's liberation. Slogans
and watchwords fill a third of the pages.(7)

These social changes were implemented to modernize the family
structure. Still other proposed changes altered the economic
structure of the community through land reform.

The PDPA's third major reform measure, Decree No. 8,
promulgated on November 29, 1978, articulated the long-
awaited plan for land reform first promised in the "Basic
Lines of Revolutionary Duties of Government."(8)   Under
this decree, all agricultural land was placed into seven categories, and ceilings were placed on the amount of land individuals were allowed to own. A maximum of five *jeribs* (1
jerib = 0.195 hectares or 0.480 acres) of first-grade land or
its graded equivalent was allowed to any individual (*Kabul
Times* December 2, 1978).

During 1979, the program of land redistribution became one
of the centerpieces of the PDPA program. This program
first was initiated in Kabul Province, then in the northern
and western regions, and finally in the eastern, predominantly
Pushtun provinces. Demonstrations celebrating land reform,
the Party, and Taraki--the "Great Leader"--were held in the
major towns and administrative centers, and frequent proc-
lamations were made as to the number of *jeribs* of land that
had been distributed under the auspices of Decree No. 8. In
April, 1979, it was announced that 104,000 landless laborers,
petty landowners, and nomads had been given 1,024,000 *jeribs*
of land; by June 30th, 248,114 individuals had been given
2,917,671 *jeribs*.(9)

Through its policy of radical land redistribution, the PDPA
intended to create a mass movement by enlisting the support
of the economically-disenfranchised segments of the population,
gambling that they could indoctrinate and mobilize sufficient
numbers of the rural poor before the inevitable backlash by

the wealthy elites. As announced in the *Kabul Times* news-paper, a new social order could not be put in place until the old order had been liquidated: "As a prelude to democratic land reforms, the Khalqi order had to annihilate those who impoverished the peasants, that is the plunderers who used to mortgage small holdings belonging to peasants and leasing these to the latter and money-lenders . . ." (*Kabul Times* February 8, 1979).

To attain this objective, the PDPA had to instill a class consciousness where none had previously existed. For the reform program to succeed, not only land redistribution had to go forward and existing debts be erased, but an ideological awareness of class and a respect for the PDPA as the vehicle for the deliverance of the poor from the oppression of the "oppressors" had to occur. At the same time, the PDPA had to liquidate the dominant landowning class before it used its existing power and influence to force the peasantry to fight against its own best interests.

To prevent or muffle an anti-government backlash, the PDPA employed a two-prong strategy: (1) the arrest and execution of those who opposed the government or who were thought likely to become critical of the government in the future and (2) the propagation of an ideology focusing on the role of what the PDPA called (in a direct linguistic appropriation) the "feudal" elements of society, the landowners and previously landless peasants.

The PDPA envisioned the initial creation of a class of petty landowners indebted to the party for its enfranchisement. In time, this class would itself be replaced, but not before it had succeeded in eradicating all of those existent social forces which were capable of mounting a challenge to the new order. Tribal leaders, wealthy or not, had to be eliminated. Nomads, by definition independent and marginal in relation to the state, had to be settled. The large numbers of the rural poor had to be mobilized for the revolution. When these goals were accomplished, the party envisioned a steady movement beyond the stage of peasant enfranchisement through the expansion of rural cooperatives. An estimated 1.1 million families (5 to 7 million people, representing between one-third and one-half of the rural population of Afghanistan) would be living on 4,500 cooperatives responsible for 45 percent of the total volume of agricultural production by 1984.(10)

Through all of these changes, the PDPA portrayed in its press reports a great groundswell of popular support rising in response to its reform program. A typical example of this kind of rhetoric is contained in the following dispatch depicting the gratitude of a peasant in the province in Ningrahar given a land deed:

Naji Nasruddin, a peasant from Balla Bagh village of Surkh Rud said smilingly, "God is with those who are helpless. Consequently the Decree Number Eight has come to our rescue. Hereafter whatever we reap belongs to us. Hereafter no feudal lords or middlemen will be able to cheat us. This all has happened with the attention of Khalqi state. We the toiling peasants have been delivered forever. Today the government is headed by those who work solely for the benefit, for the welfare of the poor and downtrodden. It is a happy occasion that we the peasants have achieved our cherished desire."

"Now with the six *jeribs* of land given to me I am sure I will become the owner of a decent living and will not die of hunger. Before the Saur Revolution the feudal lords used to loot all our products. The rules at that time sided with oppressive landlords. Fortunately the Saur Revolution has destroyed their dreams and they can no longer achieve their ominous goals" (*Kabul Times* February 13, 1979).

In communities throughout the country, the government staged rallies in which local officials passed out land deeds to newly enfranchised peasants. Inevitably, these rallies were followed by marches of shovel-carrying farmers chanting Marxist slogans. Despite all the propaganda employed and energy expended, and the existence of what were in many cases clear economic reasons for supporting the regime, the PDPA never succeeded in translating their message to the people and establishing a base of popular support.

In addressing the PDPA's failed strategy for revolutionizing Afghan society, most observers have found it difficult to avoid couching their analysis in polemical terms. Beverley Male, for example, argues that Afghanistan, was as the PDPA ideologues claimed, a nation suffering under the harsh bondage of a repressive and feudalistic social system and that the reforms were a necessary precondition to economic and social progress:

> Taraki and Amin did not make the mistake of under-
> estimating the enemy: the tribal-feudal ruling class
> and the bureaucracy that served it had, for over fifty
> years, successfully resisted attempts by the central
> government to implement reforms that represented the
> slightest threat to its power. If the Revolution was
> to succeed, if the quality of life of the vast mass of
> the Afghan people was to be improved there could be
> no half measures. The power of the old ruling class
> and the tribal-feudal authority structure on which it
> rested had to be smashed once and for all. And its
> destruction had to be swift and thorough (Male 1982,
> 101).

Other observers, including even Soviet social scientists, have taken a more skeptical view of the PDPA strategy. Gluckhoded, for example, notes that the PDPA's giving land to the landless and "land-hungry" was "not justified by any theoretical considerations or practical experience." To the contrary, "the attainment of the basic aims of the reform was made dependent on the solution of the problem of allotting land to the peasants, which acquired an exaggerated, self-contained character."(11) While Gluckhoded takes a seemingly more objective position in his criticism of the early reform program, his analysis supports the Soviet line, formulated since the invasion of Afghanistan in December 1979, that Taraki was betrayed by Amin, supposedly a CIA agent intent upon discrediting the revolution.

Though Male and Gluckhoded differ in their opinions of Taraki and Amin's strategies of reform, they agree Afghanistan was in fact a "feudal" society. This shared understanding, however, illustrates one of the profound difficulties encountered in dealing with this period of Afghan history: namely, how to ascertain the extent to which Afghanistan was a "feudal" nation and whether the PDPA program "to annihilate those who impoverished the peasants" had any legitimate basis. Concomitantly, few analyses of the Afghan viewpoint seriously consider how those who were affected by the reform program and who chose to reject it conceptualized and made sense of their political opposition in indigenous terms and forms. To understand the advent of the counter-revolution that developed in response to PDPA rule, it is necessary to understand how PDPA rule and reform were perceived by those whom they purportedly served and why a government that premised its legitimacy on the idea of giving power to the people was rejected by the very ones it intended to enfranchise.

ORIGINS OF THE COUNTER-REVOLUTION

The first rebellion against the government of Nur Muhammad Taraki began in June 1978, less than three months after the Glorious "Saur" Revolution. Arising in the Pech Valley, it primarily involved members of the Safi tribe and neighboring Nuristanis. The outbreak of anti-government violence took place considerably before the advent of the reform program, at a time when the policy direction of the new regime remained uncertain. Therefore, it cannot be argued that this uprising was necessarily motivated by the kind of anti-Marxist/pro-Islamic sentiment that has subsequently become the dominant ideology of the Afghan resistance. In the case of the Pech Valley, the reasons for the first uprising appear to have concerned local problems and personalities more than national ones. According to one informant, the people attacked government officials in the area after local residents, who had been serving as army officers when the revolution occurred, were executed for being loyalists to the old regime.(12)

An alternative story told by Pech residents involves repression by area officials motivated by economic and personal disputes, when the man appointed by the PDPA as the local administrator (*wuleswal*) for the area became embroiled in an argument with distantly related kinsmen. Taking advantage of his new-found authority, the *wuleswal* arrested his rivals and attempted to transport them to the government center at Chaga Serai. The jeep convoy in which the prisoners were riding was attacked, however, and an officer and soldier accompanying the prisoners were killed. In retaliation, the official declared his intention to bring in troops to raze Ninglam, the village from which the attack originated, leading the residents to flee that very night by torchlight toward the more secure mountains of Nuristan to the north. In response to this challenge, the government is said to have arrested and executed military officers and government workers from Pech and Nuristan who were living in Kabul. Those who escaped returned to their homes where their stories fanned the smoldering outrage. Four months after the attack on the convoy in Pech, the government centers at Kamdesh and Bargematal in the Bashgal Valley of Nuristan were attacked and seized. Throughout the following winter, the unrest spread, and by the Spring of 1979, most of Nuristan and the Pech Valley were free of any governmental presence.(13)

Uprisings broke out sporadically in other regions of Afghanistan between the Fall of 1978 (e.g., at Pasawand in the Hazarajat in October) and the Spring of 1979 (e.g., the major western city of Herat in March). By mid-Summer 1979, local rebellions had flared up not only in outlying areas, but also in urban Kabul where Shi'i protestors rose up in the Chindawal section of the city in July and mutineers briefly took over the central army base in August.(14) By and large, Pushtun areas rose up later than other areas, and even the Paktia tribes, which previously had proved the most dissident of groups in the national mosaic, remained remarkably silent.

When resistance in Paktia broke out among the Zadran tribe in the Summer of 1979, the reasons once again appear to relate more to local circumstances than to the larger ideological concerns that later would be invoked in rationalizing the struggle. One story told about the first uprising in Paktia concerns a Khalqi named Roshan who became attorney general (*saranwal*) in Khost following the "Saur" Revolution He is to reported to have placed an old family rival in prison and forced other members of his family to flee over the border to Pakistan. A second Khalqi from Khost, who feuded with his cousins who had migrated to northern Baghlan Province during the time of Zahir Shah, reportedly used party connections to have his cousins arrested by party officials in the province.

While stories of such incidents were circulated widely, serious resistance only began in Paktia after the proclamation of Decree No. 7. In Paktia, government interference in domestic relations was a far more important issue than land reform or the elimination of debts, neither of which had much impact in an area where landholdings were uniformly small and most income was derived through such enterprises as the sale of timber from tribally-held tracts of forest and smuggling. However, virtually every provision of Decree No. 7, along with efforts by the PDPA cadres to force women to attend literacy classes, aroused the universal hostility of the people of Paktia against the government.

In their efforts to eradicate traditional patriarchal institutions, officials placed restrictions on the amount of bride-price which could be asked, reportedly forbade dancing at wedding ceremonies, and decreed that the maximum amount of rice that could be prepared for a wedding party was three *ser*, sufficient for only about thirty people (whereas it was not uncommon for several hundred guests to attend a wedding). Along with other decrees such as those allowing individuals (male and female) to choose their own marriage partners and sanctioning the right of women to divorce their husbands, the PDPA quickly incurred the wrath of heretofore inactive tribes. What the government actually proposed to do mattered less than what it was perceived as proposing. Propaganda quickly spread that the government was planning on prohibiting polygamy and on making all old men who were married to younger women divorce their wives and give them to younger, unmarried men who could not afford wives. Although few literacy programs were actually in place, rumors circulated that Khalqis were going door-to-door forcing women and girls to come to classes where they sat unveiled among non-kinsmen and were taught by young Khalqi instructors of dubious background. Whether true or not, such stories circulated widely and had a tremendous influence on the development of anti-PDPA sentiment throughout the country.

THE ANATOMY OF A REBELLION: KHAS KUNAR

In the region of Khas Kunar, south of the Pech Valley, near the trans-border territory of the Mohmand tribe, a number of factors combined to cause the local people to rise up against the government in the Spring of 1979. In the following oral account, the speaker, a senior member of a local *sayyid* family, who also worked as a civil servant for many years in government posts in various provinces, discusses the attitude of the people to government programs in the region and the stages of the uprising. His personal account is quoted in full:

In the beginning, the common people of Afghanistan didn't recognize the true identity and face of the Khalqis and Parchamis as infidels (*kafir*) and communists.

And in their own slogans they said that "We respect Islam and this is a government of the working people. Everyone has equal rights. And we will save all the people from poverty and hunger." The slogans which they said were things like, "Justice (*'edalat*), Equality (*masawat*), Security (*masuniyat*), Home (*kor*), Food (*dodai*), and Clothing (*kulai*)."

Then came the announcement of the Sixth Decree which concerned interest and mortgage payments (*gerawi*). Most of the mortgage money in Khas Junar was from the 'Border Mohmands' (*Sarhad Mohmand*) who had little land in the mountains. For this reason they leased land in Khas Kunar through the system of *gerawi*. With the announcement of this decree, all of the money from the 'Border Mohmands' was eliminated.

The people of Khas Kunar have close tribal and marital relations with the 'Border Mohmands.' These tribes also had such close relations with the former governments that they even took part in parliamentary elections (even though they hadn't taken national identity cards) and had the right to vote. The majority of these people were deprived [of their land] because of the Sixth Decree, and they cut their relations with the communist government. They gave asylum to those who made *hejrat* from their areas to the mountains and helped those who were against the government. Because of the Sixth Decree, a small percentage of the people of Khas Kunar from the poorest strata supported the Khalqis and Parchamis.

The purpose of the Khalqis and Parchamis in issuing these decrees one after another was to gain supporters and loyalists for themselves because their number was very small in all points of Afghanistan. At the same time, the strata of young people had no influence among the people, and they lacked the capacity to gain the respect of the people.

After the Sixth Decree, the Khalqis and Parchamis announced the Seventh Decree concerning marriage and engagement. The gist of this decree was that a girl had to be 16 years of age to marry. Parents could not prevent a marriage if their daughter accepted some boy, and they could not take more than 300 Afghanis as bride-price.   The boy must also be 18 years old, and he could become engaged to anyone he desired.   The custom (*rasm au rawaj*) of the people of Khas Kunar is that the girl and boy have little role in the engagement, and the engagement choice is made by the parents.   The Khalqis and Parchamis took the daughters of several people by force.   Because of this action, the opinion of all of the people changed, and a profound hatred of the Khalqis and Parchamis appeared.

Decree No. 8 concerned land reform.   Since the population of Khas Kunar is very high and the land is very little, few people had more than 36 *jeribs* of land.   Their number reaches 10 or 15.   By the most shameful kind of action, they took these people's land and gave it to others.   On the land of each one of these people, they organized a march, and they invited all of the uneducated people, the students, clerks, etc., to take part in the march.   When the land was dispensed and the deeds signed by Nur Muhammad Taraki were given out, they shouted "Hurrah" and slogans like "Death to the Feudals," "Death to the Ikhwan," "Death to American Imperialism," "Death to Reactionaries," etc.   Since the slogans of the people of Afghanistan during happier times were *"Allah-o Akbar"* ("God is Great") and *"Ya Char Yar"* (Oh, Four Companions," meaning the four companions of the Prophet Muhammad who became the first caliphs of Islam), they became very unhappy and said that in addition to the other acts of the Khalqis and Parchamis, the fact that they had changed *"Allah-o Akbar"* and *"Ya Char Yar"* to *"Hurrah"* was a sign of their infidelity.

After this, Decree No. 9 about illiteracy was issued, but it was not imposed on the people of Khas Kunar because the popular uprising soon started and the Mujahideen attacked the centers of the Khalqis and Parchamis and the jihad began in Khas Kunar.

After I returned to Khas Kunar and established communication with the elders and men of influence in the region and with the elders of the Mohmand tribes, the Khalqis and Parchamis were informed of my activities, and *Wuleswal* Usman Ghani with about 50 armed Khalqis and Parchamis came to capture me. We also had about 10 armed men in the house, and when the *Wuleswal* came near my house, he was informed by the people that if he tried to capture me, fighting would take place. It was thus that the *Wuleswal* was unsuccessful in arresting me, and the next day--the eighth of Saur 1358 (April 28, 1979), a bright day--we made *hejrat* from our home to the district of Barchanchan which belongs to the Buti Khel tribe. We established a center and began our activities. Since my father...was a spiritual figure (*rohani*), all of the people of Khas Kunar, especially the Mohmand tribes, greatly respected him. My father had also taken part in the fighting between the English and Mohmand in Naqi and Khapukh (in the 1930s), and because of this, he had special influence with the Mohmand tribes.

On the fifteenth of Saur 1358 (May 5, 1970), a general *jirgah* of the Mohmand tribes was held in Gandab (in the Mohmand Agency of Pakistan), and I participated and spoke. After introducing myself in the *jirgah*, I encouraged the people [to join] the jihad by saying that our fathers fought against the English here and now in Afghanistan the Khalqis and Parchamis who are communists and atheists have taken power. Hundreds of Muslims have been killed for the crime of being Muslims, and nearly a year has gone by that the people of Kunar have been fighting the communists. We have two moral claims (*haq*) on you. The first is that you are also Muslims and jihad is obligatory (*farz*) for you. The other is that our fathers did jihad here with you, and you also must repay the debt to us by doing jihad shoulder to shoulder with us. At the conclusion of the *jirgah*, we decided as one that we must go to jihad.

At the beginning of Jaoza 1358 (late May 1979), the Mohmand *lashkar* (tribal fighting force) was prepared, and it moved from Shabqadar and Gandab in the direction of Kama in Ningrahar.

After organizing the *lashkar* for Khas Kunar, a *jirgah* was convened in which myself and many Mohmand elders participated. Since the number of the *lashkar* was very large, it was divided into two parts...The *lashkar* under our leadership entered Khas Kunar and attacked the Middle School of Mangwal which was the center of Khalqis and Parchamis. This school was completely destroyed, and the following day we again took refuge in the mountains. The next day, both groups again entered Khas Kunar during the daylight. On the eighteenth of Jaoza 1358 (June 8, 1979), I hoisted the flag of Islam over my house.

The people of the region of Khas Kunar gathered and also joined us in the jihad against the communists. We moved toward the center of the Khalqis and Parchamis, and after a brief engagement, one of the Mujahideen was wounded. We stopped there, and the next day the Mujahideen again went toward the Khalqis and Parchamis and militia. The result was that thirteen government supporters were killed, and one person from the tribe of Khoga Khel was martyred. About forty weapons were taken by the Mujahideen as booty (*ghanimat*). After this conflict, the area of Khas Kunar came under the bombardment of the Khalqis and Parchamis, and a severe loss of property was inflicted on the people of Khas Kunar.

The *lashkar* again returned to the mountains, and the other *lashkar* that had gone to Kama was defeated there and they returned to their homes. The reason for this defeat [of the Kama *lashkar*] was that the Khalqis and Parchamis had a hand inside the tribes and spent a lot of money in this way. Our *lashkar* also returned to our homes because I knew that we could not resist the government openly and in the form of a *lashkar*. Our weapons were very primitive and simple, and our enemies were equipped with artillery, tanks and planes. [As a result], we thought that we must employ guerrilla (*chiriki*) tactics against the government.

After Mizan 1358, the resistance of the Mujahideen became very powerful, [but] this *lashkar* continued for only a very short period of time because we didn't have sufficient equipment and food supplies to keep up this kind of *lashkari* fighting. After this *lashkar*, the resistance of the Mujahideen began to be of the guerrilla and party kind.

In considering this account of an uprising in one locality of eastern Afghanistan, one factor that should be noted is the dual nature of the narrator's response to the events recounted. Two levels of understanding and involvement are implicitly present in his description. The first is the response to the actual reforms the government initiated, a response which is informed, at least in part, by practical considerations. The narrator describes the steps taken by the government and the hardships which these steps caused for the people of his area. The second level of response involves the ideological background against which the description of government actions is meant to be seen.

Here, the narrator signals his moral stance relative to the events described by first framing the narrative in terms of the government's deception in claiming to be what it was not. The claim of a false identity is significant on at least two levels. First, it explains why the people of the area waited a full year before rising up against the government. Since the region of Khas Kunar is relatively close to Pech Valley and Nuristan where the first uprisings took place, some defensiveness is evident in explaining the delay. A second, and ultimately more important, aspect of the government's deceit in claiming to be what it was not concerns the moral justification for the uprising, which is one of the principal themes of this narrative. The government's premise of relations with the people on a purposeful falsehood is an act of moral outrage legitimating the act of rebellion which alone can reassert the proper order.

This is not to say that Pushtuns are incapable of deception in their social relations or that they are so naive as to believe everything the government says. To the contrary, in everyday discourse a skillful ruse is appreciated, particularly if executed in the context of a business deal or an encounter with a government official. Such deceptions, however, take place in the realm of the contingent; they are an aspect of living in the mundane world. However, the government's act of claiming to respect Islam was viewed not as a deception but rather as a deceit, which is to say, the voicing of a falsehood in the realm of what is sacred.

When the PDPA came to power, the government tried to convince the people of their shared values and common concerns, but the language used to convey these sentiments was an alien one, derived from a Marxist lexicon that had no roots in Afghan culture and struck no resonant chord among the Afghan people. Naturally wary of the motives behind changes in government policy and action, Afghans tended to view government-supported demonstrations with their grand decorations of "Justice" and "Equality" with the utmost suspicion. Even those who directly benefitted from the land redistribution were unprepared for the sudden appearance of government representatives claiming in an alien rhetoric that they wanted to help them. The problem here was not only that the language used by the PDPA was novel but also that people had not generally looked to the government for benefits, and when they had, it entailed people petitioning the government rather than the government petitioning the people.

However much landless and "land-hungry" farmers might have wanted additional land, they were prepared neither to view those with more land than themselves as "oppressors," nor to accept land from the government that had been taken away from the wealthy by means which were considered illicit in local custom and un-Islamic under *shariat* law, even though they were legal from the government's point of view. This discrepancy convinced the people not that their own notions of right and wrong should be altered but that the government itself must be illegitimate for declaring legal what was manifestly not.

Instead of loosening the traditional social and economic ties that bound wealthy and poor, the way in which the party chose to attack the "feudal class" brought about quite the opposite response to that which had been intended. By attempting to isolate the landed from the landless, the wealthy from the poor, the party tended to encourage a defensive solidarity among the group as a whole and focused attention on the wealthy as victims of a more immediate oppression than the abstract oppression invoked by the party in its attacks on the "feudal class."

Another issue is the popular perception of the march demonstrations themselves. These events took place throughout Afghanistan during the Taraki and Amin period and usually involved the presentation by provincial and sometimes national officials of newly printed land deeds to local tenant farmers who were brought to the center of the town or village and handed placards praising the government and damning its enemies. Most newspaper photographs of these events show groups of these newly enfranchised farmers carrying new shovels and their slogan-covered placards in parade ground formation. However the government intended these demonstrations to be perceived, they were viewed by local people as an embarrassment and ignominy.

Nothing in local experience had prepared them for such an event, the symbolic construction of which was interpreted as being in complete contradiction to modes of action esteemed in Afghan culture. For example, such stock revolutionary performance devices as the shouting in unison of praise for the revolutionary party while marching in formation were "read" by local people not as nascent manifestations of class solidarity but as public humiliations in which they were forced by the government to act in a way which was immodest and demeaning, since it placed the individual in a situation in which his autonomy of action was symbolically subordinated through a series of orchestrated movements and utterances. These party rallies were staged in front of the local community, and they forced individuals to compromise themselves in the face of public opinion to the end of glorifying the party as the benefactor of the peasantry and castigating a host of unknown enemies--"American imperialism," the "Ikhwan," etc.

Another factor in the political equation which is brought out in the narrative is the role of Islam in the popular understanding and articulation of dissatisfaction with the new government. As the PDPA government came to be identified more and more as an alien entity espousing an imported, atheistic ideology, Islam became increasingly central in the expression of dissent. This is not to say that Islam had previously been unimportant. To the contrary, Afghans are devout Muslims who unequivocally view Afghanistan as an Islamic nation. But between the margins of personal and national identification with Islam, religion and religious figures seldom entered the political arena, especially in rural areas. One exception to this rule comes, of course, in times of national crisis when the integrity of the country is threatened by foreign invasion and/or radical internal changes. During such periods, Islam has provided the rallying point for otherwise disunited groups and factions within the population.

This process is seen in microcosm in the narrative quoted here and, specifically, in the personal response of the narrator himself in setting aside one facet of his identity and reassuming another. Thus, the narrator of the story indicates that as the opposition to the government increased he left his government post in a distant province and returned to his home. Returning home was a fairly logical move considering the ominous perception most people shared that the time ahead would be one of national upheaval, but, in the case of the narrator who was both a government administrator and a *sayyid*, the act of return implicitly reasserted an aspect of his identity (his *sayyid* status) that, in the context of his life prior to the beginning of the resistance, had been practically subordinate to and subsumed under his role as a government official.

The narrator then had two partial identities--one deriving from his achieved position in the government, the other deriving from his ascribed descent status and his position in the tribe. As identity is indicated by terms of address, the narrator's two identities are indicated by the two terms by which he is known to non-kinsmen, namely *Modir Sahib* and *Pacha Sahib*. The first of these can be translated as "respected director" and is used to address the narrator in situations in which his status as a ranking member of a bureaucratic organization is invoked; the second is a term of address that refers to his status as a respected *sayyid*, the term *pacha* being the common regional designation for a member of a *sayyid* lineage. When the opposition to the Khalqi regime began to mount, the *modir* left his post to reassert the *pacha* side of this public identity and to assume a position of leadership in the local uprising.

In Kunar, the attack on the narrator's family served on a local level to jell anti-government sentiment and to push passive dissatisfaction toward overt resistance. For all the government's attempts to neutralize the religious factor in public perception, its efforts were meaningless without the complicity and support of established religious figures to whom the people looked for advice and consent. Since few religious leaders sided with the new regime, the government tried to eliminate all those it viewed as the potential and likely nuclei of anti-government reaction, but once it invoked this option, the religious leaders it attacked became what it most feared. As could be expected given the defensive orientation of Afghan culture, attacks against respected religious figures were viewed as assaults against the culture at large and caused what was, in normal circumstance, a recessive part of cultural identity (i.e., being Muslims) to become the dominant feature allowing otherwise disparate tribal and ethnic units to join in common cause.

When the narrator arrived among the Mohmand, his symbolic connections and their implications were understood by everyone, for however deficient tribesmen might be in their knowledge of Islam, symbolic aspects of the faith are known to all. As a representative of this faith, the narrator took on the role of invoking these sacred precedents and making them relevant to the events at hand. Through the narrator's presence in the *jirgah*, the conflict with the government could be legitimated by defining it in Islamic terms. Since the regime in Kabul had proven itself to be an infidel government, jihad was *farz* (obligatory) for all Muslims. This was not to be a tribal *jang* (conflict) but an Islamically-based jihad against "infidels."

At the same time, the context in which this first uprising occurred was still very much a tribal one; the invocation of Islam took place in a tribal *jirgah* led by tribal elders and supported by tribesmen who were not incognizant of the possibility for booty and for the chance to demonstrate their own courage in a battle that also happened to have a sacred justification. Islam provided the symbolic background and the basis for legitimization, but traditional tribal values structured the actual response, a fact the narrator also understood as he invoked ancestral memory in conjunction with Islamic law charging the tribesmen with their responsibility to God and their fathers.

The outcome of the tribal *jirgah* was the formation of the peculiarly Pushtun fighting force: the *lashkar*. The *lashkar* system of mobilizing tribesmen for battle is well-suited to the dynamics of tribal structure since each lineage unit is independent and controlled only by its elders. Its fluid, non-hierarchical/non-rationalized design also helps to channel internal tribal and personal rivalries toward the common enemy since the entire *gaum* is present in one undifferentiated body. Each can see and judge the performance and bravery of the others in his tribe, and has the opportunity to push to the front, outdoing the efforts of his rivals, and gaining renown for himself. At the same time, the *lashkar* system is decidedly not conducive to the exigencies of modern warfare, being especially vulnerable to aerial and artillery attack, nor it is practical for prolonged periods of time since it has no logistical mechanism for feeding numerous fighters. If there were such a thing as a bestiary of military organizations, the *lashkar* would be characterized as the "shark," for it is effective only so long as it moves forward and can feed itself on the prey it manages to capture.

Lashkars are not designed with practical considerations in mind; they are temporary aggregations of tribesmen and tribal segments, each intent upon outdoing its opposite number(s) and, in the process, defeating the common enemy. If setbacks occur or if circumstances necessitate long delays in initiating attacks, *lashkars* become unwieldy, unmanageable, and vulnerable. The inadequacy of the *lashkar* system is indicated by the narrator who comments that a different sort of fighting was required against the government: one that demanded stealth, mobility, logistical support, and chains of command to facilitate coordinated operations. For this kind of a system, the tribe was not the most efficient system of organization, and consequently, most tribes soon abandoned the *lashkar* system and continued their struggle under the aegis and leadership of the various political parties that had established their headquarters across the border in Peshawar, Pakistan. The advent of political party control over the jihad essentially coincided with the Soviet decision to invade Afghanistan to bolster its disintegrating client regime. These two events together signalled the end of the first "civil" stage in the Afghan conflict.

CONCLUSION

Despite government claims that the counter-revolution in Afghanistan began as a reactionary backlash of the wealthy landowners against the liberating forces of the revolution, the popular resistance to the Marxist regime was too widespread and too immediate to be so blithely consigned to the dustbin of history. Resistance to the Kabul regime began within six months following the April 1978 coup, encompassed virtually the whole of the country within twelve months, and has continued against militarily and technologically superior forces for more than eight years. Such a movement does not begin and sustain itself for this length of time because of the disgruntlement of a limited number of wealthy landowners. Over four million Afghans have not become refugees in order to aid their former "exploiters."

Whatever the objective "facts" of land tenure, indebtedness, and other factors affecting the relations of production in Afghanistan, the solution proposed by the PDPA was soundly rejected. The revolution was never seen by the people as a "liberation." A base of support was never consolidated, and this must be recognized--to use an all-too-familiar phrase-- as a failure to engage "the hearts and minds" of the Afghan people, even if, as the regime contended, it was in the best interests of their stomachs and limbs. The popular uprisings sweeping over Afghanistan after the Marxist revolution in 1978 were unprecedented in Afghan history and involved a far greater percentage of the population than did the uprising against Amanullah in 1929 or even the two anti-British jihads of the nineteenth century which had relatively little impact in the northern and western regions of the country. The uprisings that broke out between 1978 and 1980 affected the entire country and ultimately eliminated almost all vestiges of government influence in the rural areas.

As the magnitude of the popular revolt became apparent to the PDPA leaders in Kabul, their response was to fall back on the time-worn strategy of trying to rally the tribes by calling forth the foreign threat. In a speech to elders of the Totakhel and Ahmadzai tribes, Taraki made the following accusations:

Farangis (foreigners) who are our old enemies are now showing their animosity towards us in another mask. Previously they used to send soldiers and arms and massacred the people of Afghanistan but now they carry the massacre in another way. Now they have other means such as radio, newspapers and other media. Through their spies they want to translate into action their previous ominous dreams...on the mountains they tell lies to our tribal people who have not come to Kabul and who are not informed of Kabul. They say that there [in Kabul] 500 mosques have been burnt and so forth. . . . The farangis and their puppets that is Ikhwan ul-Shayateen are going round village to village and house to house and carrying out different kinds of propaganda. Previously they used to charge us with infidelity but now sometimes they say we are cruel or sometimes other things. They change their words every time, for example, they roam about in the Kuchis [nomads'] places and tell them--if you go to Afghanistan they will confiscate your sheep and also your women.--Their women are our mothers and sisters, and we had never thought of taking anybody's sheep. We will never take anybody's sheep nor anybody's woman--who is our sister. She is our honor, and we make efforts to defend them every moment (*Kabul Times* May 16, 1979).

In defending his party and government from the accusations of his enemies, Taraki focused on the issue of deception, which also was at the heart of the preceding narrative, particularly in the matter of whether or not the Khalgis were really Muslims. For both sides, the matter of honesty and deception is a critical factor mediating the relationship between ruler and ruled and, consequently, Taraki's statements should not be read simply as the response of a man answering charges levelled against him by his opponents. The moral significance of deception can be judged first in the terms which Taraki uses to describe his enemies: "farangis" (or as they are frequently referred to in Khalqi news reports, "Muslim-looking farangis") and the "Ikhwan ul-Shayateen."(15) The first of these terms of reference is of long-standing currency and appears to originate in the Anglo-Afghan conflicts of the nineteenth century when the British are said to have engaged some of their Muslim subjects to spy inside Afghanistan. The second term, "Ikhwan ul-Shayateen," or the "Satanic Brotherhood," is an inversion of "Ikhwan ul-Muslimin," the name of the radical Islamic organization, the Muslim Brothers, that originated in Egypt and had a tremendous impact on the recent development of radical Islamic political ideology in Afghanistan. Although so-called fundamentalist ideology had been taken up by many younger, educated Afghans, the Islamic ideology, political organization, and leadership style associated with the "Ikhwanis" were not a great deal more popular in the traditional rural village milieu than was Marxism, and Taraki's statement tried to play on this mistrust of the "Ikhwanis" by referring to them in a manner which is both damning and demeaning.

These references attempted to counter the charge made against the Khalqis--that they pretended to be Muslims but were not--by claiming a counter-deception: that the enemies of the regime were themselves deceivers. In both of these terms of reference, Taraki also manipulated an existent, popular animosity toward outsiders, whether it be "made in London" Muslims or Afghan Muslims preaching a foreign and innovative interpretation of an immutable faith which heretofore had not been thought subject to novel interpretation. Beyond this, Taraki also played on an even more fundamental and personal fear than that of foreigners per se, the fear of being duped, of being made to look ridiculous in the eyes of others. He stated that the enemies of his regime "think that the people accept all their lies. But now the case is not like in the past when if somebody was told that [a] dog was running away with his ear he would chase the dog. Now they touch their ear with [their] hand" (*Kabul Times* May 16, 1979). This statement can be read both as a joke, a Mullah Nasruddin-type of reference to a kind of individual oblivious to the obvious; and, to this extent, it shows Taraki trying to identify with his audience and have them identify with him in the conspiracy of laughter and shared comprehension. At the same time, however, the attempted conspiracy turns on the rhetoric of rebuke and the underlying fear of personal humiliation, and Taraki cast his attempt to enlist the support of these Pushtun elders, not in the language of class solidarity (as he does with the so-called "peasants") but in the language of honor preserved ("your women are our mothers and sisters, your honor is our honor") and dishonor negated ("don't be duped, don't be made to look foolish").

In contrast to the accusations made against the regime by the "farangis and their bowl-lickers--Ikhwanis," Taraki claimed that "whatever we have done is in line with Shariat of Islam. . . . If Shariat says so we accept it, if Shariat does not allow how can we do it by force" (*Kabul Times* May 16, 1979). While it is true that certain social reforms against usury and excessive bride-price payments were more in keeping with *shariat* law than the tribal customs they meant to replace, Taraki's defense of his regime was inadequate in its attempt to blame outsiders for internal problems. Past leaders, of course, used this tactic successfully. Amanullah, Nadir Khan, Daoud--all had effectively used a real or purported foreign threat to their advantage, but the same was not to be the case for Taraki who, however vehemently he drew attention to "Muslim-looking farangis," only served to remind those same people of the Russian "farangis" backing the regime.

All Afghans--especially those living in the north but others as well--were concerned with Soviet influence in Afghanistan, which was perceived to have increased during the reign of Muhammad Daoud and to have grown even more since Taraki assumed power. Throughout his tenure in office, Taraki sought to assure the people that Afghanistan would not become a Marxist state and that, even though the government respected the Soviets, it would retain its independence from Soviet control. These protestations were never believed, however, for the words of denial conflicted with the ideology of class struggle and historical materialism preached in every village. Though Afghans had never heard these words before in their own milieu, they were familiar with Marxist rhetoric, for like others in the region they had listened to Soviet radio broadcasts, including both the programs broadcast in Afghan Dari Persian and Pushtu as well as the domestic Soviet broadcasts in Tajiki Persian. As a result of this, when the Khalqi cadres began using the same vocabulary and same kind of slogans they heard so often on the radio, Afghans immediately recognized where they had come from, no matter how strident the declarations to the contrary. In the eyes of the majority of Afghans, the "farangis" were in Kabul, not in the ranks of the resistance. This perception that the government no longer represented Afghan interests and Afghan values provided the pivotal understanding around which Afghans generally formed their ideological and militant response to the successor Marxist regimes.

NOTES

1. For an overview of the period between the Marxist coup d'etat in April 1978 and the Soviet invasion in December 1980, cf. Chaffetz (1980), Dastarac and Levant (1980), Dupree (1978-1980), and Halliday (1978,1980).

2. The one non-Durrani Pushtun to rule Afghanistan was the Tajik "bandit," Habibullah (Bach-e Saqao), who reigned for one year (1928-1929).

3. See "The Basic Principles of the DRA," Chapter 1, paragraph 3.

4. See *Kabul Times*, May 20, 1978. The first of the publicized *jirgahs* was held on May 7, 1978, and was attended by the leaders of the Shinwari, Utmanzai, Ahmadzai, Wazir, Bangash, Turi, and other smaller tribes. On May 16, Taraki

met with elders of the Atmer Khel, Khwajazai, Khoga Khel, Utman Khel, Mohmand, Afridi, and Ahmadzai Wazir tribes. From May 20-24, Taraki met and posed for photographs with leaders of the Mangal, Zadran, and other tribes of Paktia Province and the cross-border region, along with a lesser number of representatives of tribes from other predominantly Pushtun areas and a few non-Pushtun areas as well. The majority of those attending the *jirgahs* were Pushtuns from the border provinces of Kunar (e.g., Mohmand), Ningrahar (Shinwari, Utmanzai), and Paktia (Mangal, Zadran), and from cross-border tribes such as the Wazir and Afridi. Each of these tribes played important roles in anti-government revolts, particularly the 1929 revolt against King Amanullah; and at least one tribe, Mangal, had been involved in uprisings in 1914 and 1924, as well as in 1929. One of the political gambits played in Taraki's first months in office involved the strategic reference to the border areas of Pakistan and Afghanistan as "Pushtunistan." While sure to incite the rage of the Pakistani government, which could be mollified through diplomatic channels, it enlivened the pride and fellow-feeling of the tribes toward the regime in Kabul, and advanced a cause dear to their hearts.

5. The text of Decree No. 6 appearing in the *Kabul Times* on July 18, 1978, also can be found in *The Afghanistan Council Newsletter VI*, no. 3, Fall 1978.

6. The text of Decree No. 8 appeared in the *Kabul Times* on October 18, 1978.

7. *Afghanistan: Islam and Political Modernity* was translated from French into English by the Foreign Broadcasting Information Service (JPRS-NEA-85-116/11 September 1985).

8. "The Basic Lines of Revolutionary Duties of Government," appearing in the *Kabul Times* on May 10, 1978, included the following: "1. Implementation of democratic land reforms in the interest of the toiling farmers with their participation. . . . 2. Abolition of old feudal and pre-feudal relation." Decree No. 8, promulgated on November 29, 1978, repeated the same theme in Article One in which the objective was the "elimination of feudal and pre-feudal relations" (*Kabul Times* December 2, 1978).

9. These figures were reported in the *Kabul Times*, April 2, 1979. Figures on land redistribution began to appear in the press in early February (February 6: 26,000 *jeribs* to

2,804 peasants) and continued regularly thereafter (March 12: 736,679 *jeribs* to 75,000 peasants; April 2: 1,024,000 *jeribs* to 104,000 peasants; June 11: 2.57 million *jeribs* to 224,000).

10.   The article referenced here comes from "The Basic Directives of 5 Yr Plan of DRA (1358-62)" in the *Kabul Times*, August 9, 1979.

11.   See Gluckhoded (1981, 240 and 236), cf. also, Shahrani (1984, 3-57).

12.   See Roy (1985, 84), cf. also, Schneiter (1980, 237-244).

13.   Information on the Pech and Nuristan uprisings was obtained in interviews conducted in Peshawar during 1983 and 1984 with a number of local residents who were involved in these events.

14.   Cf. Roy (1985, 85) and Hyman (1982).

15.   References to the "Ikhwan ul-Shayateen" in the press began on October 1, 1978, in an article written by Suleiman Leyeq in which "Ikhwanis" are accused of having torn up copies of the Qur'an at Kabul University in 1970 and of hollowing out copies of the holy book to carry weapons. In an article that appeared on April 1, 1979, members of the religious opposition are described as follows: "these 'brothers of Satan,' these Muslim-looking 'farangis' clad in white but not able to cover their black faces, these false clergymen who have been inspired by London and Paris...They are actually ignorant of Islam as they have only learned espionage techniques in London. They wish our people to abandon their religion and be marked with a seal from London."

2

Leadership Dilemmas: Challenges and Responses

Sultan A. Aziz

The current war in Afghanistan is in its eighth year with no prospective end in sight. The one dominant issue of this war from early on has been the controversial issue of leadership among the resistance. Journalists, academics and "old Afghan hands" have all contributed the assessment of their leaders. The overwhelming consensus by the "experts" seems to paint a less than hopeful picture. The general thrust of their analysis indicates a society so fractious that the notion of common values, so crucial to unity, and effective leadership is an unattainable goal. Their assessments too often serve as backdrop for important decisions and policies by governments supportive of the Afghan resistance.

The picture need not be so grim. After all, the Afghan resistance with or without leadership has been able to deny the Soviets their coveted goal to pacify and completely control Afghanistan. The evident staying power of the resistance seems to indicate a more robust political process than previously assumed. For better or worse the war has forced Afghans into an unenviable role. The result of which has accelerated the pace of social and political activity. The important point is to trace the origins of these activities and to investigate their roots. In doing so it is hoped that a clearer picture of political and social behaviour will emerge, one that would place the present disarray among the resistance groups in perspective; but it should be stated emphatically at the onset that resistance problems are not all attributable to lack of effective leadership among the various groups; it is also the presence of competing international and regional agendas, and of their proponents, that equally affect leaders and leadership alike.

The attempt in this chapter is to place leadership roles in a general analytic framework, one which will help explain the evolution of Afghan leadership patterns. Such patterns, though spatially remote, nonetheless, have had disproportionate influence on Afghan social and political institutions. It is argued here that the last thirty years have produced substantial change within the Afghan body politic where political tradition is adapting to the realities of a qualitatively different political and social agenda. The resultant absence of consensually based leadership merely reflects the complex dynamics of political and social realignments that are taking place in Afghan society. Furthermore, the notion that the future of Afghanistan and its people is best served by a return to a narrow interpretation of traditional political practice is not correct. The underlying assumption that traditional political systems by definition do not undergo change and so are more stable at the price of crucial adaptability is a mistaken idea. The so-called "traditional" systems display not only change to accommodate new political realities but also display a great deal of resiliencies in maintaining their own social and political identities.

THE STATIC MODEL

Historically, political leadership has been the domain of Pushtuns in Afghanistan, in part because Pushtuns formed the largest segment of the population and also exercised the monopoly of political power. From early in the 18th century until the 1978 "Saur" Revolution, Pushtun political influence in symbolic and in real terms has been dominant. This preponderance of political power obviously has not been devoid of crucial evolutionary elements. That is to say, the Pushtun exercise of political power in itself has undergone important changes, changes that reflect the infusion of new ideas and value structures.(1)

The evolution of the state in Afghan political life is not, however, necessarily synonymous with Pushtun political aspirations. Others have contributed a great deal to the integration of political thought and methods; however, their effectiveness was often muted by their insistence on parity and equality, a requirement that many Pushtun leaders were quite uncomfortable in acknowledging. Thus the paradox: political development and integration were considered suspect not only by the majority but also by the various ethnic minorities. The majority saw the conspiratorial hand of the overachieving minorities; the minorities had their political memories to turn to--as if their abject social and economic conditions were not proof enough of problems in dealing with the political majority.

The precarious mission of the Afghan state to promote modernity in Afghanistan always has been judged by its ability to mitigate and presumably extirpate such hostilities. The study of Afghan political development also has been preoccupied with the structural processes of "ethnicity and politics" where anthropological studies unravel the mysteries of a "developing" people. These conditions hindered any organized study of political change. A handful of scholars may have considered that there are viable and robust processes of political and social organization worthy of study, but their realization went no further precisely at this at this national level of analysis where the various elements of tribe, state, ethnicity and religion intersect. Also, at such a level, leaders articulate, agree, disagree, conspire, and retire. Therefore, the national political structure must be studied in depth.

The question of leadership among the Pushtuns has been dealt with extensively in the anthropological literature elsewhere. However, the interaction of Pushtuns with Uzbeks, Tajiks, Hazaras, Aimaqs, Nuristanis, Turkomans, Baluchis, and Arabs, the emergent political accommodation among these various groups, and the institutional vehicle that affects political communication among them are of interest. Communication assumes that social structures can be bridged for political purposes (Deutsch, 1976). Political objectives may vary; they need not affect the internal social environment. However, such communication in Afghanistan has been possible without the intrusive presence of the state (Kakar, 1982). As a result, leadership patterns have been constrained by their particularistic environment, with the notable exceptions of foreign and state intervention.

Moreover, it is at this level of analysis that patterns of political intervention by the state and other actors form the predispositional base for a coherent appraisal of elite recruitment and leadership roles. Consequently, the patterns of leadership run the gamut of kin-based allegiances all the way to the integrated hierarchical organizations of Islamist fundamentalist.

A HISTORICAL PERSPECTIVE

The most relevant political history of Afghanistan for this inquiry starts with ascent of King Amanullah (1919-1924). [While it is true that Amir Abdur Rahman Khan (1880-1901) shaped the Afghan state, nonetheless the institution of the state subordinated itself to the principal task of consolidating the territory for the Amir to role.] Amanullah's reign is of interest for the following reasons: a) It produced a radical break from patterns of tribally accepted norms; b) It introduced Islam into the political equation, not as a traditional dimension of state-tribe relations but in fact as the arbitrator of civil and political society; and c) It demonstrated the irreversibility of the state's presence and its coercive character.

What is true now for the Pushtuns perhaps was true at the time of Amanullah as well: the realm of social activity rests within the domain of the tribe and all political activities affecting it are by definition subject to question and debate. However, the state that idealized the King's wishes for an enlightened nation did not quite fit with the institutional notion of tribal priorities. The consequence of such incongruity was the departure of the King and the downgrading of various intrusive state mechanisms (Adamec, 1974).

The vision that Amanullah harbored for his country was formed in places other than the social setting from which he came. The alien symbols that his programs conveyed did not capture the imagination of his fellow countrymen. The fact that he sought intellectually and programatically to distance himself from their tightly held value system portrayed him as an illegitimate, exogenous symbol and not as an Afghan and a good Muslim. The tribal and non-tribal elements of Afghan society shared a deep reverence for Islam and would not tolerate what they considered to be unmistakable deviation from accepted norms. The problem of alienation was compounded further when the King referred to himself as an Afghan, a claim to universality by Afghanistan, a concept acceptable to most Pushtuns in principle but not in reality. Pushtun history, after all, was the legacy of conquests, the embodiment of Pushtun national prestige by previous Afghan kings; it was not some distant historic abstraction. For the Pushtuns it meant a level of commitment by "their King" (*de moong badshah*) to ideals that in real terms, at best, did not include equality of position with a non-Pushtun. Pushtun tribesmen recognized the rhetorical value of their claim, but often had settled for less in terms of totally dominating national politics (Adamec, 1974).

The King was a Durrani, a Pushtun, but in the constellation of Pushtun tribal symbols, he had fallen from grace. The Durrani King had ceased to behave like a Pushtun (*Pushtu Kawool*). The distance he maintained was not only rationalized toward the Pushtuns by his universalist approach, but his sin was the more grevious for ignoring Pushtun honor. The national leader had to go!

Durrani rulers from the time of Amir Abdur Rahman implicity placed trust in their brethren among the tribes to provide them with security in periods of national emergency. The psychological dimension to the crisis response is perhaps unique. The Durrani rulers always have suffered from a paradox: on the one hand they have been the proponents of a strong, centralized state; yet on the other hand they have always wished and longed for their particularistic tribal identity. The movement toward universality stripped them, in their eyes, of a historic claim to rule. Tribal identity, given the realities of their own experience, formed their instinctive desire to find refuge in a mythical tribal past that they themselves had rejected. Political genies once unleashed are rarely contained. The inevitability of change and challenge became the ghosts that haunted Durrani leaders until the "Saur" Revolution of 1978.

TRADITIONAL LEADERSHIP STRATEGIES AND THE "STATE" (HOKUMAT)

Normative leadership strategies of Pushtuns and non-Pushtuns alike rested on their perception and ability to influence the "State" or "Hokumat." Beyond the states' principle of non interference with tribal areas in general, the institutional nature of state intrusion were felt by all. For example, compulsory conscription into the military, a tradition continued from the time of Amir Abdur Rahman, notwithstanding a brief hiatus during the rebellion in the reign of Amir Habibullah (1901-1919), was reintroduced under the rule of King Nadir Shah (1929-1933) (Adamec, 1974). The practical effect was to integrate further the disparate population and to provide a continual source of raw manpower, a tradition that continues. Compulsory enrollment for military service is an example of a tradition that continues and is all too real at the present time.

Afghan governments from the period of Nadir Khan to the present have sought to use the leverage of the state's legal and moral mandate to effect programatic change in all facets of social life, with the notable exception of Islam. In Afghanistan, Islam etched in the mind of adherents the message that the realm of civil society and political society were coterminus. Whether the more complicated definitions of what constituted civil and political authority were addressed by the state did not matter. What mattered was the practical application of policies by the state. The legal argument for the presence of the state was that the person of the King through his very position, as the defender of the faith, was consistently qualified under Islamic law. However, the Muslim scholars, or *ulama*, who for the most part were patrons of the state, did not argue with such a claim, despite the fact that in Islam the concept of monarchy is firmly rejected. Despite this seemingly important contradiction, Afghan monarchs enjoyed the support of the religious establishment.

The relationship between the state and the religious establishment goes back to early years of Afghan monarchy. The *ulama* or scholars were always present and accessible to the state to dispense advice on variety of matters. Their legal standing rooted in Islamic law *sharia* went beyond their role as scholars. The *alim* by definition was a person who had mastered Islamic law, a position that allowed him considerable latitude in the political sphere. A possible contributing factor might have been that most if not all the *ulama* were employees of the state. The remaining members of the religious establishment were the mullahs. Interestingly enough the mullahs were for the most part considered 'uneducated' by the *ulama*, a fact that the French scholar Olivier Roy considers a contributing factor to the mullah's political militancy (Unpublished monograph, 1985).

The mullahs on the other hand, were to be found at all levels of social organization. The mullah was involved in the day to day affairs of the population, where all matters of social and political importance were discussed. However, the level of social and political leadership on part of the mullah nevertheless was constrained by by the presence of others such as tribal leaders (Khans) or other charismatic religious leaders (Pirs). The tacit support of the *ulama* by the government did not always find popular expression among the people in the countryside, partially because policies sanctioned by the *ulama* failed to come to grips with the realities of rural life. Unresolved issues in rural life were not of a judicial nature (an area of traditional activity of the *ulama*) but were in essence political. The state's increased involvement in rural life elevated the standing of the mullah. Problems of political nature were to become the domain of the mullah, as such, for he was better suited to interpret government policies, at least from the local perspective. Additionally, the mullah, by the virtue of his religious station in life, was the natural arbitrator of communal values. The only exception to this customary role was found among Pushtun tribes.

Among the Pushtuns, the mullah performed a more defined role, in which his realm of activity is restricted to his clerical duties including marriage, the collection of *zakat* (alms), and leading prayers. The only exceptions in subscribing to these duties has been in times of war. The leadership role at such moment shifts from the Khan to the mullah. The role of the mullah among tribal and nontribal peoples has been basically to provide the legal sanction (*fitwah*) to move against the would-be enemies of the Muslim community (*umma*), be they fellow tribesmen or foreign invaders. The legal concept of jihad in Islam, quite narrow by definition, nonetheless has been liberally used by its practitioners to invalidate a potential foe's standing among the community's would-be believers. By declaring an enemy a *kafir*, all the institutional requirements of resistance against the declared evil are met. The elasticity in leadership roles pits the mullah and the Khan against each other

on a competitive course. Such competition is usually mitigated, however, by the fact that extraordinary circumstances
have prevailed during times of crisis when the Khan cannot
marshall the material resources demanded by his role and
has deferred to the temporal authority of the mullah
(Lindholm, 1982).

The potential for control of rural political alliances was
obviously not lost on the government. The periodic meeting
of the *Loya Jirgah*, a traditional practice of convening a
national council representing all segments of the population,
was one of the many avenues used by the government to
legitimize its national programs. *Jirgahs* in general and the
Loya Jirgah in particular served a useful political function.
Aside from being a consensus-creating device, in most
instances it served as a neutralizing vehicle. The social
rules of Pushtun tribal conduct emphasized the conciliatory
nature of *jirgahs*. As a consequence, the supposedly binding
agreements that emerged operated from the premise that it
was the sole repository of legal action and that not all
agreements undertaken at *jirgahs* necessitated compliance.
These events, in turn, forced many would-be leaders and
Khans to pursue other channels of communication with the
central government. The use of money by local leaders to
influence the government's representative was one of many
methods used. In some instances leaders would directly
contact the royal court for an audience with the King and
later on with the President, Daoud; in fact as late as
Taraki's regime such communication channels were effectively used.

The result of government's social and programmatic
activity created alternative methods for local leaders to
pursue: those local leaders who insisted that the state deal
with them on a bilateral basis found the state to be quite
unaccommodating. The alternative was either to pursue
their concern through the maze of bureaucratic structures
or to retrench and pursue a more localized network. These
tactics were partly successful because the government lacked
the material resources to make its full presence felt on the
entire population. Additionally, this seemingly contradictory
partial vacuum of authority also may explain the occasional
challenges to government projects in rural areas.(2)

For some leaders the prospect of government recognition
meant the possibility of increased aid and help to their

communities. Such recognition also required the leader to be physically present in the capital, if only to keep an eye on the interests of his constituencies. The broker role for some of the leaders was also a launching pad to tap into the elite network that dominated the state apparatus. Personal rewards existed for promoting the government's agenda. A common practice was to enroll a leader's son in the local military academy. The prestige of such undertakings favorably affected the population at home. These events also underscored the political affiliation and standing that the leader or group enjoyed vis-a-vis the government.

The "live and let live" policy of the government towards the rural population occurred principally because of its preoccupation with consolidating itself in the larger cities. By extending the arm of the state to the larger metropolitan area the government intruded further and promoted its programs in more remote areas. The construction of a highway network, for example, also hastened the process of bringing the outlying area into the grid of regional economic (not to mention political) activity. The modernizing efforts of the state were not devoid of political content. Nevertheless, the expression of its political character became a major liability, a political liability that future generations were to bear.

AGENDAS AND LEADERS

Elite roles, political participation and the emergence of intermediate political structures did not take place till the latter part of Zahir Shah's tenure. The activism of the period was intitated by none other than the King's own cousin, Daoud Khan. Daoud initially ruled as Prime Minister for a decade (1953-1963). The various policies that he undertook were quite radical and uncompromising. His vision of bringing Afghanistan into the fold of modernity implied a quantum leap. The sudden political and philosophical shift in state action strained the delicate balance traditionally maintained between the center and the periphery. This shift does not suggest Afghans were xenophobes for they tried to understand the world around them from their own unique cultural and historic perspective. Daoud's vision did not accommodate their world view. His understanding of the world was a curious mix of national chauvinism coupled with a sincere desire to help build a modern Afghanistan.(3)

As a leader Daoud displayed confusing tendencies; while correctly assessing the needs for a structural change in the economic sphere, he neglected to understand the impact of his plans in the social realm. The rationalizing of state intrusion, into areas which until that time had constituted private activity, became a symbolic issue for Afghans to resist government encroachment. The relations between the traditional "center" (*hokumat*) and outlying areas (*atraf*) became hostile and antagonistic. The task of implementing reforms and projects became difficult. The government's response was to dispatch more bureaucratic experts. Opposition to Daoud's plans resulted in the appearance of leaders and elites who for the most part had remained either underground or just simply uninterested in participating in a system that was closed to them. There were many instances of opposition to government policies, prior to Daoud's rule. What they lacked was the institutional character that distinguished them from personal or intratribal feuds.

Daoud's irredentist preoccupation with the Pushtunistan issue, whereby Afghanistan would gain support for claims to land inhabited in present day Pakistan by Pushtuns and Baluchis, became the focal, if somewhat muted, point of protest by mostly non-Pushtuns and clerical elements within the country. Minorities such as the Tajiks and Uzbeks saw themselves as major contributors to the national economy. Yet, their political influence was quite limited. They saw the government's increasing commitment to a cause that would sap the resources of their country, with uncertain results. The symbolic issue of Pushtun political priorities in itself was seen as a sign of their political arrogance. The clergy always had approached the government's modernizing political initiatives with ambivalence and suspicion. The Pushtunistan issue was even more vexing to them because the alleged "antagonists" were Pakistani Muslim brethren. The legal Quranic basis for political and military sanctions against fellow Muslims did not exist. The problem for most of the clergy therefore was found within the Pushtun tribes. Among the Pushtuns the clergy adopted a relatively lower profile, given the issue of kin-based alliances and tribal connections. In retrospect, evidence suggests support among tribal elements on the Pushtunistan issue was lukewarm at best.(4)

To justify his claim to territory lying to the east of the British-imposed Durand Line, Daoud undertook a more ambitious stance on the Pushtunistan issue. He chose to demonstrate symbolically the depth of his conviction on the issue by stirring the majority versus minority argument. By creating a national debate without the benefit of politically relevant institutions, he further stirred regional animosities and suspicions. The question of the Pushtuns being a majority had very little to do with Pushtunistan, and quickly regressed to such symbolic issues as language. Among the minorities the Pushtunistan issue was recognized for what it was, namely, a political prop from another stage in Pushtun political dominance. Yet, the minorities' response was subdued and generally supportive and low key. The minorities aquiescence indicated a desire to continue their participation in political life. The majority, except for the traditional Durrani Pushtuns, most of whom did not speak Pushtu, in many ways did not share the benefits of political power. They felt even more bitter and ready to embrace Daoud's symbolic gestures. The cumulative effect was to force the King to sideline Daoud (in 1963) and introduce basic political change.

The introduction of the 1964 constitutional reforms and the declaration of freedom of speech and political activity introduced a new dimension for would-be leaders. The institutional mechanisms of party officially were not in place, but that did not matter much. Overnight twenty or so publications appeared with editorial staffs to follow. Almost all of the tabloids professed a particular ideology. The pace of political activity was even more brisk among the students. The elements representing the religious establishment were mostly students or faculty members in the theological college at Kabul   University. Left wing groups of all ideological shades were also among those pressing for a more rapid pace in the reforms.

The result of these political changes was division, not national unity. The constitutional experiment suffered from some inborn ailments from its very birth; the institutional character of Afghan political life did not quite square with the arbitrary separation of civil and political society. Social matters formed the principal layer of political values. The debate that lasted for fifty years about Pushtun domination, linguistic hegemony, and disproportionate neglect of the minority would not be resolved by simply dressing it another political garb. The argument by the disenfranchised political elements was that the new political arrangement did not fundamentally alter the political power equation and as consequence was seen to be even more disruptive, while the imposition of modern political practice was considered hostile to religion and traditional education.(5)

The reform period saw three types of basic leadership strategies: first, the leftist agitational and confrontational style, that would further polarize the centers of political power, allowing them to operate with relative ease; secondly, the emergence of ethnic based leaders whose social agenda would be limited to their respective ethnic constituencies; third, the fundamentalist or religious leaders trained in different *madrassahs* (religious schools) that would maintain extensive ties to the rural population. The center *markaz* or *hokumat* versus *atraf* or "periphery" dichotomy that always has been part of the Afghan political scene once more figured into the strategies of would be leaders.

The leadership strategies of those who chose to operate in the rural areas have been of principal concern and importance. Among the religious groups there was a loose organization of students and pupils (*talaba*) from various religious institutions. Although, some like Olivier Roy have argued that their principal philosophical outlook was much more radical than the traditional network of *mawlawis* (clerics of some legal standing) and mullahs, during this period a certain amount of political retrenching seemed to take place. Most of the religious students found themselves operating within the confines of tribe or ethnic rules, and as such their programmatic approach took account of the traditional sensibilities of the people among whom they lived. However, their message to the rural elements was received quite readily when they combined religious teaching with social analysis of their political condition.

In contrast, the principal leftist leaders who chose to return among their fellow villagers were the Khalqi and *Shula-i-Jawed* groups. The Khalqis were predominantly Pushtuns, and their ability to influence their fellow tribesmen mostly played on the relative economic imbalance that existed within and outside of the tribe. The approach was

novel: first   the   would-be   tribesman   saw   himself   as
exploited by another co-equal, the Khan, and so the egali-
tarian notion of equality formed an important part of Pushtun value structures; second, the idea was promoted that
others, namely non-Pushtuns, were acquiring more than their
share   at   his/their   expense   (Roy,   1985   Unpublished
manuscript).

The potential to mobilize disgruntled Pushtuns through
such tactics has to be viewed in the broader context of
tribal relations.   Among the Pushtuns, the majority of the
Khalqis were school teachers; this fact in itself tended to
isolate the Khalqi, given the anti-secular view of education,
and tribal hostility went a long way to check the influence
of the teachers.   As a consequence of such local hostilities
a number of clashes between students representing the
fledgling Islamic movement, and the Khalqi teachers were
reported.   In the southeast, matters got so bad that the
provincial government sent troops to extract the embattled
teachers.

Strategy on the part of the *Shula-i-Jawed* leaders was to
concentrate in the northweastern provinces.   The *Shula*'s
Maoist ideology played on the simple disparity between
peoples in the northeast and peoples in the other parts of
the country.   Therefore, the Shula was able to mobilize
successfully people in the northeast.   Eventually, with the
turn of events that the country would take they, as well as
all other groups and leaders, reassessed their strategies.

Between the constitutional period and the fall of Daoud
in 1978, most political leaders, with the exception of the
Marxist-Leninists, discovered the limits and the possibilities
for change in Afghanistan.   The fundamental agenda of the
country remained essentially unchanged; what had changed
was the experience of the various leaders and elites.   Too
often seen by many would-be leaders, on either side of the
political spectrum, was that the prospects for a meaningful
transition meant fundamental change, a break with the past.
The irony in this approach was that they had forgotten
their collective history.   Leaders neglected to understand
that the years of forced and social experimentation had
deeply affected the so called traditional population.   The
Afghan people, regardless of their ethnic affiliation, had
access to a more meaningful set of rules and political
ideology, Islam.

Islam was not an archaic construction for the rural population of Afghanistan. Islam embodied a concrete set of rules that Afghans understood and above all had practiced for millenniums. The change visited on the rural people was the ideological dimension of Islam, a concept quite alien to most Afghans who understood Islam in its concrete social aspects. But political Islam was a new idea, an idea to be lived and understood, an idea that would accelerate with the Marxist coup and the Soviet invasion of Afghanistan.

CURRENT LEADERSHIP AND
THE CHALLENGE OF RESISTANCE

The traditional elites chose to watch the events unfold after the Soviet invasion. Many reasons were cited for the traditional elites' dearth of activity; the principal one was a lack of credibility among the people. Their involvement in the Daoud regimes and their acquiescence to accepting the new order were marks against them. The traditional rural elites were more effective in organizing the promoting resistance; however, they also found the tribal and traditional cleavages to be too much to overcome. The religious leaders had a better chance, for they pointed to the un-Islamic character of the newly installed regime, and in doing so legitimized the universality of the war in the form of jihad.

The beginning of the jihad saw some confusion, no doubt inevitable given the programmatic and philosophical outlook of a young and fledgling resistance effort against a superpower. The various realignments basically fell in two categories: the so-called fundamentalists and the traditionalists. The assumption about the two groups capabilities indicated their respective leadership, and the personal qualities of the leaders themselves became the focus of debate.

Much has been said about the resistance leaders in Peshawar; not all that is said is complimentary. The resistance's social organization at the leadership level may account for this attitude. The transition from a political milieu in Afghanistan, where personal relationships reflected and for most had replaced the institutional requirement of individual accountability, was the operative political culture. Institutional development in Afghanistans always has had a comparable rival, that of family, clan, tribe, and ethnic group. The theoretical argument that stratification is inevitable as a consequence of economic integration has had a limited application in Afghan society.(7) However, in this study reviewing the importance of social structures is not necessary in order to explain them.

What is remarkable is the degree of resiliency and resistance that Afghan society has shown to the change that accompanies economic and political integration. The implicit trust placed in political society and the state, as the corner stone of modern government, has not been felt by Afghans. The argument is made that a people's collective historic memory is the best guide to its political future. The people within the resistance and within Afghanistan reflect this reality, as people once again have accepted their responsibility to fight an aggressor who poses as extreme danger to all. The personalization of institutional political relationships is a reaction to the relative disintegration of traditional and religious values.   To reverse this trend, the personal values implicit in an ideal Islamic society have been reintroduced.   Afghans rarely distinguish between their traditional ties and their commitment to Islam. To make a distinction is to impose unnecessary distance between the two.

The popular understanding and rationalization of Islam may be one thing; the current political symbols it embodies among the resistance is quite another.   The ideological dimension of Islam has surprised many would-be leaders within the resistance. Nearly all leaders of the resistance groups rationalize their affiliations to the resistance through some mode of religious association, and the realm of political action includes all the politically relevant maximizing strategies, and the fundamentalist believes in an active, viable, and ideologically committed Islam, where political interpretation obviates the need for a learned Muslim scholar.(8) The fundamentalist also seeks to reorder the political variables from the strictly mechanistic and legally bound tradition of Islam. On the contrary, this reality does not necessarily imply that there exists an alternative to the exhaustive legal and judicial components of Islam. The tradition merely infuses the sphere of politics with the neglected aspect of Islamic activism.

On the other hand, the traditionalist Islamic groups place

more emphasis on the legal aspect of social justice. The war is interpreted in terms consistent with that view, namely that the Prophet and Quranic scripture are the legitimate sources to guide them. This view fits quite well with the more salient aspects of tribal and ethnic affiliations, through which the practice of a traditional Islam is sanctioned in legal practice. The principal exceptions, of course, are the Sufi orders and millenarian movements that still have a sizable following among the Afghan population. Within both the traditionalist and the fundamentalist leadership there is above all the understanding that Afghan society by its very historic and cultural circumstances tends to be quite conservative. The relative issue of Islamic activism must be understood to reflect those values that conform to an ethical system--one in which all actions undertaken by Muslims are in harmony with *sunna* of the Prophet.

While the resistance has been portrayed by many as weak and ineffectual, it nonetheless enjoys the wide support among the Afghan people in and out of the country. The lack of management and coordination among the resistance can be attributed to leadership style and administrative abilities.

This style is attributed to personality factors. Personalities of leaders are important in that they set the tone of their specific agendas. Among the traditional leaders Gulbuddin Hekmatyar, who heads the Hizb-i-Islami, conjures up various images. Most tend to be negative given his alleged tendency to deal harshly with his critics. It may well have something to do with his philosophical priorities, which are said to be somewhat different from those of the other resistance leaders. In any case, he is credited with creating a very efficient organization in and out of the country. His popularity is mainly among young fundamentalists and certain Pushtun groups. His style, though confrontational, is characterized by a quick wit and a keen memory for details. Although some critics have suggested that his popularity is waning and his base of support is shrinking, he does retain a considerable following among Afghan refugees in Pakistan.

Other leaders' styles are very different from Hekmatyar's. For example, the head of the Hizb-i-Islami faction, Yunus Khalis, is a dedicated mullah with humble roots. He is looked up to and is considered a pragmatist, with a successful war record. Professor Abdul Rasul Sayaf, with his extended Arab supporters, does not have a very large base of support and is increasingly considered as an opportunist in some quarters.

Professor Burhanuddin Rabbani, the leader of Jamiat-i-Islami, one of the largest groups, is a theology professor who formerly taught at Kabul University. His style is one of consensus and coalition building, as far as it is possible; his principal source of support is among the Tajik people and groups in Paghman and the north.

The traditionalists include Sibghatullah Mujaddidi, a former professor at the University of Kabul and head of Jabha-i-Nejat-i-Melli-Afghanistan. Mujaddidi was credited with having carried on a personal crusade to stop Daoud's efforts at proximity accommodation with the Soviets. He spent many years in prison as a result of his anti-Daoud activities. He currently has a sizable base of followers, which does not necessarily translate into a large military contingent. His ties to the old regime detract from his popularity among other segments of the rural population. His principal aides and advisors tend to be his immediate relatives and cousins. His organizational abilities are considered quite modest. Nevertheless, he commands considerable respect among traditional tribal leaders.

In contrast, Mawlawi Muhammad Nabi has probably the largest organization among those in the resistance, the Harakat-i-Inquilab-i-Islami. His group is made up of all segments of Afghan society, although the majority tend to be Pushtun. A charismatic figure, he is a good orator and is considered the common man's leader. His organizational abilities leave a lot to be desired, however. The unwieldiness of his organization has limited his fighting ability in more recent times.

Finally, there is the leadership of Sayyid Gailani and his Mahaz-i-Melli-i-Islamiye Afghanistan. He is considered a royalist with limited fighting and organizational zeal. Despite the fact that he has some able people, he has chosen to maintain control in his own limited style. Although he commands a traditional following among the tribes, his base of support is considerably smaller because of his ineffectual administrative style.

The limitation on style and organizational efficiency is part of a greater problem that faces the resistance. A good number of the people with logistical and management abilities who joined the resistance came from the bureaucratic elements of the Afghan civil service system. Many of these refugees operated under private directives of the resistance leaders, thus making the waging of a major war against a modern enemy quite difficult. The problem was exacerbated further by the bureaucrats themselves. Their new role in the resistance did not change their old bureaucratic habits. The ability to move efficiently laterally and horizontally within the administrative structure requires a level of managerial expertise that counters petty bureaucratic and inefficiency, an ability many leaders lacked.

This inablity to perform and manage efficiently the day-to-day operations of the war has had two important consequences. First, it has too often involved leaders in basic decisions that could easily be handled by the person in chrage. Second, it has unnecessarily forced the resistance leaders to make decisions that are ultimately translated into personal grudges. The result is strained relations between leaders and followers, in the process creating distractions that are time consuming and often unproductive. Additionally, the cumbersome bureaucratic network is creating an image problem for the resistance, who are seen to behave very much in the same manner that previous government officials behaved. In a sense not much has changed. Behavioral patterns reflect historical patterns.(9)

THE INTERNATIONAL PERSPECTIVE

The resistance's ability to project a positive international image is viewed as its principal problem in communicating its version of the war. The various representatives of the resistance in Europe and the United States are not familiar with even the most basic concepts of public relations. The problem seems to stem from a profound misperception and reading of European and American public and private reaction to the Soviet invasion. It is taken as an article of faith that the people in the West understand and support the Afghan cause. Such an assumption is all the more damaging as it distorts the resistance movement's relative political weight in relation to the resistance's perceived material and political support. The resistance would do well to strengthen its ability to communicate its side of the war in symbolic terms by calling attention to values and ideals it shared with the west.

The resistance faces yet another challenge in its ability to consolidate itself, namely that it operates politically in a host country, Pakistan. Many resistance leaders have privately conceded that the limitations placed on them by the Pakistanis needlessly hinder their cause. The Pakistanis are, to be sure, in a difficult position, but it is equally clear that Pakistan's willingness to control the resistance is tied to a greater local political agenda. A resistance that operated with impunity in Pakistan is assumed to be a liability for Pakistan. The Pakistanis take increased Soviet intimidation seriously. Their alternative is equally grim; capitulation to Soviet demands would eventually create the very outcome that Pakistan has sought to avoid. Where the Afghan Mujahideen, facing a decision to lay down their arms and return to Afghanistan, are politically forced to reclaim their right to stay and fight, they will be co-opted to carve out a piece of Pakistan, given the regional and ethnic autonomy issues that exist in the area. Furthermore, such a situation would be a signal for other irredentist movements to challenge the government. The point is that these possibilities are potentially real insofar as Pakistan is willing to accept accommodations with the Soviets and the quisling Kabul regime.

The United States' policy toward the resistance suffers from an equally difficult dilemma: the institutional ideological differences among various departments of the government and the Congress are creating policy problems that will be difficult to undo in the long run. There are those within the administration who are increasingly critical of the resistance's ability to carry on the war. Some are bothered by the eventual character of leaders who will replace the present regime. This criticism tends to be most visible among the liberal establishment. In contrast, the conservatives, operating on their own agenda of fighting communism regardless of its effects on the resistance, are happy to meet an occasional freedom fighter for a photo session. The resistance's image problem can be improved substantially if the U.S. adopts a less ideological view of the situation in Afghanistan, and plays a more active role in the support of the resistance, materially and politically.

CONCLUSION

The problem of the resistance in many ways is a micro-cosm of Afghan society. However, one need not condemn the Afghans to a anachronistic past or present. Are Afghans a society in transition? Are they "prior" to or "after" societal development? These questions confront Afghans and the Afghan resistance. Whatever the answer, there is a particular strain of logic that ought to be avoided, one that looks at the world in terms of mechanical analogies or concepts that are at their core weighted with values that are alien to the study of the subject at hand. If social science can avoid such pitfalls, perhaps an explanation of the Afghans and their attempt to create viable leadership is possible.

This study has shown the historic basis for leadership roles pointed to the various constraints within that process. Change is a constant aspect of the human condition and change has already taken place among the many institutions of Afghan political life. The degree of change ultimately will decide the extent of the resistance and the leadership within it.

NOTES

1. Olivier Roy [Unpublished Manuscript]; September 11, 1985, pp. 8-13. JPRS-NEA-85-116; AFGHANISTAN: *Islam and Political Modernity.*

2. R. Newell, [The historic precedence suggest control by the government was primarily to make its presence felt.] p. 83.

3. A. Arnold, p. 12.

4. Ibid.

5. R. Newell, pp. 170, 174.

6. Olivier Roy, p. 6.

7. Cohen, p. 87.

8. Roy, p. 6.

9. Tapper, [Rob Hager cited in p. 114].

3

Arms Shipments
to the Afghan Resistance

John G. Merriam

BACKGROUND

This chapter should possibly be entitled "The Egyptian Connection," though it deals not with narcotics, as the title might suggest to some moviegoers, but with arms transfers. Egypt's initial role in the Afghanistan conflict as a conduit for arms has been little recognized, perhaps because these transfers have been largely covert operations.

This study focuses at the outset on Egyptian shipments of Soviet arms warehoused or manufactured in Egypt. Destination of these arms is the Mujahideen, the resistance movements consisting of Afghan guerrillas who receive some of their weapons through Pakistan.

What this chapter shows is how Egypt and the United States have worked together to become a key supplier with Pakistan as the principal conduit. It then goes on to identify other key suppliers. A caveat is in order: As this chapter explores a covert activity, accurate information is simply not available in the public domain from which the research material presented here is derived. Indeed, arms shipments are such a tangled web that no one knows with certainty the number, nature, and origin of the arms that actually reach the Mujahideen from outside sources, and this includes those for whom the arms are intended.

There are many unanswered questions. Who are the foreign arms suppliers? What do they supply and how much? More importantly, what are the political objectives steering the arms suppliers' efforts? Finally, what is the ratio of externally to internally derived arms?

In an interview conducted in May 1984, guerrilla leader Ishaq Gailani commented that weapons from internal sources constituted 80 percent of all arms, whether furnished by Soviet occupation troops or by DRA (Government of Afghanistan) troops through capture, desertions, or even barter.(1) Deserting Soviet troops, particularly of Central Asian origin who share language, religion, and ethnic characteristics with the Mujahideen, have found greater acceptance if they bring their weapons with them at the time of surrender. Numerous, though unverifiable stories, speak of troops bartering weapons and ammunition for hashish, copies of the Qur'an, or food. Most guerrilla leaders in Peshawar and inside the country itself echo the same 80-20 ratio, although some guerrilla leaders such as General Ramatullah Safi have maintained that they receive none or little in the way of foreign-supplied weapons.(2)

The Mujahideen have taken up their struggle against the supporters and troops of the Soviet Union, whose invasion of their homeland came to world attention in the closing days of December 1979. Less than two years later the Egyptian connection was revealed. President Anwar Sadat, shortly before his death October 6, 1981, made known to a foreign correspondent and to the world that Egypt was funneling Soviet or Soviet-type light weapons by way of Pakistan to aid the Mujahideen in their struggle against the Soviet occupation. Coordinating and funding for this operation, he revealed, came from none other than the American Central Intelligence Agency.(3)

Several questions arise. Why was Egypt chosen for this covert operation? Who initiated the plan, Egypt or the United States? Why, in any event, did Sadat engineer this deliberate affront to the U.S.S.R.? More difficult to ascertain would be why Egypt's leader chose this time and this means to publicize the operation. And then there are other questions: How secret has this arms flow been all along? Why is it useful for Sadat's successor, Hosni Mubarak, to continue? If the Russians have long known about it, why the discomfiture over Sadat's seemingly inopportune disclosure?

In attempting to answer these questions and others that follow, it should be pointed out that no officials in the United States or Egypt will talk freely. Frankly, to ask questions about covert operations is not wise and certainly not productive in any country, and there may be entirely legitimate reasons for withholding information about operations from public scrutiny. Also, the Afghan resistance, comprising a proud and determined people, is unlikely to acknowledge dependence on weapons not captured by their own efforts. With regard to the externally derived arms, there is the question of whether the sources of arms supplied to the Mujahideen who are actually doing the fighting are known at the point of delivery.

HISTORY

The external flow of covert arms began as a trickle in those first months following the Soviet incursion, but by October 1980 the Carter administration and key Muslim states committed themselves to a substantial increase in aid levels.   The arms' passage through several hands can obscure or erase the supplier country of origin, especially when that is the very aim of covert operations.   Arms passed out in Mujahideen camps are usually said to have come from defectors when in reality at least some of them have moved through the pipeline established for such clandestine purposes (Bernstein 1981).

Though Peshawar is the principal conduit for Egyptian and almost all other external weapons sources, especially small arms and ammunition, some experts off the record indicate shipments are also being ferried by the CIA via Oman to the Baluchi coast. Such arms are going through Iran and Pakistan, probably without Pakistani permission. Baluchistan is run by its own mullahs apart from the rest of Iran; it would not be difficult therefore to carry something through.(4)   With this background in mind, we should explore the actions and reactions of the Chinese, Americans, and Egyptians to understand the arms flow problem.

THE CHINESE CONNECTION

According to some accounts, most of the externally supplied arms are of Egyptian origin. Others maintain that more recently Chinese arms predominate. Though Chinese arms continue to arrive in sizable numbers, the earlier sealing of the Wakhan Corridor for a time hindered P.R.C.

supply efforts. The bulk of them are now routed through Peshawar.

In January 1980, just days after the Soviets invaded Afghanistan, U.S. Defense Secretary Harold Brown, then visiting in China, obtained an agreement with their government which permitted overflights of Chinese territory for planes carrying arms destined for the resistance. The P.R.C. would supply Sam-7s and RPG anti-tank rockets. In the event the Pakistan-Afghanistan border was sealed the agreement would even allow unloading equipment in China and would facilitate the difficult transshipment by overland personnel. A Chinese arms supply was thus assured. Yet, the P.R.C. did not agree to a joint operation but rather, as one participant in the discussion put it, to "do things in parallel" (Bernstein 1981).

(Note: On January 30, 1985, Afghanistan's ruling PDPA or People's Democratic Party Of Afghanistan expressed grave concern at Beijing's supplying the resistance with arms. In a letter addressed to its counterpart, the Chinese Communist Party, the PDPA accused Beijing of what it referred to as "terrorist activities.") According to this letter, published in the official Afghan media, "training camps are set up in Xinjiang province for 'counter-revolutionary bands,' as the Kabul regime styles the Mujahideen." Furthermore, it went on, "several hundred Chinese instructors are engaged in training Afghan bandits in the training centers inside Pakistani territory." It further alleged that the Chinese have supplied "approximately 2,000 heavy machine guns, 1,000 anti-tank rockets and nearly half a million rounds of ammunition."

Chinese weapons, particularly rockets and anti-aircraft guns, are known to be available to the Mujahideen in sizable quantities. More effective than the heavier, costlier equipment from the West, Chinese arms effectively supplement the Soviet weapons captured by the resistance; and, in most cases, the parts and ammunition are interchangeable.(5)

THE AMERICAN REACTION

The American commitment to the liberation of Afghanistan spans the Carter and Reagan administrations. Commentators tend to label Jimmy Carter as the humanitarian and Ronald Reagan as the ideologue, which may not adequately characterize either individual. The question is not whether there is a sustained commitment but rather what is its depth and what measures are to be taken to achieve what goals. Jimmy Carter, during whose presidency the Soviet invasion occurred, established the American arms supply commitment and is the key to understanding the endorsement and indeed the expanded role by President Reagan.

Anthony Hyman labels Carter's reaction to the Soviet invasion as one of "overreaction and bluff at the same time."(6) Carter accused the Soviets of a "blatant violation of the accepted rules of international behavior," which indeed the invasion was, and went beyond this denunciation to call it the most serious crisis since the end of World War II, a premise belied by the less-than-dramatic steps the Administration actually did take.

Expanding the President's tough State of the Union message to Congress on January 23 in the month following the Soviet thrust, special U.S. envoy Clark Clifford told reporters in New Delhi that "The Soviet Union must understand that if they move toward the Persian Gulf, that means war." The very same day, during testimony before the Senate Armed Services Committee, Secretary of Defense Harold Brown sounded a more cautious note: "We can't assure you that we would win a war there. . . . But to cast doubt on our ability to deter or fight effectively is . . . unnecessarily damaging to U.S. security."(7)

A major concern was and is whether the Soviet invasion marks the first step toward what are invariably called the "warm waters of the Gulf," the reference and concern being of course the vulnerable oil lanes through which now pass several million barrels a day (MBD). Though down from the onetime high of 18 MBD, the Gulf oil shipments will always be important. Significantly, Afghanistan's southern border is less than 300 miles (500 km) from Iran's port of Chah Bahar. From there the distance to the Strait of Hormuz, the so-called "choke point" through which all shipping must pass, is not great.(8)

While the 1979 Soviet invasion disrupted the move toward detente, Carter's responding acts were carefully measured. The U.S., it was decided, was not going to launch World War III over Afghanistan. It was, however, ready to send a strong signal to the U.S.S.R. indicating American displeasure and the concern of the Western allies. Carter took the following actions: The Senate's debate on the SALT II agreements, whose ratification prospects were far from good in any case, was shelved.   The possibility of eventual reconsideration pending positive Soviet behavioral modification remained.   A highly visible gesture was the boycott of the Olympic Games scheduled to be held in Moscow--ironically enough--a boycott in which the West Germans, Japan, and the P.R.C. joined.

Other actions included a partial embargo of grain sales that probably had more repercussions for American farmers than for Soviet policymakers.   Then there were the revocation of fishing rights for Soviet trawlers in American waters and the suspension of cultural affairs.   Of perhaps more military significance or at least relevance was the shipping embargo of high technology goods to the Soviet Union.

But nagging, unanswered questions remain.   U.S. government officials close to the situation who must remain anonymous have indicated to me that the White House knew of the Soviet buildup at least three months before the invasion and unquestionably a month prior.   Surely, the time to talk tough in private or to inform the world was before the event.   One is tempted to think that the image of American decisiveness or certainly preoccupation with the Teheran hostage crisis which had taken place the previous month gave the green light to Soviet adventurism.   The U.S.S.R. calculated correctly that the United States would take no significant military action following the invasion of Afghanistan.(9)

THE EGYPTIAN ARMS CONDUIT: PAST AND PRESENT

Egypt became a crucial part of these arms shipments. What the U.S. was prepared to do was to make the Soviet behavior costly by providing military aid to the resistance. While Pakistan was the natural route for arms from Egypt and elsewhere, the very act of funneling CIA-initiated arms through Pakistan necessitated a redefining of relations between the United States and Pakistan, whose authorities feel understandably vulnerable with America distant but the Russian bear to their immediate north and now to the east in occupied Afghanistan.   It is true that every effort has been made to keep the arms traffic secret so as not to incur Soviet wrath, which Pakistan would be the first to feel. Nevertheless, mention and even pictures of Egyptian and other foreign-supplied weaponry appear from time to time in publications worldwide; and these weapons can be seen in Peshawar.

Why has Pakistan's President, General Muhammad Zia-ul-Haq, given personal approval for the arms shipments from Egypt? Military largesse for the government of Pakistan's own forces offered by the Carter Administration was originally rejected as "peanuts," but a substantially larger sum was accepted under Reagan who originally pledged more than three billion dollars in long-term military credits. This agreement has eased restrictions on the trickle of arms coming through Pakistan and across the border into Afghanistan.

When all is said and done, the Pakistani government's commitment to an independent Afghanistan is absolutely and certainly genuine. Not all members of Pakistan's ruling elite share this view, however. Zia faces complex and many-sided challenges even from among his own supporters. The March 1985 elections in Pakistan, despite setbacks for some of his colleagues, may be regarded as a general endorsement of his commitment to a free Afghanistan.

As a matter of political realism, Pakistan's leader cannot readily alienate the Pushtun majority in the NorthWest Frontier Province (NWFP) who form the backbone of the Peshawar-based resistance to the Soviet-backed regime in Kabul. Then, too, like Sadat, Zia has sought to refurbish his legitimacy and in some quarters his not always popular rule by helping a troubled neighboring Muslim people. It should be added that the Islamization trend received a setback in the elections. The purpose was apparently to increase legitimacy for the regime that came to power with the 1977 overthrow of the charismatic President Zulfiqar Ali Bhutto. The generally popular Bhutto was hanged on April 4, 1979, only months before the Soviet invasion of Afghanistan.(10) This widely condemned act only increased Zia's need for legitimacy and his support for the subsequent Afghan resistance struggle. Nevertheless, the resistance groups will need to continue to convince the people of Pakistan that this struggle is their struggle.

With regard to Afghanistan itself, the Soviet entry in December 1979 did not mark the beginning of domestic resistance to the central government nor to the arms traf-

fic.   While there has always been resistance to central
authority, the April 27, 1978 "Saur" Revolution marks a
useful modern starting point.   This revolution put the PDPA
in power with Marxist leader Muhammad Taraki as President.
At this time organized resistance occurred, and refugees
began to flow into Pakistan, though slowly at first, particularly into the provinces of Baluchistan and the NWFP, while
armed fighters moved in the opposite direction.   Taraki's
lieutenant, Hafizullah Amin, replaced him only months before
the Soviet incursion and indeed was the principal reason for
it. Neither man's embrace of an alien ideology was acceptable to the devoutly Muslim and anti-Soviet population.   The
American arms flow to the resistance did not, however,
become   a   factor   until   after   the   December   27,   1979,
takeover.(11)

Policy shifts in any case take time.   This might be an
appropriate moment to take note of the fact that the United
States government had been, in a very small way, an arms
supplier to a Marxist government in Afghanistan.   In the
course of his research, Michael T. Klare found that the
Office of Munitions Control (OMC) of the U.S. Department
of State licensed sales of police--as distinguished from
military--hardware by U.S. corporations to Afghanistan, as
part of the so-called "police-industrial complex" of relatively
small specialty firms. Checking into the granting of export
licenses under the Freedom of Information Act provided the
possibly startling finding that one of the recipients has been
Afghanistan.   As an ally of the Soviet Union it is of course
ineligible for purchases of U.S. military gear but foreign
police agencies such as Afghanistan's have been sold American security gear (Klare 1985).

What kinds of weapons have been made available to
police agencies of a country like Afghanistan?   Typical
items have been tear gas grenades, canisters of Mace,
carbines, rifles, submachine guns, pistols, revolvers, and
ammunition. Klare learned that between September 1976 and
May 1979 the government of Afghanistan received for its
police force use of 36,000 pistols and revolvers and 10,000
rounds of ammunition.(12)   Using data from the U.S. Arms
Control and Disarmament Agency, *World Military Expenditures And Arms Transfers, 1970-1979*, he affirms that the
government of Afghanistan received $478 million in arms,
ammunition, and related equipment, excluding services and

construction, $450 million of which was supplied by the Soviet Union while sources for the remainder are not indicated. Pakistan, by way of comparison, received $875 million during the same period at that time, principally from France followed by the United States.(13)

Several observations are in order regarding Klare's findings. Great powers are notoriously casual about small arms traffic. The Soviet supply of clearly military equipment, including the dreaded Mi-24 helicopter gunships to the government of Afghanistan, has recently played an increasing role in the Afghan people's survival. Nevertheless, those who have suffered at the hands of the KHAD, Afghanistan's secret police, whether in Kabul's dreaded Pol-e Charkhi prison or elsewhere, do not lightly dismiss small arms sales, as countless issues of Dr. Sayd B. Majrooh's *Afghan Information Centre Monthly Bulletin* (AICMB) and the *Report From Helsinki Watch* attest.

The issue becomes a question of whether the United States should ever permit shipments of small arms to an ally of the Soviet Union. Notwithstanding Afghanistan's historical efforts to be neutral, the policy that succeeded so well, despite repeated pressures from both sides in World War II, began to unravel. In January 1955 Prime Minister Muhammad Daoud turned to the Soviets for military aid after having been rejected by U.S. Secretary of States John Foster Dulles (Hammond 1984). Most commentators agree that Daoud's action, whatever its justification, opened the door to Soviet penetration. Subsequent events which with the benefit of hindsight might have given pause to the sales of even small arms were Soviet development of highways, bridges, the Bagram airport to the north of Kabul, and the strategic Salang Pass, which later facilitated the December 1979 invasion. The murder of Daoud and the coming to power of the Marxist leaders Nur Muhammad Taraki and then Hafizullah Amin were in retrospect causes for considerable concern. Presumably no police arms were shipped after the bizarre killing of U.S. Ambassador to Kabul Adolph Dubs in February 1979, although the termination date cannot be determined from the data made available to Klare.

Of greater consequence today are the arms that the Mujahideen can bring to bear against the forces of the government of Afghanistan and the Soviet Union. The Pakistan arms conduit plays a special role.

What have the arms flow policies of President Zia been since 1980? According to information available he has required that the countries supplying arms to the resistance not publicly acknowledge such a role--a requirement violated by Sadat on the eve of his assassination in a bid to refurbish his tarnished legitimacy. In addition, Zia required that arms arriving in Pakistan move immediately across the border, thus avoiding storage or warehousing, and that the quantity of arms moving across Pakistan's territory be limited to the equivalent of two planeloads a week (Bernstein 1981). With these requirements the political consequences of arms shipments are supposedly minimized.

Current reports indicate the weapons arrive in Pakistan as air cargo in planes whose markings are continually altered. Then, under the direction of the Pakistani Inter-Services Intelligence Directorate, the arms are transferred to the Mujahideen who get them across the border. Thanks to the concealment afforded by the rugged topography and the guerrillas' familiarity with the mountain paths, they carry them on their own backs or on pack animals to distribute them to resistance groups in the interior.

Egypt, then, has been a major source of externally supplied weapons for the Pakistani conduit. Which weapons and in what quantities is not always ascertainable. At the outset, the AK-47 Kalashnikov was the mainstay. Although more sophisticated weapons, including a limited number of surface to air missiles are now being supplied, the weapons clearly remain in the small arms category.

What are the findings about Egypt's present role? To begin with, it was Sadat who, according to some accounts, approached the American authorities almost immediately following the Soviet incursion, and the United States quickly and readily responded. Egypt was a logical choice for the covert arms flow. It had a large supply of aging Soviet weaponry dating from the Nasser years that was increasingly less useful as Sadat had boldly expelled the Soviet technicians from his country in 1972. These arms were being replaced by modern American equipment following the 1974 resumption of relations. Furthermore, Egypt, with the oldest and most experienced military establishment in the Arab world, was beginning to manufacture spare parts and ammunition not only for its Soviet arsenal but also for export. Indeed, tons of replicated armaments have been manufactured on the outskirts of Cairo.(14)

Whether or not Egypt's President initiated the arms shipment idea or not, his unequivocal endorsement stemmed from genuine dislike of the Soviets and admiration for the heroic Afghan resistance. But was it unbridled opportunism? Nasser confidant and Sadat critic, editor Mohamed Hassanein Heikal, asserts that in 1980, the year after the invasion, Egypt's President faced allegations of corrupt deals in high places. To counterattack, he sought to mobilize the Egyptian people to the cause of Afghanistan, a fellow Muslim nation. Such a diversionary tactic was, in Heikal's view, ineffectual, counterproductive, and probably dangerous:

> Committees for aid to Afghanistan were set up throughout the country, but they never achieved anything. If Afghanistan was to be helped in the name of Islamic solidarity, that was playing into the hands of the unofficial Muslim groups which were in a much better position to exploit it (Heikal 1983, 214).

To visitors Sadat lamented that the Shah had fallen and the Soviets had "captured Afghanistan in broad daylight." In his view, American "timidity" over Afghanistan had been very dangerous" (Hirst and Beeson 1981, 345, 348). The public expressed support for Afghanistan. In a wide ranging interview, Defense and War Production Minister General Kamal Hassan Ali expressed Egyptian support but dodged questions on arms shipments as the following text makes clear:

> The Afghan people have asked for help from the United States. We are against the Soviet intervention in Afghanistan. If the Afghan people request such facilities from the United States, the situation would be different.
>
> Asked if the shipment of arms to Afghan rebels (sic) had begun, he said: 'I have no comment.'
>
> Asked if any contacts were held with officials in Afghanistan concerning the training of Afghan volunteers in Egypt, the Egyptian defense minister again said: 'I have no comment.'
>
> Regarding the announcement by the minister of state for the presidency, Mansur Hasan, that Egypt

was studying the question of offering military aid to Afghanistan, General Ali said: 'I do not want to enter into details. The offer stands, and we are fully convinced that what happened was a Soviet occupation of Afghanistan (FBIS 1980).

Several comments are in order. The term "rebel" is in my view not appropriate for labeling the Mujahideen who were fighting against the Soviet occupation and the puppet regime of Babrak Karmal which came to power on a sea of bayonets and through mass murder of Hafizullah Amin and an estimated 3,000 of his supporters. Having come to power illegally, in no sense could the Karmalist regime claim what has been termed "legitimacy by procedure."(15) The Mujahideen were not "rebelling" against a duly constituted government.

Second, the offer to aid and train the Afghans of course refers to the resistance (the Mujahideen), not the Soviet-backed nominees. Willingness to train Mujahideen has no doubt undermined the covert arms shipments' operational asset which is termed "plausible denial."

The last comment should rest with Mohamed Hassanein Heikal:

> On 3 September 1981 journalists had been arrested . . . political opponents as well as Muslim fundamentalists were being rounded up. On 3 September the same day, Sadat gave an interview to the NBC, "Today" Programme in which he referred to Egypt's sending arms to the guerrillas in Afghanistan 'because they are our Muslim brothers and in trouble' (Heikal 1983, 214).

The timing of Sadat's revelation is most significant for it helps to explain why he chose to go public on a covert operation, and it opens him up to Heikal's implied charge of political opportunism. In that very month reports and indeed published lists in the ruling National Democratic party mouthpiece *Mayo* indicated 1,536 persons were initially arrested including Mohamed Hassanein Heikal himself.

The Western press expressed concern over the incarceration of such distinguished opponents to the regime as university professors, journalists, and television and radio

producers who were allegedly engaging in activities "detri-
mental to public opinion." These foreign observers mistak-
enly overestimated the impact of the articulate, accessible,
though not particularly politically powerful, left wing intelligentsia. These commentators failed to recognize until the
assassination of Anwar Sadat only a month later the scope
and intensity of Muslim repudiation of the Egyptian leader,
particularly in the wake of Camp David and the 1979 signing
of the peace treaty with Israel.

Sadat, however, was keenly aware of, if rather fatalistic
about, the challenge to his person and his rule following
previous assassination attempts. The disclosure of Egyptian
arms aid to the Mujahideen and the CIA role in these
shipments could only underscore the fact that his need for
restored legitimacy, to be gained through the helping of a
fellow Muslim country, was greater than his fear of American reaction to the politically compromising disclosure.(16)

The perceived need for such a politically risky act
deserves to be placed in context. Sadat's dramatic November 1977 Jerusalem trip in search of peace resulted in
ostracism from most of the Arab world. The Soviet arms
shipments to Egypt ended with the 1972 ejection of their
technicians, but the 1973 October War was to have brought
with it the promise of a massive infusion of Arab oil money
which would have enabled Sadat to recover from the war
and to distance himself even more from the U.S.S.R. The
prospect of the loss of Arab aid was not sufficient, as it
turned out, to prevent the Egyptian President from signing
a peace treaty with Israel.

The Arab strategy, which was later aborted, had been to
finance food production in the Sudan and arms production in
Egypt. The Gulf States (Saudi Arabia, United Arab Emirates,
and Qatar) at the same time put up $1.04 billion. Their
purpose: to establish the Arab Military Industry Organization
(AMIO). Contracts amounting to some $1 billion were there-
fore concluded with Western companies for local assembly
and co-production in five major factories, mostly near
Helwan, the former spa now industrially polluted located to
the south of Cairo.

The January 1977 food price riots in Cairo and other
major cities seemed to have revived the Arab financial
commitment, but the November peace initiative of that year
with the State of Israel reversed that favorable monetary

flow (Merriam 1979). By 1979, as a result of the concluded treaty, Egypt was expelled from the Arab League, and the Gulf Arab contributors withdrew from the AMIO.

However, the loss of Arab funds was to be made up by American (overt) foreign military sales (FMS) credits of $1.5 billion (1979) and a further $1.5 billion in 1980 spread over two years, to be followed by $800 million for the following three years.

As a consequence of Sadat's ostracism, Egypt needed Western and above all American support. Today contracts have been signed with the United States, France, and Great Britain but also with the People's Republic of China and Rumania. Once again, Egypt has projects under the AMIO and is capable of manufacturing increasingly sophisticated weapons, some of which are finding their way into the hands of the Afghan resistance.(17)

ARMS SOURCES

While Egypt remains an important source of arms and part of the American geostrategic plan, "the primary source of weapons deployed by the Mujahideen," maintains John Fullerton, "is the Soviet Union itself."(18) Fullerton therefore reflects the position consistently held by the Mujahideen themselves. Defectors from the Afghan army have been more readily accepted by the resistance when they have come over with weapons. Although each year as the weather turns warmer and the mountain passes once again become usable the military campaigns waged by both sides increase in number, attacks during the winter are becoming more commonplace as the war intensifies. The attacks directed at, but also launched by, the Kabul regime and the Soviet occupier often result in defections. An estimated one-third of the Afghan government forces has deserted, leaving 30-40,000 to serve Soviet purposes. The DRA has resorted to tough forced draft or press gang methods to rectify the situation. To be a service age male in Afghanistan is not an enviable lot. Young teenage males are no longer immune. The already poor morale, as Kerry Connor documents, has worsened with consequently high numbers of deserters.

Into the resistance hands have come thousands of small arms and lesser numbers of mortars, mines and, from time to time, artillery pieces, all manufactured in the U.S.S.R. Particularly prized are the newer, high velocity AK-74 mm assault rifles, a lethal improvement over the better known veteran model,(19) the AK-47 Kalashnikov. Mujahideen arms needs are still far from being met, but since 1981 antiquated bolt action .303 Lee-Enfields have not been the mainstay they once were. To eliminate government troops as a resistance weapons source, the Soviets no longer provide the soldiers or even the supposedly loyal party cadres with, for example, the RPG-7 anti-tank grenade launchers that have proved so effective for the Mujahideen in ambush situations.

Egypt and China provide the largest part of the externally supplied weapons of Soviet design. Guerrillas in the interior, particularly in some northern and western areas, must rely on what they can take or capture from defectors. Yet, Soviet-style light weapons and stores do come to the insurgents in the northeast from China, despite severe logistical problems. Egyptian arms come through Pakistan's NorthWest Frontier Province. Egyptian and Chinese versions of the Kalashnikov are well known. Recoilless rifles, reports Fullerton, such as the Chinese 82 mm B-10 and 75 mm Type 56 were first seen in resistance hands in early 1981.

In addition, the Mujahideen have captured 82 mm (Soviet) mortars and 60 mm Type 63 (Chinese) mortars. British manufactured 2-inch mortars are presumably supplied from Gulf sources. Such light anti-aircraft weapons as the Chinese copy of the Soviet ZPU-2, a twin-barrelled 14.5 mm heavy machine gun, also have been seen.

Anthony Davis found that Ahmed Shah Massoud's forces in the Panjshir Valley were armed with Soviet-manufactured AKM and AK-74 automatic rifles plus some of the latest Soviet "Krinkov" 5.45 mm submachine guns. Other weapons expectedly included rocket launchers, heavy machine guns, and recoilless rifles, all of Soviet Bloc design, but the ammunition appeared to be primarily Chinese in origin (Davis 1984).

Fullerton asserts that these weapons are often incorrectly employed and therefore cannot provide the "mainstay of the guerrillas' wholly inadequate air defense capability," even though that is the avowed purpose (Fullerton 1984). While there is no doubt some truth to that finding, an American authority claims that the much publicized Mujahideen commander, Ahmad Shah Massoud, fighting in the Panjshir northeast of Kabul, had brought down more enemy aircraft--above all the much feared Mi-24 "Hind" E armored helicopter gunships--with machine gun fire than with the much sought after surface-to-air missiles.(20)

Much of the controversy about the covert American role centers around the quality as well as the quantity of CIA weapons actually reaching the Mujahideen. Some accounts of CIA successes in this regard have been overblown.(21) But according to a reliable Washington, D.C.-based source, Sam-7s and 82 mm medium range Soviet-made mortars are much less suitable than the more accurate "Redeye," the later "Stinger," or British "Blowpipe" surface-to-air missiles, and the longer range British or Finnish 81 mm medium range mortar. Furthermore, such weapons as anti-tank and anti-personnel mines have arrived unusable, without their demolition components. What are useful are the 12.7 mm and the 14.5 heavy machine guns, but ammunition is often so scarce that what might have been contests favorable to the Mujahideen often result in failure. The resistance controls 90 percent of the land, but the enemy controls 90 percent of the air, a crucial factor (Erulkar 1984).   Nevertheless, wars have ultimately been won, history tells us, by the force controlling the land not the air alone.

What the resistance and villagers alike fear is, without doubt, the Mi-24, or "Hind," to use its NATO designation.(22) Inspired by the American use of helicopter gunships in Vietnam, the Mi-24 has been inadequately powered by American standards, at least in the earlier versions. It uses the same engine as the Mi-8 "Hip" which is used for transport purposes. But the engine supplied 40 percent less power in relation to its airframe. Soviet enthusiasm for the attack helicopter evidently has not been tempered by the American experience in Vietnam, where nearly 5,000 helicopters or about one-third of their total force was lost each year. As Cockburn points out, helicopters are inherently slow, unmaneuverable, and highly vulnerable to any kind of damage, particularly to the whirring rotor blades, which in the Mi-24's case span nearly 60 feet.(23)

The Soviet version of the "Hind" F, but less so the version available to the DRA, is armored to protect the crew and parts of the engine. This formidable helicopter is equipped with a 12.7 mm multi-barrelled gun mounted in a chin turret and 128x57 mm rockets carried in four pods and four launch rails for "Swatter" or "Spiral" anti-tank missiles and also with bombs that can be carried on weapon pylons.(24) Though terrifying in appearance it is nevertheless vulnerable and has been brought down on numerous occasions by heavy machine gun and cannon fire.

Verifiable monthly accounts indicate the resistance is bringing down fixed wing aircraft as well as the vulnerable helicopters.(25) The level of sophistication is clearly improving on both sides. What can the Mujahideen do about the Soviet supremacy in the skies? Paul Moorcraft (1985) indicates the principal antiaircraft weapon has been the 12.7 mm DShK, called the "Dasheka." Curren and Karber (1985) estimate that "99 percent of the air-defense assets employed by the resistance are heavy machine guns captured from the Soviet forces or received as 'gifts' from Kabul army deserters." There are reports that Massoud's forces have disabled or destroyed the dreaded gunships by, in some instances, firing down on them when they swept into the Panjshir. On the other hand, some sharp shooting resistance fighters prefer to wreak havoc on the gunships with so-called elephant guns--.455 caliber weapons that can inflict lethal damage on the rotor blades without the telltale flash and smoke that give away the attacker's position (Cockburn 1984).

A report published in September 1984 by an authority on arms use in Afghanistan found a NIFA camp equipped with the 12.7 DShK heavy machine gun or "Dasheka" which possessed Soviet factory markings, vintage 1966; Chinese versions are also known. Although these tripod-mounted guns are the backbone of the Afghan resistance air defense, a smaller number of single or twin 14.5 Zp-1 "Ziqriats" and Chinese-made 23 mm's are also known (Isby 1984).

Will surface-to-air missiles nevertheless play a larger role? The British author Gerald Seymour in his carefully researched account has SAS agent Barney Crispin go into Afghanistan with eight aging American "Redeyes" in order to bring back the electronic system of an Mi-24 (Seymour 1984). The attack abilities of the craft as mentioned in the story are perhaps exaggerated, but the troubles encountered in effectively using the "Redeye" probably are not. In reality, NATO forces can hardly need information on this well-seasoned helicopter. Recent accounts indicate two helicopters were flown by their defecting crews across the border into Pakistan (*The Blade* July 15, 1985). These particular models contained the most advanced electronics, a lucky intelligence break.

While some Western supporters have called for wide-spread introduction of the "Stinger," a more advanced shoulder fired heat seeking missile, a few of these weapons have reportedly found their way to the Mujahideen. According to *The Times*, however, a new version of the Soviet weapon, the Sam-7, has been created by forces sympathetic to the resistance. Paid for by the United States, anti-DRA forces in late 1984 were reportedly being trained in Egypt on the missile's use, employing manuals written by American experts. The Soviets have increasingly resorted to air strikes and less so to ground forces. Furthermore, they are reportedly relying more on jets than helicopters, relatively speaking. To counter the growing Soviet threat, resistance organizations had purchased some ancient Sam-7s from the Palestine Liberation Organization after it was forced to withdraw from Lebanon. Priced at a hefty equivalent of 26,000 British pounds each (U.S.$1.51=1 pound), few worked and most were unserviceable. The new upgraded version is being manufactured in Egypt and will reinforce the Egyptian connection.

First used with some success in the 1973 Arab-Israeli War, the Sam-7 should be the perfect weapon as it is light and can be carried by a single Mujahid; it is shoulder fired and relatively simple to operate, unlike the more complex "Stinger." Ideally, the Sam-7 missile, using an infra-red detector, homes in on its target, but the old systems were easily fooled. A campfire or the sun itself could prove to be a problem. As decoys to mislead the missiles fired by the guerrilla forces, the Soviets, like the Israelis, use flares and metal foil strips to deflect the missiles from their intended targets. Sometimes the old system simply does not work, but the new systems being developed in Egypt can reputedly detect a helicopter almost four miles away and are less likely to be diverted from their intended targets.(26)

The Soviets, troubled by technology lag, poor troop morale, inadequate or unsuitable training, excessive centralization of decisionmaking authority, and low levels of adaptability have dealt poorly with the insurgency in a country characterized by mountainous topography and a resourceful, determined indigenous population. Although others have bemoaned the lack of Mujahideen training and indeed their apparent indifference to the need for it, bravery and extraordinary stamina have seemed to be more important values than unnecessary troop losses and well thought out and coordinated strategies. Signs indicate that both sides have in fact become more effective in combat situations and are fighting with more appropriate and indeed more lethal weapons combined with more suitable strategies. Crack Soviet troops recently have shown that they have learned to launch surprise attacks and lay ambushes in the style of the resistance. Some Soviet raids have taken place at night with specially trained troops, the "Spetznaz," using infrared equipment (*Afghanistan Forum* July 1985).

What armaments are the Mujahideen working with? Indications are that they have been able to seize 76 mm mountain howitzers and 122 mm field guns, but they may lack the training to make use of some of the more sophisticated weaponry.

Journalist Mike Martin, accompanying a Hizb-i-Islami group (Gulbuddin Hekmatyar), was shown a 122 mm D-30 field howitzer, with a range of 15 km (approximately 9 miles). The men had learned by a process of trial and error how to fire it. They had also developed an ingenious method for obtaining shells by barter as well as by capture. As mentioned earlier DRA troops are most willing to exchange shells for such basic necessities as hashish and food. On this particular occasion the Mujahideen commander, having concluded a deal and obtained the much needed shells, turned the gun on the post "with devastating results." Quite typically the Soviets responded by bombing the local villages for a full two weeks (Martin 1984).

Other reporters have been brought to inspect captured BTR-60 armored personnel carriers (APCs) and also BMP armored fighting vehicles (AFVs). Interestingly, tanks have also been captured in working order but are then stripped of useful parts. Soviet invasion troops are known to have T-62s and some of the newer T-72 tanks which are more effective in controlling urban areas or relatively flat parts of the countryside. However, they are of little use in mountainous terrain in contrast to the helicopter gunships and so are stripped to make better use of the parts (Furlong and Winkler 1980).

While the Mi-24 is the principal source of concern to the

Mujahideen, the Soviets have found they cannot rely on DRA ground troops. To cut their own troop losses they have to rely increasingly on their aircraft. The Sukhoi Su-25 (NATO code name "Frogfoot") can provide close support in operations against the Mujahideen and, by using flares, can defend itself against infra-guided Sam-7 missiles fired by resistance forces. Also used are the older Sukhoi Su-24 "Fencers" and the Tupolev Tu-16 "Badgers" employing close support tactics to reduce danger from Mujahideen-fired Sam-7s. The high altitude bombers, based at Termez, Uzbekistan, just across the border in the U.S.S.R., can attack while keeping out of range of any antiaircraft weapons the Mujahideen possess, but the use of decoys and flares makes possible the low level and therefore more accurate release of drogue shoots carrying bomblets by such high speed strike fighters as the Mikoyan-Gurevich Mig-21s and the Sukhoi Su-25 (Gunston 1984).

It is well known that the Mujahideen have successfully brought down helicopters and planes. "About 700 Soviet and Afghan aircraft [have been destroyed] since the insurgents began fighting," according to verified figures provided to *U.S. New & World Report* (September 23, 1985). *Afghan Update* (Washington, D.C., September 30, 1985, Issue XIX) does not question the figures but does question the supposed effectiveness of CIA-provided air defense weapons. Their remarks are worth quoting at length:

> In Vietnam, North Vietnamese and Viet Cong gunners downed 3,000 U.S. aircraft during a similar time frame. Although most Soviet weapons to the Vietnamese were the same type the CIA ships to the Afghans, the Soviet deliveries were a dozen times greater in numbers, ammunition quantities and training.

> The two main helicopters the Soviets use in Afghanistan are the Mi-24 and the Mi-8. . . . Soviet factories build them ten times faster than the guerrillas knock them down with current CIA-provided weapons.

The same source, quoting Ishaq Gailani of NIFA and spokesmen for Jamiat-i-Islami (Rabbani) and Hizb-i-Islami (Yunis Khalis), reports that matters are now more serious as the Soviets have introduced the Mi-28 "Havoc" helicopter. Smaller, faster and armored on the underside, it cannot be harmed by the guerrillas' heavy machine guns. The Su-25 "Frogfoot," a single seater attack plane, is also well-armored and maneuverable, packs lots of firepower, and is capable of coming in low against Mujahideen on mountainous ridges with devastating effect (*Afghan Update* September 30, 1985). In view of these developments the quality and quantity of covert arms shipments need to be reassessed with a view to upgrading.

THE SHI'ITE RESISTANCE

Though the levels and effectiveness are less than adequate, arms and money continue to flow from the P.R.C., the Gulf, and Egypt. Less information is available regarding arms going to the Shi'ite resistance. Names of known pro-Iranian organizations are found in Franceschi (1981) and Centlivres.(27) Mostly from the Hazarajat in west central Afghanistan, they are derived from the Shi'a community.

But the Shi'a minority (approximately 11 percent of Afghanistan's predominantly Sunni population) is far from united and mirrors factionalism within neighboring Iran to which they necessarily turn. The Harakat-Islami of Sheikh Assef Mohseni is a revolutionary group backed materially by Iran in its fight against the Soviets. Another is the extremist Hazara Nasr party. Also armed by the Khomeini regime it draws its recruits from the young Hazaras working in Iran.(28)

The draft pool may consist in part of Afghans employed as guest workers in the Iranian economy, plus 1.5 million refugees in East Iran between Mashad and Zahedan, according to sources located in the Swiss Embassy in Iran and in the U.S. State Department.

These refugees are reportedly living in fenced in, heavily guarded camps (1983 data). Other sources indicate border crossings are restricted by Iran, in contrast to the porous Afghan-Pakistan border. Nevertheless, Iranian-backed guerrillas are a source of concern for the Kabul regime. The KHAD, which presently numbers close to 30,000 persons, apparently has successfully infiltrated these groups and provoked internecine conflict (ARIN March/April 1985). Reportedly, many Hazaras, put out by the treatment received in Iran, have broken away from these pro-Iranian groups and have formed their own smaller groups inside.

Christina Demeyer, an American journalist who spent October and November of 1984 in Iran, confirms that the Iranian newspapers, radio, and television provide more coverage of the events in Afghanistan than does any other country. Rhetoric is strongly pro-resistance and anti-Russian though also anti-Western. Nevertheless, she said "the Afghan freedom fighters were not free to move and did not seem to be supported at all."(29) According to knowledgeable sources the Soviets quickly discouraged any Iranian show of active support by bombing villages in 1980 cross border attacks. Iran was advised to concentrate on the revolution within. Largely isolated from the community of nations and still in the early stages of its internal upheaval, Iran had little choice but to comply and to address itself to the domestic priority.(30)

Ismail Khan, commander of the resistance forces from the Jamiat-i-Islami fighting in the city of Herat, not far from the Iranian border, has denied receiving the Iranian military or financial support so critical for the fighting in the border provinces. Iran does provide some backing to two small Shi'a groups, as Olivier Roy has pointed out. These Mujahideen organizations are Jamiat-i-Islami, led by Burhanuddin Rabbani, and Gulbuddin Hekmatyar's Hizb-i-Islami. Both are permitted offices in Iran. However, Jamiat sources have complained about guerrillas facing obstructions from Iran's Revolutionary Guards when crossing the border to mount raids into Afghanistan (Haqqani 1985).

In recent attempts to break out of its isolation, Iran has made overtures to the Soviet Union. In April 1985 Iran's Deputy Foreign Minister Kazembur Ardebili met in Moscow with Soviet Foreign Minister Andrei Gromyko. (Significantly, in 1986 Iran has shown willingness to resume gas deliveries.) Indications of the slight warming of relations may include, according to diplomatic sources, an agreed upon slowdown of Iranian supplies to the refugees now living in Iran, some of whom have been slipping across the border to confront the Soviet occupiers. Nevertheless, not too much should be read into this piece of information. Trade flows often signal foreign policy thrusts, but the indications are that the most dramatic growth in trade has not taken place with the U.S.S.R. but rather with Pakistan, though it is considered an American ally. And Iran, for its part, would want to have good relations with any future Afghan Islamist regime.

In Iran, with an Afghan refugee population second only to Pakistan, editorials appearing in the government-controlled newspapers find fault with Islamabad for being "too soft" on the Soviet occupation of Afghanistan, although it could be argued that Pakistan, not Iran, shoulders the greater risk. In any case, the thinking is that Iran will not go too far out of the way to accommodate the Soviets who after all provide arms to their Iraqi adversary. A Soviet breakthrough is not therefore imminent. In fact, says James Glad, a Teheran-based reporter, "Contempt for the Soviet Union is voiced through a steady stream of ridicule and invective," through not only the newspapers but the Voice of Islamic Revolutionary Afghanistan (VOIR) (Glad).

Therefore, Peshawar remains the principal conduit for externally supplied arms. Iran is preoccupied with the war with Iraq and troubled by an arsenal of aging American materiel. (Recently, in 1986, the P.R.C. has indicated a readiness to supply Iran with the Chinese version of the Mig-21, although not in numbers sufficient to overcome Iraqi air superiority. The point is the Chinese have become a significant arms supplier.)

One other source, though not an important one, is the gunsmiths who have operated historically in Pakistan's NWFP and who can, particularly in Darra the "town of guns" located twenty-five miles from Peshawar, make in a month's time a Soviet-style Kalashnikov automatic rifle for 10,000 Pakistani rupees (PRs. 13.476=US$1, 1983-84 average).(31)

CONCLUSION

Covert arms shipments from the United States via Egypt, the P.R.C., and some of the Muslim and European suppliers through the Gulf continue to show material and indeed politically symbolic commitment to the liberation struggle. Generally speaking, the United States views its support in terms of the Cold War struggle and not as a means to aiding a beleaguered people who happen to be Muslim. Islam--like Judaism and Christianity--may have sprung from the same cradle, but Americans possess little understanding or even awareness of this fact. U.S. arms are but a fraction of what the Soviets provided Ho Chi Minh's forces in the Vietnam conflict with which the Afghan conflict is sometimes, though not especially usefully, compared.

Americans can be wonderfully humanitarian. Supporters range the political spectrum though they are dominated by the right wing. Indeed, it is the liberal, now called moderate, wing that questions the wisdom of, as they term it, "fighting to the last Afghan" to serve our superpower goal, tying the Soviets down in a protracted conflict which is unpopular with the increasingly aware public in the U.S.S.R. and the world at large. The Soviets are expending political capital as well as their own human and financial resources. American conservative and moderate positions on the Afghan conflict, the one supportive, the other obliquely critical, reach their conclusions for the wrong reasons, in my view. The resistance effort should be judged on its own merits, but that is probably not possible for us Westerners who have other global priorities.

The questions arise: in pursuit of an arms control agreement, would the United States "sell Afghanistan down the river"? What about the *quid pro quo* arrangement linking Soviet pullback from Nicaragua to cessation of American covert arms shipments to the Afghan resistance? Would the United States, independently of Central American priority, promise a cessation of covert arms shipments as a pre-condition to a meaningful Soviet timetable for withdrawal to be presented at the Geneva "proximity talks"?

Will the P.R.C., concerned by cross border violations by its Soviet neighbor, consider a rapprochement to be in its national interest? Will Pakistan, with its unswerving support for the Afghans, grow weary and wary of repeated Soviet military incursions and the threat of political destabilization? And what about Egypt? Recent interviews (32) indicate undiminished support levels. Yet the Egypt-CIA link in the wake of the EgyptAirliner interception following the Achille Lauro affair may make the partnership politically dangerous for President Hosni Mubarak. It is perhaps not insignificant that the Egyptian leader is once again moving closer to fellow Arab states and the Soviet ambassador has returned to Cairo. But nothing is ever predictable in the Middle East. The September 1986 Alexandria meeting between Hosni Mubarak and Israeli prime minister Shimon Peres over the Taba dispute opened the door for the return of the Egyptian ambassador to Tel Aviv. The thinking here is that continued support for the Mujahideen would have the double advantage of serving American purposes (pressure on the Soviets) and Egyptian needs (mollifying Arab critics by helping a Muslim people).

In all likelihood, the bottom line is that Soviets will not be negotiated into a withdrawal, the covert operations will continue, and the Afghans will fight on for they see no other choice. Will there be an increased commitment by the United States and perhaps other supplier states? The argument, again by American liberal/moderates, is that such a move would result in a "horizontal escalation" in Afghanistan and Nicaragua alike and therefore be counterproductive. That line of reasoning might of course prevail, though it shows no signs of doing so at this writing.

It is my conviction that commitment to the Afghan struggle should transcend American ideological boundaries. Nevertheless, when all is said and done, the final solution, whatever it may be, will be found in the political arena as much as in the armed struggle.

POSTSCRIPT

Some recent developments indicate contradictory trends. Fierce fighting was reported in the Spring of 1986 when a force of 12,000 to 15,000 troops, mostly PRA overran Zhawar in Paktia province on the border of Pakistan. A major stronghold, the Mujahideen have preferred to store weapons there on the Afghan rather than the Pakistani side of the border. The Soviets have known about these arms caches and have sought to destroy them and seal the border flow of arms and guerrillas. In neither case have they ever been totally successful, and the capacity of the resistance to continue the struggle remains considerable. Though some observers feel time is on the side of the DRA and Soviet troops, the resistance feel favored by history, topography, and sheer determination.

Do the recent DRA-Soviet efforts presage a heightening of hostilities for bargaining advantage in the ongoing Geneva talks, or do they mark a determined effort by the Soviet leader, Mikhail Gorbachev, to end the military stalemate once and for all? Or are the parties involved--

the Soviets in particular--seriously interested in peace negotiations?

On May 4, 1986, the day before the seventh round of "proximity" talks resumed in Geneva, Major General Najibullah, until December the chief of KHAD, the dreaded state security agency, took over as effective leader of the People's Democratic Party of Afghanistan (PDPA). Babrak Karmal resigned the country's key post, ostensibly for health reasons.(33) The rise of Najibullah (he goes by the single name) has been interpreted by some as a Soviet effort to further the negotiation process with the Pakistanis who would not engage in direct talks with Karmal, whom they regarded as a Soviet puppet. Yet the one-time doctor is a known hardliner, and I might speculate that he was chosen as least as much for his effective leadership skills and perhaps ruthlessness as he was to aid the negotiatory efforts.

The Soviet commitment to withdrawal is ambivalent at best.   The sticking point in the talks is reputedly the setting of a timetable for the withdrawal of Soviet troops, but no Soviet government will accept full or partial withdrawal leading to the downfall of a pro-Soviet Kabul regime.

Pakistan for very different reasons is also ambivalent. The war in Afghanistan brings conflicting pressures but also benefits to the government and people of Pakistan. As a case in point, the downing of a Soviet-built Afghan SU-22 aircraft and the disabling of a second 15 km (9 miles) inside Pakistani airspace by American-built F-16s which took place during the May 5-16, 1986, "proximity" talks presaged higher tension levels.

Kabul complains that Pakistan is being used as a sanctuary for guerrilla forces and is the major conduit for the arms flow.   Islamabad for its part has repeatedly protested such airspace violations (over 160 in the first four months of 1986 alone) but has not previously responded militarily (*Pakistan Affairs* June 1, 1986). In the background is the presence of as many as 3.5 million refugees whose wishes and needs cannot fail to be taken into account.

Arms aid to the Mujahideen, my central concern, cannot fail to affect Pakistan. Clandestine in nature, its size is difficult to determine.   Authorities agree that recent increases from the United States alone are substantial and therefore significant. The *EIU* reports $250 million in aid for fiscal 1986-87 and agrees that the "revelation" of covertly supplied "Stinger" missiles on top of this aid to the Mujahideen could have grave consequences for Pakistan. These more sophisticated hand-held heat seeking missiles with their greater range, accuracy, and reliability may be seen as a response to the more lethal weaponry and tactics employed by Soviet-DRA forces. Certainly, "plausible denial" becomes more difficult and the pressures on Pakistan may well mount.

A proposal to bypass the Peshawar conduit with C130 air drops inside Afghanistan would not reduce Soviet pressures but would in fact increase them, in my view. The use of C130s for this purpose is not likely, but the "Stinger" commitment, if it is genuine, marks the first time the United States has formally introduced American-manufactured weaponry. (Some sources indicate the British "Blowpipe," not the "Stinger," was in evidence in the Zhawar battle, and that it is the British not the Americans who are playing a key role in this type of weapons supply.)

Most important is the sheer size of the aid package. Congressional and other sources apparently approved $470 million in the Spring of 1985 for the fiscal year. Subsequently, Congress was said to have approved a $300 million supplemental aid appropriation ovet two years. Whether this supplement was in addition to the $470 million čould not be determined. The question remains: Does the White House want to achieve a decisive Afghan resistance victory or merely to conduct a low-level conflict to harass the U.S.S.R.?

While the evident increase in funds and sophisticated weaponry could adversely affect Pakistan, it continues to be the recipient of substantial assistance. Congressional approval of $15 million in AID-administered assistance plus $10 million for Department of Defence shipment of nonlethal items such as clothes and blankets to Pakistan for Afghan refugee use would ease the refugee burden (Ottaway 1986).

Despite the Gramm-Rudman budget-cutting bill, the reinforced commitment to the anti-Soviet struggle explains much of the March 24, 1986, agreement to provide strategically important Pakistan with $4.2 billion between now and 1993, in contrast to the 1983-1987 $3.2 billion package (*EIU* 1986).

Nevertheless, peace talks could in time result in a settlement which could partially dry up funds for Pakistan and totally end the CIA-supported arms flow, a requirement clearly implied when the U.S.S.R. demands the end to all outside "interference." Resistance stockpiling of arms in areas under their control and more careful use of guerrilla forces indicate steps are being taken to prepare such eventualities.

The greater likelihood is that the conflict and foreign arms support will continue. The widely publicized Soviet pullout of some 8,000 troops in mid-October 1986 marks a hardening of Moscow's stance rather than a move toward peace. The removal of anti-aircraft regiments which are hardly necessary and their eventual replacement by troops and equipment more appropriate to combatting a guerrilla insurgency will only serve to strenghthen the Soviet military presence.(34) The need is greater than ever for maximizing Mujahideen effectiveness, particularly in dealing with Moscow's mastery of the air.

NOTES

1. Mr. Gailani is part of the National Front For The Liberation of Afghanistan (NIFA) whose umbrella organization is Islamic Unity (more completely the Islamic Unity of The Afghan Mujahideen, or IUAM). Led by his highly respected uncle, Pir Syed Ahmad al-Gailani, it operates in the south and southeastern part of the country, but with only moderate military effectiveness according to most observers (see Fullerton, page 197).

2. Highly respected, the former brigadier general in the Imperial Afghan Army more recently has run a training camp for the Mujahideen (see Wheeler, page 26). [A similar assertion was recently made by Abdul Qadir Karyab, a leader of the Hizb-i-Islami resistance organization which plans to open an information office in New York in order to win diplomatic recognition and Afghanistan's seat in the United Nations.] (see Keshavan, page 3).

3. See Roy, page 284. See also Bonosky.

4. This reference comes from an interview in Washington, D.C., on April 19, 1984. For a probably inaccurate and overblown account of CIA activities, see *Time* (June 11, 1984).

5.   See Haqqani (1985, 24-25), cf. Rieser (1983, 12-19). Some useful data on what the Mujahideen are fighting against may be found in Cordesman (1983, 34-69). See also Cordesman (1984) and Isby (1984, 1523-1528). Some of these findings were confirmed in an interview with Prof. Dr. Sayd B. Majrooh, Afghan Information Centre, Peshawar, Pakistan, on May 14, 1984.

6.   Anthony Hyman (1982), pp. 170-172; (1984), pp. 170-171, provides a useful summary from which the following summary is drawn. The analysis is mine.

7.   Quoted in R.D.M. Furlong and Theodor Winkler, p. 168.   A fuller treatment may be found in Bradsher (1985, Chapter 10). See also Hammond (1984), especially Chapter 12, "The Carter Administration and the Soviet Invasion."

8.   See Marfleet (p. 13).   Some interesting foreign interpretations are found in Tahir Amin, Bhabani Sen Gupta, Kuldip Nayar, Fath-ur-Rahman, Bashir A. Qureshi, and Sayed Qassem Reshtia.   Some clearly pro-Soviet views are in Mikhail Ilyinsky and Boris Petkov.

9.   Among the sources that may be consulted for an analysis of the Soviet invasion are the contributions in Rubinstein (1983).

10. Stories surfacing of instances of repression under Bhutto apparently have not tarnished his image. The fact that the Pakistani government placed Benazir, the politically astute daughter of Bhutto, under house arrest (August 28, 1985) angered American authorities as well as local opposition leaders (cf. *Far Eastern Economic Review*, September 12, 1985, page 13). She has since been released.

11. Among the many useful accounts of the Saur revolution are by John C. Griffiths and Thomas M. Cynkin.

12. See Klare (1985, 263).   The source cited is Export Licenses issued to U.S. arms firms by the office of Munitions Control, U.S. Department of State.

13. See Klare (1985, 210-211), using data from the U.S. Arms Control and Disarmament Agency, *World Military Expenditures* (1982).

14. See Perera (1984, 14-16).   Bernstein disagrees that Sadat was the initiator and maintains that "[p]lanning for the operation was personally ordered by President Carter and carried out under the direction of his national security advisor, Zbigniew Brzezinski, and his CIA Director Stansfield Turner." In fact, Bernstein says the President affirmed a

"moral obligation" to arm the Afghan resistance at a meeting of the National Security Council only hours after the Soviet incursion (cf. "Arms for Afghanistan").

15. "Legitimacy by procedure" is a concept customarily applied "to the manner in which a government, ruler, or officeholder has obtained office," according to Deutsch (1980, 13). Interestingly enough, the Soviets have attempted to twist the facts. The disinformation they are circulating, according to A. Rasul Amin, former Dean of Social Sciences at Kabul University, is the "claim that it was the Afghans and not the Red Army who killed Amin" (cf. fn. 2, p. 60, in "A General Reflection on the Stealthy Sovietisation of Afghanistan").

16. See Merriam (1982). Some information comes from an interview with Milad Hanna on August 15, 1983, and November 11, 1985. Dr. Hanna, a contributor to the left wing *Al-Ahali*, a publication critical of Sadat, was among those arrested.

17. See Perera (1984, 14-16) and Saikal (1984, 103-106). Pictures of Mujahideen using heavy weapons were provided by British reporter Ken Guest as early as 1980 on his first trip to Afghanistan. See Gearing (1985, 18).

18. Much of the following summary except where otherwise noted is drawn from Fullerton (1983, 103-105).

19. See Brown (1986, 56).

20. This interview took place in Washington, D. C., on April 12, 1984. A good number of intrepid reporters have gotten to Afghanistan's Panjshir Valley. The fact that the Panjshir straddles Kabul's link to the Soviet border and the Massoud has been the object of such international attention has prompted Soviet offensives to control this strategic area. Accounts listed by year of publication are Patrice Franceschi (1981, 1984); William Dewell (Autumn 1982); Sandy Gall (1983); Nigel Ryan (1983); and Christophe de Ponfilly (1985).

21. See *Time*, June 11, 1984, for a somewhat apochryphal article.

22. For the number of Mi-24s and other craft deployed by what is euphemistically called "the limited contingent group of Soviet forces in Afghanistan" and by the DRA (again euphemistically, The Democratic Republic of Afghanistan), see issues of *Jane's Defense Weekly*: July 7, 1984; September 21, 1985; and October 5, 1985.

23. See Cockburn (1984, 242-243). See also Seymour's (1984) well researched novel which pits man (a British intelligence agent) against the Mi-24; and also an emotional account of the human cost (Ferri 1984, 19).

24. See P. G. Harrison et al., *Military Helicopters*, pp. 87-88 and Fig. 6.9.

25. See *Crisis & Conflict Analysis Team, Afghanistan Report* (Islamabad, Pakistan: The Institute of Strategic Studies [monthly]).

26. The Sam-7, also designated as the SA-7 or "Strella," to use the Soviet nickname, is used by the Warsaw Pact forces. See Samuel Beloff, page 76, and also Chapter III, "The Soviets in Afghanistan: Lessons Learned?" pages 133-177.

27. Consult Franceschi (1981, 264-265) and Centlivres et al. (1984, 246). They also provide information on the more numerous Sunni groups. Fullerton provides only the latter, listing the seven major resistance groups under their umbrella organizations, the Islamic Alliance and Islamic Unity (1984, 196-197).

28. For an indepth treatment, consult Roy's *L'Afghanistan: Islam Et Modernite Politique* (Paris: Editions Du Seuil, 1985). See the citation for Roy for an English translation.

29. This information is listed as it was reported in *AICMB*, nos. 44-45, November-December 1984, pages 12-13.

30. This report comes from an interview conducted in Washington, D. C., on October 31, 1985.

31. See Fullerton, page 78; Roy's article in *Le Monde Diplomatique*. See also David M. Hart (1985).

32. This information is based on interviews made in Washington, D. C., from October 31 - November 1, 1985. See also Magnus (1985).

33. See *AICMB*, no. 62, May 1986 (Peshawar, Pakistan); James Rupert (1986); and *Economist Intelligence Unit*, no. 2-1986, Country Report: Pakistan, Afghanistan (London).

34. See Erwin Franzen, "Soviets Begin 'Pullout' From Afghanistan Widely Viewed As Cosmetic, A Ruse," *Middle East Times* (Egypt), Vol. IV, No. 40, October 19-25, 1986, p. 5.

4

Afghan Refugee Women and Their Struggle for Survival

Kathleen Howard-Merriam

INTRODUCTION

On a dusty tent-filled plain a mile and a half from the Afghan border, a group of black-clad women, their faces marked with weariness yet full of dignity, communicate through sign language their plight of having been raped and of having lost as many as ten or twelve members of their families at the hands of the Soviet occupiers of their country. One of the women, Sultana, related how she herself had escaped only by pretending she was dead in the apparent rush of the Soviet soldiers to get on to the next village.

These women poignantly conveyed to me in this scene the key role women play in this courageous struggle against the communist regime in Afghanistan now propped up physically with the presence of 120,000 Soviet troops. The women's appearance revealed the dark reality of the refugee situation more vividly than did the scene of the better dressed crowd of men patiently seated around the grass lean-to where I conversed with the tribal leaders.

Refugee women must cope with the trauma of enforced idleness and isolation brought about by being separated from their agricultural domestic work and crowded into refugee camps or among the host population. An added burden is making do with the meager rations received from the relief organizations, which they award first to their men, followed by their children, and only finally to themselves.

Tradition plays an important role in the Afghan refugee women's contribution to the resistance effort against the Soviet-backed Afghan regime. Women's separateness and invisibility from the public world outside the home characterize Afghan traditional society, a society engaged in a struggle against the Soviet-controlled, purportedly modernist regimes of Babrak Karmal and now Najibullah. This freedom struggle is being waged within and supported from centers just beyond the Afghan borders, with Peshawar and the NorthWest Frontier Province (NWFP) in Pakistan serving as a major center for more than three million Afghan refugees. The Afghan freedom movement is characterized by a number of different groups formed on the basis of family, tribe, or religious (Islamic) ties typical of a traditional society. The harsh conditions of refugee living and the help provided by outside or host country agencies to ameliorate these conditions with such amenities as clinics nevertheless have brought about certain social changes in the lives of the women.

Scholars of Afghan affairs have paid little attention to the role women play in the freedom struggle, despite the fact that women and children constitute three-quarters of the refugee population, and the Mujahideen (holy warrior) leaders recognize women's importance to the jihad (or holy war) with their exhortations to preserve women's honor through the continued practice of seclusion. The reinforcement of this tradition, most Westerners have failed to notice, serves to strengthen the men's will to resist. Why have women received so little attention? Is it another case of "out of sight, out of mind"? Merely because women are out of sight does not excuse scholars and others concerned about the fate of the Afghan people from facing the fact that the liberation struggle cannot be won without the support of the women. How they are supporting this struggle, "behind *kala* walls," must be addressed as well as how the struggle is impacting upon the women.

The functional separateness of the Afghan women's world and the way it performs for the strength of the Mujahideen or freedom fighters' struggle are two issues crucial to this study. Has this separateness assumed new meaning in the special circumstances of the refugee and resistance presence in Pakistan? Is it a condition more stringently imposed by the men in these changed conditions? And how do the women cope with their separateness and added burden of responsibility for the survival of their family? In curious, unsuspected ways, the very separateness of women can and perhaps does meet the physical and psychological needs of the Afghan freedom movement, through the maintenance of informal networks among women, strengthened by the new access to meeting places such as clinics. Other research has found that such separateness "provides women with the opportunity to develop leadership skills and to accumulate resources for leverage and coalition building with other groups" (Staudt 1980, 58). To what extent does this hold true, if at all, for Afghan women refugees and their relationship to the freedom movement?

The basic characteristics of Afghan culture governing the women's role must be outlined first. Then a picture will be presented of the current conditions of Afghan refugee life in Pakistan, primarily in the NorthWest Frontier Province's capital of Peshawar, which I was able to visit. Finally, this study will explore the interaction of tradition and environment of refugee conditions upon the contributions of a publicly neglected majority of the Afghan refugee population, and the refugees' struggle to regain control of their homeland. Data is from a personal visit in May 1984 to Peshawar as well as the scant secondary sources on women's roles in Afghanistan.

PUSHTANA (THE HONORABLE AFGHAN WOMAN)

The code of Afghan behavior is permeated by the *Pushtunwali* or code of the Pushtuns, the major ethnic group in Afghanistan, comprising over 50 percent of the population, and 7 percent of the population in Pakistan. The code possesses three core elements: hospitality, refuge, and revenge. Other key values are equality, respect, pride, bravery, purdah (seclusion of women), pursuit of romantic encounters, worship of God, and devoted love for a friend. Focus here is on the traditional values more directly affecting women which they themselves manifest. Purdah is a key element in protection of the family's pride and honor (Knabe 1977). This seclusion from the world outside the family walls is customarily justified by invoking Quranic prescription and by the notion that women are basically

licentious and tempt men. Therefore, women must be protected from cuckholding their husbands or fiances. This
protective role underscores a means of male control over
women.(1)

Women are regarded as men's property. As noted by
Boesen, men exercise control over women in two crucial
ways: their control of marriage and of property, as illustrated by the institution of bride-price, the Pushtun prohibition of divorce (despite the Quranic allowances, primarily
to the men), and the taboo of land ownership for women
(again contrary to Islamic law and the actual practice in
many other Muslim countries). Women normally are viewed
as subordinates dependent on their husbands, as further
exemplified by women never asking the men their where-
abouts or expecting marital fidelity. The women also are
expected to give all the meat, choicest food, and the best
clothing to their husbands, as well as their personal wealth
if so demanded.(2)

Since the woman's standing is maintained primarily
through bearing sons to continue the family, she of course
must marry, for only through marriage can one's basic needs
be legitimately fulfilled. A certain stoicism characterizes
the women's expectations of marriage. The choice of husband most often is made by her family with its own concerns of lineage maintenance or gain and property. The
best she can hope for is a handsome and kind cousin or
close relative she has known and with whom she has grown
up. The worst is an old man from another village whom she
has never seen and who is unkind. In either case he is
obliged to provide for her materially and, it is to be hoped,
father her children who will in turn endow her with status
in her new home.

If the husband treats her unbearably she does have
recourse to breaking out and returning to her own family or
seeking *nanawatia* (refuge) with another family. Such an
action would bring dishonor to her husband's family as well
as to her own, the very threat of which therefore serves to
some extent as a brake on the husband's behavior. This
weapon is not used often, however, as her natal family has
given up rights to her through the customary bride-price at
the time of marriage. Moreover, since she is married to
one of equal standing or higher, her family would not have
much leverage and would cause an undesired conflict

between the two families (Boesen 1983).

The prohibition against divorce has given the women a sense of security to be balanced against the disagreeable situation of marriage to a man who mistreats her or takes on a second wife. This bittersweet "security" perhaps has contributed to the wife's resilience and cultivation of her role as wife-mother *par excellence* and mistress of the *kor*, or house. When her daughters are very young she transmits to them these skills of preparing bread and food, washing clothes, cleaning the house, and caring for the animals and vegetable garden within the compound, or *kala*.

In view of her world as defined by the *kala* walls, the woman must learn to cope with the demands generated by the social relations among the household women: the mother, sisters, mother-in-law, and sisters-in-law. The physical closeness of the household and the culture of purdah, throwing the women together for long periods of time, has in general made for an atmosphere of peacefulness and cooperation. However, this closeness has the potential of creating tension among women, as they are all dependent on men for survival and contact with the outside world. Women must develop their own resources of strength of personality and sons' loyalty if they are to improve their situation.(3)

Another means of dealing with her rivals and erring husband is the practice of magic (*djardu*). A woman will place amulets with verses from the Qur'an and key names in strategic places such as her husband's tea or in places frequented by her female rival in order to cast spells to exact the desired appropriate behavior (Boesen 1983).

The *goder* (watering place or proverbial meeting place) is another route of escape for women, as are the romantic fantasies acted out in poetry (*landays*) in which the *goder* figures prominently. It is at the *goder* that women may hope to meet other women, and other men. The institution of the *goder* has changed its form in the refugee environment in Pakistan as medical clinics have to some degree sup-planted the watering place as a meeting ground for women.

In Afghanistan, the very suspicion of a woman's search or pursuit of extramarital affairs is done at great personal risk. Traditionally, the husband or fiance is bound to kill her and her alleged lover. Yet, she may resort to such a dangerous means to escape if she sees this as her only hope for an improvement in her life. More likely, however, will be her acceptance of the *kor* (house), and purdah, relieved by periodic visits to the *goder*.

Should the woman engage, however, in a flirtation or affair at the symbolic *goder*, she can at least count on the support of her fellow female household members. Women's solidarity against the men is broken only by household lines. Conflicts between the women of the two households are dealt with only by the women, as the men are not brought into the disputes at all.

As beings set apart and excluded from the public, women are united in their hostility toward men as "bad, ugly, and cruel." The women find comfort among themselves during the gatherings over domestic chores performed together or for pure entertainment. In any case, the men have no expressed interest in women's affairs, in keeping with their assumption of superiority. On the other hand, women have no compunction about openly criticizing their husbands. Moreover, since women do not hold land in Afghanistan they are not subject to the rivalry that develops among men. Although competition exists among women over possessions, the hostility is not as severe as it is among men, perhaps because women are thrown together more often.

The women's sense of harmony and community of feeling also can be attributed to the relatively low level of their expectations, in contrast to their men's higher and often unrealistic ones of world conquest. Women have the defined boundaries of the house over which they can exercise control, but men realistically cannot hope to rule the world. Moreover, women have the luxury generally of remaining in private and being able to express themselves openly without fear of public reaction and loss of face. The women, therefore, have been much more accepting of their fate (Lindholm 1982).

The male Pushtun "must present to the world the image of the hawk, the bird of prey. What he must conceal is the dove, the sensitive victim" (Lindhom 1982,189). The values of equality and pride develop survival traits of struggle, cruelty, and at times betrayal. Pride and the hostility toward the opposite sex to compel the Pushtun to conform to the outward norms all the time, and any deviation from the social norms is ridiculed by peers. Therefore, custom can lead men to act against their inner feelings--as, for example, a family will keep their daughters from attending school for "fear of what the neighbors would think."

Whereas the Afghan men's world may be conflict-ridden in the quest for individual independence and honor, the Afghan women's world is characteristically more cooperative, born out of the recognition of their isolated common status as bearers of the family's honor, food, and children. How have these worlds changed in the context of the flight from a foreign force bent on changing the basic cultural values of the Afghan to an environment undergoing its own processes of change, though within the familiar cultural framework of Islam? How different are the women's lives in the refugee conditions in Pakistan? How are these differences affecting their traditional role as silent but essential preservers of Afghan men's and family's honor, and indeed the honor of the Afghan people? An examination of the refugee conditions in Pakistan in the area of greatest concentration, the NorthWest Frontier Province, is the focus of this study. I will not deal with the internal refugees, or with the refugees in Iran.

NANAWATIA IN PAKISTAN

In April 1978 the "Red" Prince turned President, Muhammad Daoud, was overthrown by his erstwhile, now impatient, supporters, the communists comprising two factions: the Parchamis and the Khalqis. The successor regime was led by Nur Muhammad Taraki, a Khalqi, and his colleagues, Hafizullah Amin, a fellow Khalqi, and Babrak Karmal, a Parchami.

The Taraki regime soon embarked on a program to modernize the country rapidly, first by putting through a land reform law, as David Edwards indicates in Chapter 1, and then by limiting the bride-price practices and raising the minimum marriage age. Both of these so-called reforms struck at the heart of the key traditional patron-client relationships in the rural areas. The Taraki regime also thought, erroneously, that it could win support from the "oppressed" tenants by abolishing rural indebtedness to the rich landowners. Taraki, despite his nomadic origins, failed to understand rural Afghan society and its bonds of mutual dependence and resistance to outside intervention (Bradsher 1985).

The bride-price limitation and the minimum marriage age laws as well as the promotion of girls' education, whether or not genuinely intended to promote the status of women, were resisted equally by most Afghans. Rural economic relations were based to some degree on bride-price payments, and furthermore these payments were regarded as women's social security. Whether the Khalqis were genuinely interested in what they considered to be reform or whether their purpose was to break up rural power relationships can be subject to debate, but these self-appointed reformers in retrospect clearly needed to understand the reason these seemingly archaic customs existed and the full range of social purposes they served. It was serious enough that the new Marxist regime failed to recognize the vital social function performed by the much maligned concept of bride-price. Worse yet, this regime and the subsequent Marxist regimes of Hafizullah Amin, Babrak Karmal and presumably Najibullah have coopted the women's liberation issue.

Despite the strong and often blunt resistance to these new laws by rich and poor alike, these laws were forcibly implemented. The regime's determination to move ahead with its reforms contributed to the birth of the Afghan resistance movement, the activation of the traditional principle of refuge or *nanawatia* in neighboring and culturally affiliated lands, and the re-emphasis of purdah in exile.

Most members of the small, urban, non-Marxist elite who might have supported genuine social reform have fled to distant countries. The vacuum has been filled by the predominantly rural and traditionally oriented mullahs who have reinvoked their customs in a show of resistance solidarity. By the end of 1978, the first year of the communist regime, 25,000 had fled across the border to Pakistan. In 1984, the year I visited the NWFP, the Afghan refugee population numbered worldwide about five million, with more than three million registered in Pakistan, mostly in the NorthWest Frontier Province (Bradsher 1985).(4)

The growth of the refugee population is, of course, a product of the Afghan communist regime's difficulty in gaining popular acceptance and of conflicts within the leadership which contributed to the rise in brutality by the regime and the increased and direct Soviet involvement in

the communist rule of Afghanistan. This Soviet rule cul-
minated in the December 27, 1979 armed invasion of the
country in an attempt to save "face" and their investment
pursuant to the Brezhnev Doctrine.

After Hafizullah maneuvered himself into, and forced
Taraki out of, power in the first year of communist domination, he proved to be even more brutal in the exercise of
this power. His ruthless response to the growing opposition
to communist rule in the rural areas served only to harden
the Afghan resistance and to embarrass the Soviet sponsors.
This resort to armed intervention in December, 1979 and the
forcible replacement of Amin with the Soviet-preferred
Babrak Karmal were seen as more accommodating to both
themselves and the Afghan people. The resistance to communist rule now turned to resistance to the Soviet armed
presence in Afghanistan and has continued unabated, with
far-reaching consequences for Afghan women.

With the Soviet invasion and the paradoxical Soviet-
demanded release of thousands of prisoners held by the now
deposed Amin regime, the refugee population in Pakistan had
increased to 300,000. Each month 25,000 had been leaving
their homes in Afghanistan to seek refuge, primarily in
Pakistan (U.S. Committee on Refugees 1983).(5)

Most of the refugees belong to the Pushtun tribes who
comprise the majority in Afghanistan and a considerable
minority in Pakistan.(6) Other groups represented in the
refugee population are the Tajiks, Uzbeks, Turkomans,
Badakshanis, Hazaras, and Nuristanis. Regionally, the refugees have come for the most part from the central and
western sections of Afghanistan. Eighty percent of the
refugees have flocked to the NWFP (International Labour
Office 1983).

Debate exists over the exact number of refugees in
Pakistan as some contend the numbers are underestimated,
though others contend the reverse (U.S. Committee on
Refugees 1983). Certainly some refugees are living with
their kin who have resided on the Pakistan border for some
years--testimony to the political rather than physical or
natural border between Pakistan and Afghanistan. This
border, the Durand Line established in 1893, ignored the
dominant presence of the ethnic group, the Pushtuns, who
comprise 51 percent of the Afghan population and who
considered the border area their home long before the Great

Powers sought spheres of influence and favorable boundary definition in the late nineteenth century (L. Dupree 1980a). Since then Pakistani-Afghan relations have been marked periodically by disputes over the "Pushtunistan" issue. In the recent attempts by the Karmal and Najibullah regimes to secure popular Afghan support, the issue may well be used again to divide the Pushtuns and reduce their involvement in the resistance.

The great majority of the refugees are women, children, and elderly males who cannot participate in guerrilla operations inside Afghanistan. A third of the refugees are women and 48 percent are children. Almost three-quarters of the refugee households are headed by women (Overseas Education Fund 1984). The average number of persons per family as registered with the authorities is seven (York 1980). In terms of occupation and geography, the majority of the refugee population has come from the agricultural areas and are primarily agriculturalists (U.S. Committee on Refugees 1983).

The Pakistan government has taken the initiative in assuming responsibility by providing the Afghans a refuge for humanitarian and political reasons. Understandably, they wish to control the migrant situation in view of the common ethnic population shared by both Pakistan and Afghanistan-- the Pushtuns, the influx strains they are bringing on the local society and resources; and the security considerations vis-a-vis the Soviet presence in Afghanistan.

The Pakistan Government has increasingly had to appeal to the international organizations that have responded chiefly through the medium of the UN High Commissioner for Refugees (UNHCR). As aid from abroad has increased, the Pakistani government has reduced its own contributions of monthly stipends to refugees. Presently the Pakistani government provides a cash supplement of 50 rupees (PRs. 14.05 = $1.00, 1984 average) per refugee per month to a limit of 500 rupees per family, and it transports food and supplies from Karachi to the hinterland. To reduce the pressure on the local Pakistani population, the government has stipulated that the refugees must remain in the refugee villages to qualify for monthly stipends (Azhar 1984). The particular effect of these refugee policies on women's development merits further study.

The refugees are housed in approximately 330 villages,

most of them in the NWFP. While each is designed to house 5,000, several villages comprise as many as 12,000. In Baluchistan, the village populations average around 14,000. Refugees in that province have concentrated in the districts of Pishin, Chazai, and Quetta and in the NWFP in Peshawar, Kurian, Mardan, Baaner, North Waziristan, Kolat, and Abbottabad (International Labour Office 1983).

The middle class urban Afghans about which Grant Farr writes elsewhere in this volume are not to be found in the camps. Rather, members of those classes who came as refugees live among Pakistanis, usually in Peshawar or Islamabad, if they have not moved on to Europe, the United States, or elsewhere.

Settlements are basically of two kinds: the refugee tent villages (RTVs) and the older, more stable structures of mud and brick. The second type is more likely to indicate the sedentary culture of the refugees and their earlier arrival in Peshawar, while the tent villages represent the nomadic style of life of some of the refugees with poorer economic status.

The mud-brick housing units are characterized by the high-walled family compounds which provide the security sought by the families, particularly for their women whom they are determined to protect from the outside world. Two or three rooms usually surround the open-walled space, depending on the size of the family and their economic resources (International Labour Office 1983). One room typically is used for receiving guests and for family living activities; it is customarily furnished and decorated with the family's handicraft of embroidered hangings and coverings. The open space or courtyard is used for vegetable gardening, stabling the livestock the family managed to bring with them from Afghanistan, water and fuel storage, or a well.

NANAWATIA LIFE FOR WOMEN

Within these walls, once the families have been able to construct them, the women lead their lives, performing the household tasks of baking bread, cleaning, tending the children, and, when conditions permit, practicing their skills in handicrafts.

The division of labor in the family is clearly drawn on the basis of age and sex, whereby the older women are responsible for maintaining the stoves and cooking. Depending on the number of women in the household, the various other tasks are allocated to the daughters and daughters-in-law. Fetching water can be time-consuming. Since it involves leaving the house the older women may perform this function, provided the family (particularly the men if there are any present) feels it is in a "safe" environment (York 1980). Otherwise, little girls of five or six are delegated to go to the river or water source to wash the dishes and collect the water (Christensen 1984). The younger women will be left at home to do the handiwork as their eyesight may be better.

Purdah, the institution of female seclusion, has been reinforced in some cases and relaxed in others. Because of the crowded conditions in the tented villages and the frequent absence of the men who are seeking work or are working, fighting, or dead, the traditional notions of modesty have been mitigated somewhat as the women have to perform some of the tasks originally done by men, such as the marketing and dealing with bureaucratic institutions. Again the older women more likely assume these tasks. Differences in ethnic background, migratory practices, and occupation account for the variations in the practice of purdah. For example, some of the non-Pushtun women engage in itinerant trading of cloth and the very poor women without male support must earn their own living, primarily as tailors for other women (International Labour Office 1983).

Purdah, it should be noted, is supported not only by men for their own religiously attributed reasons of social control but also by women who view it as a convenient excuse for not performing tiresome tasks. Some women also cling to purdah as a way to preserve their privacy in a now more alien world. As Christiansen aptly notes, purdah provides the opportunity for preserving one's own identity and a certain stability in the face of external pressures (1984). Westerners who have been quick to impose their own ethnocentric perceptions should note the value of this seemingly anachronistic custom for a people under siege whose very survival is at stake.

Three basic groups of refugee women can be identified in the NWFP. One group is found in the Refugee Tent Villages (RTVs). These refugees have not obtained resources by finding a job and housing, enabling them to move in among the Pakistanis. The women and their remaining male providers (brothers, sons, cousins, uncles, fathers) are compelled to live in these villages in order to qualify for the rations awarded by the UNHCR through the Pakistani agency responsible for refugee affairs.

The second group of women are those who have just arrived from Afghanistan, and the bureaucratic processes for registration as refugees have not been completed. I visited such a camp, established as a result of the Spring, 1984 Soviet offensive. Comprising 5,000 families, this tented camp is situated 1.5 miles from the Afghan border, 40 miles northwest of Peshawar in the Mohmand Agency. I met with some of the women, most of whom were widows who had lost the greater part of their families from Soviet bombs and napalm.

Basic villager concerns were for survival. Between eight and ten individuals occupied a tent; approximately a quarter of the families at that time had no tent covering--a disturbing fact. The tent village survived on the gifts of fellow tribal members who had arrived earlier. A water truck, but no relief agency food, arrived perhaps once a day: the explanation for this gap was that the paperwork authorizing food allotments took up to three months to complete.(7)

In this camp it was evident that the tribal community spirit was very much alive and held in control by the male elders. The women were quartered in a section of the camp an appropriate distance from the center with an improvised lean-to or *mehmakhana* made of saplings, which must have been brought some distance to that barren, windswept plain.

While the distance between the women's quarters and the male quarters established a modicum of traditional separateness, the women did not shy away from gathering to relate their plight to me, a female stranger, accompanied by an Afghan male, a member of our group. They were still visibly shaken from their ordeal of having lost many members of their family and in some instances having been sexually assaulted by their Soviet attackers.

In contrast to this group, the third group of women refugees comprises those who have managed to arrive with sufficient financial resources or who earn enough income to live in the city among the Pakistanis so that they are not dependent on handouts from the host government.

The three groups of women refugees necessarily differ somewhat in their adjustment to and role in refugee life and in their support of the freedom fighting effort.

For the first two groups, basic issues of survival intermesh with support for the Mujahideen. To begin with, food and nutrition affect the long-term survival of the Afghan people. But food distribution reflects the secondary status of women and children and the role women's honor plays: women do not go to the marketplace on their own to obtain their rations if there is a male relative in the extended family. As a result, women heading households are not as likely to receive their fair share from the men. Indeed, this is evidenced by incidence of anemia among the adult female population (Hunte 1986).

Moreover, the provided foodstuffs are often unfamiliar and there is an inadequate supply of wood for cooking (Overseas Education Fund 1984).(8) The responsibility for distributing the food is given to the representatives of the refugee villages who are often religious leaders or mullahs who in turn distribute the food to male heads of households. Quite frequently food given to the refugees is diverted to the local markets, apparently as a means for generating income to support the Mujahideen's return to Afghanistan. The sacrificers are, of course, the women and children (Report on Refugee Aid 1981).

On the other hand, some tribal leaders may well have become sensitized to the women's needs. At least in the camp I visited, the male tribal leaders were respectful enough of the concerns expressed about the women to verify that the women had been given the financial donations as we requested.

In general, however, even when the food is delivered, the custom of serving the men and guests first means that women eat whatever remains. Nevertheless, availability of some food is evident, with bread being the staple. In one study it was observed that women of the household consumed about four loaves of bread in contrast to the men's six or more. According to reports, men usually saw to it, however, that an adequate supply of the food was left for the women and girls (Christensen 1984).

Health is also a problem for the refugees. Although the women are in the habit of maintaining themselves and their homes with particular attention to cleanliness, and continue to do so even under the difficult refugee conditions, problems of adequate sanitation remain. In some cases, crowded conditions and the improvisations of the dwellings have resulted in inadequate latrine facilities. Communal latrines have been built in some camps, but the drainage could be much improved. This lack of sanitation has been cited as a major cause of gastro-intestinal diseases prevalent among the refugees (N. Dupree n.d.).(9)

Although the refugees need good medical care, a shortage of medical care in the camps is caused by the reluctance of Pakistani physicians and health workers to serve under such difficult conditions, even though they are less adverse than those found among Ethiopian famine victims. The medical units in the refugee villages nevertheless are poorly equipped, and mothers seeking treatment have been turned away by the local unit with the advice that they could be treated only in the hospital in the nearest city, an unrealistic recommendation given the refugees' logistical problems and lack of money (Report on Refugee Aid 1981).

However, the provision of modern if modest health services in the camps is providing a new opportunity for the informal gathering of women, just as fetching water at the local well in the past helped serve women's social needs in the home village back in Afghanistan. In my visit with one of the few Afghan women physicians in Peshawar I was told how the clinics swell in numbers at night as women come to care for their relatives and find shelter and what might be termed a "social refuge" in the process.

Some women come to the clinics describing their own sickness symptoms, "weakness" or "fever." Often the physicians find no clinical basis for these symptoms, only psychological ones: the sense of frustration with their refugee status; their separation from their fields, their families, the memories of forced flight from their villages; and the loss of family members through burning and other acts of terror.

A hospital operated by one of the resistance organizations has six women physicians and fourteen female nurses on the staff, two of whom are Afghan women physicians. They are faced with 350 women per day seeking medical advice, only ten of whom are admitted to the hospital as inpatients. One of the two Afghan women physicians, Dr. Syeda, revealed that most of the others came for moral support in either caring for relatives admitted to the hospital or the opportunity to share experiences and facilities with their fellow women suffering the plight of crowded conditions, uncertainty, little or no work, and lost male providers.(10)

The women living among the Pakistanis rather than in the refugee camps are as isolated, in many cases, as those in the RTVs, if not more so. They must rely on their own families, what remains of them, for moral and economic support. If urban but uneducated, they do not venture out of their compounds unless they are within close walking distance of their relatives.

Both in the RTVs and outside, these women may be engaged in some kind of productive enterprise, such as embroidery or weaving. The products then are marketed by the male members of the family. On the other hand, depending on the economic-social status they have been able to acquire or retain, these women may be involved in an activity outside the home, earning the money for the family in a service occupation or working among the Afghan refugees, contributing their skills as teacher, physician, or nurse. These positions, however, have been scarce because of the ready availability and successful preemption by Pakistani personnel.

For the majority of the Afghan women in the Pakistani community, their major problems are coping with the uncertainties of their immediate surroundings: tension with their Pakistani hosts and neighbors who have discovered the advantages of manipulating for their own benefit a dependent population. Rental agreements, for example, are broken when a Pakistani landlord discovers he can get a higher rental fee by threatening or claiming he can get a higher fee from another renter. The Afghan family either must keep moving their quarters or pay even more.

How do the women maintain their spirit in the face of this unfriendly new environment where they may be deprived of the daily work to which they were accustomed in Afghanistan? The cultural sense of fatalism combined with innate resilience serve them well. Both men and women have been imbued with a basic sense of acceptance of "the will of God" and in particular the women have internalized this profoundly held belief.

While in Afghanistan, a woman was not given many life

choices other than accepting or rejecting her parents' or brothers' selection of a husband for her. She was not trained to expect much from life. The best she could hope for was perhaps a few years of schooling, then a husband who would provide for her and give her sons so she could acquire status within her husband's family as soon as possible after marriage.

Now she hopes that those male members who have been left behind in Afghanistan have not been killed by the Soviet-backed regime, that she can find a suitable wife for her son who must carry on the family name--a goal that may involve trading her daughter in marriage, and, finally, that there will be a return of some semblance of security to her life, both mental and economic.

The uncertainty is perhaps the most trying for the women who are now dependent on the few remaining male members of the family with whom they fled to Pakistan. As an example, one interviewed household of eight was dependent on a single male member for its livelihood as the women whose husbands were left behind received no support from them. The rent, equivalent to $150 per month, for their house ate up most of whatever income the male breadwinner brought in from his store.(11)

At the other extreme is a group of widows separated along with their children from their male relatives and visibly housed in an area near the VIP helicopter pad. The reasons for the establishment of this particular camp remain unclear as the Pakistani authorities claimed the widows requested this separation, but the widows rejected this claim and complained that the male headmen and administrators were trying to use and control them in this fashion. Certainly, this camp's strategic placement within easy reach of prospective VIP donors would suggest the male headmen and administrators are using the women to elicit charitable donations.

Whatever the reason, this kind of situation promotes a dependency syndrome which is all the harder on the women when "temporary" assistance dries up completely (N. Dupree 1984).(12) The male headmen were apparently concerned that the widows' condition, which did not seem to be ameliorated by their male relatives' household environment, would lead the women to pursue certain unacceptable and nontraditional occupations in order to survive.(13) With the establishment of this camp, a kind of institutional separation was deemed to be in the widows' "best interest."

The renewed importance of *pushtunwali* and the male leaders' perceived need to enforce purdah also have adversely affected whatever progress had been made in women's and girls' education in Afghanistan. The Soviet-backed regime loudly proclaims its commitment to educational reform for women. Whether the motivations are genuine or simply the means to more effective political socialization remain unclear, but these exogenous forces (exogenous because they are both foreign and urban) are rejected out of hand by the more traditional society. School for refugee women and girls has suffered as it is seen as threatening for their essential seclusion. In 1983 the adult refugee female literacy rate reportedly stood at 1 percent and the male literacy rate at 5 percent (International Labour Office 1983). The literacy rate nationwide is usually cited at between 10 and 11 percent. Notwithstanding these constraints, literacy rates will probably climb in Afghanistan, especially in the controlled urban areas, and also in the better established refugee camps. Yet constraints do remain for many as the very idea of girls' education has been taboo among refugees in the early post-1978 revolution years.

Ironically, education may now be preferable to women's enforced idleness which so alarms some Afghan male leaders and the international agencies. Schools have been established for girls, among them 19 primary schools in the NWFP refugee tent villages.(14) These institutions have the potential for providing alternative centers for women networking.

For instance, in the Darsamand Camp in the Kohat District, a program to train midwives has been established by the International Rescue Committee. Some of the trainees were traditional midwives (*dai*) interested in learning modern methods while others were widows seeking self-support. Financial incentives of 400 Pakistani rupees per month during training and PRs 900 upon graduation encourage the women to join the program which also is geared to comprehensive maternal and child care. Despite some difficulties, the program generally has been accepted, and prenatal visits to clinics have increased, as has improved health for children under five (ARIN January 1985).

In another area, a school for girls has been established by the Union of Afghan Mujahid Doctors. Named the Naheed Shaheed School, it serves the urban refugees but also the camps by providing bus service. The staff is reportedly energetic and the environment for women provides a healthy alternative to the crowded and often unsatisfactory camp conditions.(15)

Self-help programs are also being developed, spurred on by international agencies' investigation, to encourage women to practice and benefit more directly from their skills in handicrafts. Settings non-threatening to men are customarily the traditional home, but the clinic and the separate schools for girls could provide a healthy substitute *goder*, or meeting place for women.

CONCLUDING REMARKS

The conditions of refugee life for Afghans have reinforced the code of *pushtunwali* as applied to women. The strengths of the Afghan people--bravery, singlemindedness, pride--are being exercised in the struggle against a Soviet-backed regime. Although this regime claims to be modernist and to address itself to the liberation of women through aggressive education and social reform policies to eliminate the institution of bride-price, it is perceived by the Mujahideen to be destroying the treasured fabric of Afghan culture, of being, in a word, cultural imperialists. One suspects that the primary regime goal is to establish political, social, and economic control.

The other core element of *pushtunwali*, the honor of the family as maintained by the women who therefore must be protected by purdah, also has gained significance in this situation of *nanawatia* in Pakistan and revenge or *badal* against the foreign rulers in Afghanistan.

Women's seclusion, mandated by the Afghan refugee situation as they are away from the familiar and relatively freer village environment, serves the freedom fighters' need for a core of stability. The women's stoicism, resilience, acceptance of, and indeed pride in their respected role as maintainers of the home may well be crucial to the jihad if the religious leaders' claims of the need to reimpose the seclusion of women for their protection can be taken at face value.

Or is the real reason an extension of the male's need for security? In a time of enormous social and geographic dislocation the traditional Afghan male may not feel he controls much, but he may console himself with the belief that at the very least he controls his women. As noted elsewhere, the shelter of the home, protecting the pre-servers of the family--the women, is particularly important in a world perceived by both sexes to be dangerous. The notions of peril and refuge are generally important in Middle Eastern society. *Refuge* is sought within the *kala* walls from a dangerous and unpredictable world outside. The dangerous conditions in Afghanistan and the resulting splitting of families thus reinforces the Afghan's under-standing of the world as dangerous. *Refuge* has been found in Pakistan to a certain extent but must be aided by the more conscious "protection" via seclusion, of the women.(16) But wars are by their very nature catalytic--engines of social change. Afghan women have had to take on new roles in the absence of their menfolk. They have emerged with new strength.

The adherence to purdah among the refugees varies in degree depending on their living situation. If the women find themselves in camps controlled by the fundamentalists, they are almost forced to comply with the custom, whether or not they had observed it in Afghanistan. The term "fundamentalist" is a relative one as all those involved in the resistance movement are profoundly Muslim. In con-trast, educated, predominantly urban middle class Afghan women who live away from the camps may not be accus-tomed to stricter interpretation of purdah although they still will pursue a conservative lifestyle. Certainly, adherence to tradition is viewed by the traditionalists and religious leaders as a demonstration of their commitment to jihad.

The larger question of whether the war for the liberation of the Afghan homeland is in turn a liberating experience for women is a matter of much controversy. The women's separateness under refugee conditions, devoid of their customary work and opportunities for freer social interac-tions in the familiar surroundings of village life, also is testing this frequently cited strength of character. This strain is exemplified in clinics which offer possible treat-ment for nervous ailments, and are sources of comfort and opportunities for otherwise unavailable social communication.

Whether this separateness is providing an opportunity for women to "develop leadership skills and to accumulate resources for leverage and coalition building with other groups" is an open question at this point. Because of their profession or husband's organizational position with the Mujahideen, educated Afghan women in the NWFP feel constrained about exercising any overt leadership role among women because of political considerations and pressures, especially from the conservative religious leaders gaining power in the movement.

Afghan professional women who have been lucky in gaining positions in the Mujahideen-operated institutions such as hospitals provide an informal leadership role of counselor in their professional capacity, but their work load and their additional "natural" role of keepers of the home fires necessarily limit their activities among women.

On the other hand, at the widows' showcase camp of Nasir Bagh, these women demonstrate a lively patriotism and energetic enterprise as they seek sewing machines and weaving looms, and consider setting up shop. They point out "as 'heads' of the families we have many responsibilities. When we return home to Afghanistan, people will discover there are many more adults among the women than among the men. The task will be tough; we must start preparing right now for the day we rebuild our country" (U.S. Committee on Refugees 1984, 22).

Although the women's role in the freedom struggle inside Afghanistan has not been mentioned, it is a subject worthy of study but beyond the realm of possibility at the present time. The accounts which have filtered through from returning Mujahideen indicate that women have been playing a key role in the struggle from distributing night letters (shabnamas) in Kabul, as objects of arrest and torture, to simply baking bread under siege for the Mujahideen. An Afghan Mujahida exhorted, "Though there are individuals who never paid respect to the rights of women, I would just like to mention that women and girls today play an important role in the independence struggle against Communism in our Motherland" (*Afghanistad Jehad* March 21, 1983).

The above observation certainly should apply to Afghan women in refuge as they cope with uncertainty, enforced idleness, loss of family, and new demands on their honored status as upholders of the family and identity and their dignity and resilience.

NOTES

1. See Lindholm (1982), page 211; Boesen (1983), page 119. See also Knabe (1977), page 333.
2. See Lindholm (1982), page 210. See also Ahmad (1980), pages 202-203; Boesen (1983), page 109.
3. See Boesen (1983), page 116. See also Lajoinie (1980); Ahmad (1980), page 204; Delloye (1980).
4. See also Tavakolian (1984).
5. More recent reports put the flow rate per month at 6,000.
6. There are between eight and ten million Pushtuns in Pakistan, or ten percent of the Pakistani population.
7. See also Denker (1985), page 788.
8. See also Christensen (1984), page 60.
9. See also York (1980), page 34. Our interviews in Peshawar confirmed these findings.
10. This information comes from an interview with Dr. Syeda in Peshawar on May 17, 1984. See also Dupree (1986), "The Afghan Refugee Family Abroad: A Focus on Afghanistan."
11. The family of engineer Seyid Habib Rahman was interviewed in Peshawar on May 17, 1984.
12. See also Dupree's "The Women's Dimension Among Afghan Refugees in Pakistan."
13. Various Mujahideen were interviewed in Peshawar on May 16, 1984.
14. See Dupree's "The Woman's Dimension Among Afghan Refugees in Pakistan" and ARIN, *Newsletter*, No. 14 (June/July 1984). The latter notes that "Private, non-party, educational initiatives have become less difficult in Pakistan since mid-1983 when a new Commissioner for Afghan Refugees in the NWFP, Rustam Shah Mohmand, was appointed, an open minded man in contrast to his fundamentalist-inclined predecessor."
15. See ARIN, *Newsletter*, No. 17 (March/April 1985, page 7). The school is named after a young woman student imprisoned by the Taraki regime in 1978 for distributing leaflets against the regime. She had been tortured by her captors in the effort to secure information about her colleagues. In a last ditch effort, the prison director called her into his office and did with her sexually. Unable to face her cellmates or herself with this indignity to her honor, she thereupon slit her throat with her fingernail and scraw-

led the word "liberty" on the wall.   This account was related to me by the Mujahideen in Peshawar, May 1984.

16. Dupree (1986) used the framework from Gulick's (1976) book to describe the scenario of peril and refuge.

5

The New Afghan Middle Class as Refugees and Insurgents

Grant M. Farr

The emphasis in the Afghan conflict up to now has centered on the countryside where the insurgency has had its greatest successes and from which most of the refugees have come. Many of the Afghans from the cities, primarily members of the new Afghan middle class, now find themselves on the sideline of a war that desperately needs their help. This study deals with the role of this new Afghan urban middle class. It includes a brief history of the development of this class in Afghanistan and the political activities of members of this class before the Coup of 1978, examining how the middle class deals with the present situation, how and why they leave Afghanistan, and which conditions they face in exile. Finally the study examines the future of the new Afghan middle class, both as refugees and as insurgents. Despite present attention paid to the traditional religious groups, many members of this class have participated in active, although secret, secular elements of the Afghan resistance. It is the new urban middle class that will assume greater importance as it shapes the future of the Afghan conflict.

I gathered data for this study in Peshawar, Pakistan, in the Winter and Fall of 1983 from Afghan refugees, as well as from Afghan refugees in the United States. While in Peshawar data were collected in open-ended taped interviews with many members of the new Afghan middle class who were then refugees in Pakistan. In addition, a more systematic survey was conducted in and around Peshawar using a fixed questionnaire for statistical information. Other secondary and archival resources were also consulted.

DEVELOPMENT OF THE AFGHAN NEW MIDDLE CLASS

While students of social change in the less developed world have focused heavily on class development and class conflict, class analysis has been largely resisted by scholars of Muslim countries. This lack of information occurs to a great extent because the social structure of Islamic societies appears to be built around vertical organizations such as kinship, tribe, or ethnicity, structures that intersect horizontal or class lines. As a result the development of class consciousness and consequent social change, as experienced in other parts of the world (Europe and Latin America, for instance), has not apparently occurred in the Middle Eastern countries.

A class is a group of individuals united by common economic interest, usually a similar mode of employment. They usually, but not always, share the same amounts of power and a common lifestyle. Historically, scholars have divided Islamic societies into anywhere from two to seven classes (Bill and Leiden 1983). The basic three classes are the peasants, the bazaar keepers, and the ruling class, usually some kind of royalty. To these a clerical class of powerful *Ulama*, a bureaucratic class of government scribes and officials, the nomads, and a traditional working class are often added. With some exceptions, these classes historically have seldom exhibited "classlike" characteristics, specifically the development of some type of collective consciousness or collective action that would make these class distinctions useful in understanding forces of social change in Islamic countries.

Two new classes, however, have emerged that have changed this picture: a new industrial working class and a new middle class. The new middle class especially has been important in less developed countries, including Afghanistan.(1) The new middle class, as distinguished from the old middle class, are those employed in the modern sectors of the economy, no matter how small, and in the state bureaucracy. The modern middle class is composed of Westernized intellectuals, civil servants and white-collar employees, and Western-oriented merchants, while the old middle class is composed of small landowners, officials of traditional pre-Western bureaucracies, traditional shopkeepers, and the clergy (Chirot 1977). More specifically this new class is drawn primarily from "teachers, bureaucrats, professors, students, technocrats, engineers, physicians, writers, artists, journalists and middle ranking army officers" (Bill and Leiden 1983, 123).

The size of the new middle class varies directly with the size of the modern sector of the society. In some Middle East countries, such as Egypt, the new middle class may constitute over 15 percent of the population, while in other countries, such as Afghanistan, it may amount to less than 1 percent. In addition, since the state controls most of the development of the modern sector in emerging societies, most of the members of the new middle class are employed by the government in one way or another. This scenario is true in Afghanistan.

The rise of a new middle class presents several challenges to traditional societies as this new class finds itself in direct competition with other classes, especially the traditional ruling class, for societal power and influence. Being a product of modern education, this new class prefers to advance through merit, education, and professional skills, and is often critical of the traditional ways of ruling through personal influence and patrimonialism. The members of this class tend to prefer universalism to particularism. While they may disagree strongly, even violently, among themselves over ideology and strategy, they usually favor political and economic reform, generally emulating some foreign model. Following their class interests, segments of the new middle class may try to capture the reins of government. Many segments have succeeded, as members of this class now rule many Muslim countries, including Afghanistan.

The new middle class also represents a horizontal layer in a largely vertically structured society. While the transition is less than complete, members of this class tend to form allegiances toward occupation, profession, and lifestyle among people at the same level. The traditional symbols of allegiances in Islamic societies are to vertical structures including family, kin, tribe, ethnicity, and religion. As class awareness develops, this new middle class begins to find itself in conflict with these traditional social structures. In Afghanistan the new middle class found itself in conflict primarily with tribe and religion.

Early in its development the Afghan new middle class

split into three political orientations, each with many sub-factions. One of the factions of the leftists came to power, and another group, the fundamentalists, fled to Pakistan to lead the insurgency against the new government. The rest, the Western-oriented liberals and much of the remaining left, were pushed aside. This study depicts and analyzes these events.

EDUCATION IN AFGHANISTAN

While the members of this new middle class are not all intellectuals, in any real sense, they are nonetheless an intelligentsia, in that they are the members of the society with modern education. They are distinguished from the traditional middle class whose education was in the traditional *madrassahs*, or religious schools. In Afghanistan, university education was important for entry into this class, and also was important in shaping its nature. Afghanistan historically has only two means to receive higher education: to go abroad for education or to go to Kabul University.

For training beyond the baccalaureate level an education abroad was necessary, and several hundred Afghans did so each year. However, students could earn a baccalaureate degree at home.

Kabul University was founded in 1932, in the second year of the rule of Nadir Shah, and began as a medical faculty (L. Dupree 1980a). By 1978 Kabul University had grown to a student body of around 6000, offering baccalaureate degrees in a wide range of subjects including engineering, law, and agriculture as well as the usual liberal arts topics.

In the 1950s and 1960s when Kabul University grew rapidly, many of the departments, called faculties, were supported and staffed by foreign universities. The faculty of medicine, for instance, was aided and staffed early on by Lyon University, France, agriculture by the University of Wyoming, from the U.S.A., and economics by the University of Bochum, Bonn, and Germany (L. Dupree 1980a). However, by the mid-1970s there were generally enough Afghans with advanced degrees in most areas to replace much of the foreign staff. In addition, by 1978 at the time of the coup, there was also a polytechnic school for training in science and engineering and a medical school in Jalalabad.

The students at Kabul University in the early years were primarily children from relatively well off Kabul families, including the children of the traditional upper and middle class: land lords, well-to-do merchants, and officials in the government.   Since a large segment of the students came from Kabul they were mostly speakers of Dari, a Persian dialect.   Since the emerging middle class was heavily Dari-speaking Kabul residents, while the traditional ruling elite was from Pushtun backgrounds, the government made several attempts to incorporate the Pushtu speakers into this emerging class by bringing students from Pushtun tribal areas into the campus.

In 1959 dormitories were built at the University to house students from rural or outlying areas.   In addition, a quota system was implemented in 1964 that fixed the rural/urban ratio at 60%/40% for entering students at Kabul University. The direct purpose was to increase the proportion of non-Kabuli students, primarily Pushtu speakers, in part because the government felt that the growing campus unrest that began in the late '60s and '70s could be dampened by the infusion of "country boys."   The imposition of the ratio, however, was also part of a plan to incorporate the dispersed and largely independent Pushtun tribes into the national framework by bringing to Kabul the sons of tribal leaders for education.

This process was furthered by the building in Kabul of two tribal boarding lycees (high schools), Rahman Baba Lycee and Khushal Khan Lycee.   Rahman Baba Lycee was built for the Pushtun tribes on the Afghan side of the Afghan-Pakistan border, while Khushal Khan Lycee was built for the Pushtun tribes on the Pakistan side of this border. While the notion of bringing rural tribal students from the most remote corners of Afghanistan into Kabul for education was perhaps naive and produced, by some accounts, mixed results, it began to change the Kabul-Persian speaking bias of the University.

Another change that altered the ethnic and rural/urban balance of Kabul University was the introduction of a college entrance examination in the early 1960s.   Before that time any student with the time and money could go to the University, and it was able to accommodate all comers. However, the increase in the number of lycees as well as

the imposition of the new rural/urban quota made it necessary to restrict admission. The test ironically had two
contradictory effects--it put entrance into the University
onto a merit system, and, in combination with the imposition
of the urban/rural ratio, it lowered the quality of the
incoming students. Students from the rural areas were at
an academic level considerably below the urban students' at
entry level. But they usually did as well if not better than
the urban students, once they entered college, because they
were more motivated.

The faculty at Kabul University was largely foreign
trained, some with Ph.D.s, more with Master's degrees, and
a few with B.A.s. Foreign staff continued to constitute a
part of the faculty, but the numbers by 1978 were down
considerably from a high in the mid-1960s when several of
the faculties were held together by the presence of large
foreign teams. A cohort of Afghan scholars began to
emerge to take over the teaching and research duties.

Being on the faculty at Kabul University held considerable prestige even though the children of the upper class
generally chose other occupations with greater power or
monetary rewards. Since it was an occupation based at
least to some degree on merit in a society where inside
connections and nepotism dominate, it was attractive to
those in the new middle class who saw it as one of the few
opportunities for upward mobility.

In addition, the pay was considerably higher than other
government jobs, salary being on three criteria: civil service
rank, diploma, and academic rank. The University had six
academic ranks, from *pohyalai*, somewhat equivalent to a
teaching assistant, up to *pohand*, full professor. A teaching
instructor with an M.A. would begin at approximately 3,000
Afs., or about $60.00, a month.(2) A *pohand* with consider-
able seniority and a Ph.D. made close to 10,000 Afs., or
about $200, a month. While this seems a paltry sum to
those accustomed to Western salaries, it is a decent salary
in Afghanistan where the per capita GNP is probably not
much over $100 per year.

By 1978 thousands of students had passed through the
University, many had studied abroad, and nearly one thousand taught at the University itself. The approximate size
of this emerging educated middle class was about 50,000 by

1978, or less then .3 percent of the population.(3) This educated group constituted an emerging segment of society that, while small, represented a potential power group whose allegiance and ties were less with either the traditional rural tribal-based power structure or with the Kabuli ruling elite. Certainly they were still rooted in an Afghan society where kin connections and tribal allegiances dominated, as it would be impossible in one generation to shake all vestiges of the traditional society from which they came and in which they lived.

Employed largely in the government agencies as well as at the universities, the emerging new middle class represented the technical bureaucrats and professionals that students of modernization posit to be vital in the role of national development. Being urban in a predominantly rural society, being educated in a country of overwhelming illiteracy, and having been exposed to Western styles of life in a country of strong traditional culture, the new middle class began to find itself estranged from its traditional ties. Although efforts were often made to maintain contracts with traditional, rural, ethnic, and tribal roots, nonetheless a sense of isolation, however small, was beginning to grow.

This nascent isolation manifested itself in several areas. Marriage arrangements were altered so that Afghans could have more choice in selecting mates. People began to cease speaking their native language, primarily Pushtu, and to speak Dari. Tribal obligations were less often attended to and tribal ties weakened. Contact with the relatively large foreign community in Kabul and extended stays abroad led many of the new middle class to acquire a lifestyle that was out of step with the more traditional customs of the rest of Afghanistan.

This process was less than uniform, however. Those who had come from the rural tribal areas, who entered the educational process through the tribal lycees or came from rural lycees, in most cases still had family and kin in the hinterlands. Being only a few years removed, their ties remained stronger to the traditional life. For those from urbanized Kabuli families the educational experience only accelerated a process started a generation ago. This bifurcation between those who maintained their rural/tribal roots and those who lost them would assume great importance following the events of 1978.

THE NEW MIDDLE CLASS TO 1973

The period between 1963 and 1973 was pivotal in the course of events in Afghanistan. The so-called democratic experiment was started in 1963 by Zahir Shah, who voluntarily surrendered to a constitutional monarchy. He also doomed the democratic experiment to failure in the eyes of some by not giving it his full support. The events of this period were chaotic--at times amusing, at times bloody, and ultimately unsuccessful. The attempted democracy and its constitutional system eventually did not work, perhaps because Afghanistan was not yet ready to go from tribalism to parliamentarianism in a mere ten years.

However, the period of the new democracy was a period of considerable political activity, and probably more people than ever before participated in Afghan politics during this period. For the first time the new middle class began to assert its influence, directly confronting the traditional tribal-based ruling elite. By 1978 this traditional ruling elite relinquished control of Afghanistan to a segment of the new middle class.

Three political orientations began to develop among the new middle class during this period: leftists of various sorts, including pro-Soviet Marxists, Maoists, and other non-Marxist elements; fundamentalists, primarily made up of religious students and faculty from the department of religious law at Kabul University, but including some enlightened *Ulama*, Islamic clergy; and Westernized liberals largly oriented toward social democracy.(4)   All three of these orientations represented a common goal at the broadest level--a goal that expressed their class interest. Namely, all three advocated some type of change of government, be it violent or gradual, based on a foreign model. In other words the middle class, whose training had been largely influenced by foreign institutions and ideologies, advocated and worked politically to move Afghanistan in a new direction. In this way the class interest of the new middle class ran into direct conflict with the traditional ruling elites during this period.

Since political parties were banned, much of the political activities of this period went into publication of various newspapers. More than thirty papers in Kabul alone started and folded in the period of press freedom in 1966, some lasting for only weeks while others lasted until 1973 (L.

Dupree 1980a). All three orientations were represented by newspapers.

However, the political parties with the strongest ideological stance attracted the largest following. The groups to emerge from the sixties with the most adherents were the leftists, both pro-Moscow and otherwise, and the Islamic fundamentalists. Other groups tended to focus more on particular narrowly defined issues, or to be largely personality cults.

Some centrist liberal reformist groups flourished briefly among the new middle class commonly referred to as *Afghan Mellat* (The Afghan Nation), started in March of 1966 in Kabul at a meeting of prominent or retired business and government officials at the home of Ghullum Muhammad Farhad. Farhad had been mayor of Kabul, a one time member of parliament and twice a member of the *Loya Jirgah*, the national tribal assembly. By national democratic socialism they meant a democratic parliamentary form of government, land reform, a guided economy, and the return to a greater Afghanistan. This last point, a greater Afghanistan, has come to be substantially synonymous with the Pushtunistan issue, the argument that all of Pushtun areas of Pakistan should belong to Afghanistan, or at least be independent, claiming that a large chunk of Northwest Pakistan belongs rightfully to Afghanistan.

The Pushtunistan issue had been an important item in Afghan politics for years. Many liberally-oriented members of the new middle class who might otherwise be attracted to the social democratic reforms suggested by the *Afghan Mellat* party were kept away by the party's strong emphasis on the Pushtunistan issue and the association with Pushtun culture and language. Many of the members of the new middle class, who were Persian-speaking Kabul residents, found the Pushtunistan issue to be a dead horse with little appeal and with strong racist overtones.

Another major centrist party of that period was the Progressive Democratic Party of Maiwandwal, which also had a following among the moderate liberals. Widely viewed as a "cult of personality," the party largely collapsed when Maiwandwal reigned as prime minister in 1967.

As the period of the monarchy came to an end in 1973, the new middle class grew in influence and participated actively in the political events of the era. Split into three basic orientations, they had served in parliament, published newspapers, and formed the political organizations that would shape the next decade. By 1973 it was also becoming clear that the moderate or reformist positions were being pushed out by groups at both ends of the political spectrum advocating more violent political activism. Out of the three basic orientations, four important political groups had arisen among the new middle class and the students at Kabul University that would shape the events of the next decade. The Parcham and Khalq were pro-Moscow Marxist parties with roots in the new middle class, although the Khalqi branch had close ties to rural tribalism.(5) Both had been influenced by the Soviets, and their coming to power in 1978 would also bring the presence of the Soviet Union and over 100,000 Soviet troops.

Other leftist parties had also grown among the new middle class during this period. These included the *Satam-i-Melli*, National Oppression Party, and the *Shola-i-Javid* (Eternal Flame). Both parties had followings among the new middle class as well as in some rural areas, the *Satam-i-Melli* especially being popular in the North as an anti-Pushtun party.

The *Shola-i-Javid*, usually called simply *Shola*, had a large following on campus and in the late '60s and early '70s dominated student politics, shutting down the University at times and organizing student strikes. The *Shola* had been labeled Maoist, non-aligned Marxists, and reformist, among other things, but the party in fact had a following among various groups possessing a variety of political ideologies. It had some following also among non-Pushtun ethnic groups who resented Pushtun dominance in Afghanistan. For instance, some Hazaras participated in *Shola* activities, because they saw it as a vehicle for airing their ethnic grievances, not because of a commitment to any leftist ideology.

The third group to develop among the new middle class during the period from 1963 to 1973 was the Islamic fundamentalists. Islamic fundamentalism has several origins, but it has found strong support among a segment of the new middle class in most Islamic societies. The rise in Islamic fundamentalism in Afghanistan was in part a reaction to the leftist and nationalist groups. It was attractive to members of the new middle class who still had strong religious sentiments, while the rest of the new middle class had largely become secularized. This group also desired radical change in Afghanistan, but they were not attracted to the modern ideologies of socialism, Marxism, or capitalism. Yet they found the views of traditional Islam equality wanting. They resented the growing Westernization of Afghanistan, the use of alcohol, Western movies, miniskirts, and other aspects of the Western culture. This group thus identified and joined with other fundamentalist groups throughout the Middle East.

The fundamentalists' original connection was with al-Azhar University in Egypt where the modern fundamentalist movement had started, and which had helped start the Department of *Shariat*, or Islamic law, at Kabul University. Al-Azhar sent Arabic teachers to Kabul University in the 1950s and the 1960s, and many from the the Department of *Shariat* at Kabul University went to Egypt for religious training, including Sayyaf and Rabbani, who were members of the faculty of that department at that time and who are now leaders of fundamentalist insurgent groups in Peshawar. Through this connection the faculty became aware of the writing and thoughts of the fundamentalists in other Muslim countries.

Among the students at the University the early connection with the fundamentalist movement came through Qom, the religious center in Iran. Intimidated by the vocal and aggressive leftist students, the religious students found the work of some of the fundamentalist writers had been translated in Persian in Qom. Hekmatyar Gulbuddin, a powerful figure in the present insurgent movement, emerged from that student organization.

THE COMING OF DAOUD

On July 17, 1973, Sardar Muhammed Daoud Khan, the first cousin and brother-in-law of the king, and a former prime minister (1953-1963), came to power in a bloodless coup while the king was out of the country. He abolished the monarchy, declaring Afghanistan a Republic, and himself Prime Minister and President. Political parties were banned, and this time effectively, except for Daoud's own party, the National Revolutionary Party.

Political activity did not cease, however, and some

members of the new middle class participated in Daoud's government. The Parcham branch of the pro-Moscow Marxist party had participated in Daoud's takeover and members of that party were given cabinet posts and appointed to the Central Committee of the National Revolutionary Party. As a consequence their activities were more or less allowed, at least in the first few years of Daoud's rule. The members of the new middle class active with the *Afghan Mellat* were also allowed to continue their political activity and that party was asked to join the ruling National Revolutionary Party, Daoud having long been a strong supporter of Pushtunistan nationalism.

Members of the new middle class of the other ideological orientations were not so fortunate. The two parties selected for the harshest attack were the *Shola* and the fundamentalists. By 1973 these two groups represented the most serious threat to the Daoud government, both representing important and opposing ideological positions of the new middle class.

Fundamentalists were arrested and as many as 600 were killed by Daoud (Amin 1984). As a result other fundamentalists fled to Pakistan, including Gulbuddin and Rabbani, early leaders of the fundamentalist movement in Afghanistan and now of fundamentalist insurgent groups in Pakistan. With the help of the Bhutto government they began a campaign of insurrection against the Afghan government of Daoud.

The *Shola* and the other leftists groups were driven underground. They were to emerge later, reorganized in other forms, about which more will be said later. This segment of the new middle class, however, would not again have the influence it had before 1973. The leftist and many members of the new middle class of liberal or socialist views from this point on found themselves in retreat against the growing strength of the Soviet-supported Marxist groups on the one hand and the fundamentalists on the other. While these groups, especially the *Shola*, had had great popularity in the late sixties and early seventies, they had never come to power in Afghanistan. In part their failure was that they shunned foreign connections and thus never developed a foreign sponsor. When the Soviet Union actively supported the pro-Moscow Marxists groups, the other leftists had no foreign power to which to turn.

When the Marxist coup came in April of 1978, there was actually a sense of relief on campus and among the new middle class. By the end Daoud had become isolated and estranged, and his government had grown more and more repressive. The first proposals of the Marxist government seemed reasonable. Of the two Marxist parties that came to rule in 1978, Parcham (flag) and Khalq (people), the members of the new middle class much preferred the Parcham. Not only did their politics seem more moderate, but they were largely Persian-speaking Kabuli residents, whereas the Khalq branch of the party was made mostly of rural Pushtuns recruited largely through the tribal lycees and the military.   The members of the Parcham party were well known to the other members of the class. As the power of the Khalqi branch of the Marxists grew, the situation of the members of the new middle class began to deteriorate rapidly, and eventually many were jailed or killed.

Although some of the members of the new middle class sensed the danger immediately and began forming plans for counter measures, most adopted a wait and see attitude. The first few months after April, 1978, were taken up with orchestrated speeches, demonstrations and marches, praising the new government. While at Kabul University the faculty were required to attend, many simply would slip away and go home. As one former professor at Kabul University at that time reports, "when we were supposed to march, I marched home."(6)

Other faculty members tell of an amusing incident from that period arising over confusion between the English word "march" and the Persian word *mash*, meaning salary. A clerk came into the social science faculty offices saying something about *mash*, meaning that the salaries of the faculty were now ready. But instead, some thought that the clerk had said "march" and, dreading another weary parade, they sneaked away only to miss getting their paycheck.

It was soon clear that the situation would be serious. In Louis Dupree's description of that period, he describes six overlapping purges, during the period from April 1978 to December 1979, most of which were directed at the new middle class (1980b). The University came under heavy attack. The heaviest crackdown at Kabul University occurring after November 1978, soon after the split between the Parcham and the Khalq, came to a head and many Parcham leaders were either shipped abroad as ambassadors or arrested and jailed. In late November and December of 1978 a sweep resulted in the arrest of many professors and students of Kabul University as well as at Ningrahar University in Jalalabad. By late 1979 over ten thousand political prisoners were estimated to be in Afghan jails. When Amin took power on September 15, 1979, he announced that the Taraki regime had jailed over 12,000 people, a large majority of whom were of the new middle class (L. Dupree 1980b).

At Kabul University many tried to stay out of trouble by adopting a neutral stance. But the Marxist government used a number of tactics to extract ideological commitment. At first they attempted to persuade people to join the party by offering high government positions. Since party membership was relatively small, most party members, including students, were given high government positions. At times more direct threats were used.

Many members of the new middle class were caught in a trap. They could flee, and many did, mainly to Pakistan. They could stay and attempt to be neutral, even though non-commitment was a risky game. Or they could organize secret cells to plan subversive activities. Several attempts at such organizations were made. Despite great care and secrecy they almost were always discovered and the members arrested and killed.

THE NEW MIDDLE CLASS AS REFUGEES

To many the only alternative was to leave. Since the middle class lived primarily in Kabul, where many worked in government jobs and were thus highly visible, escape was difficult and dangerous. There were essentially two ways out of the country: one by air, flying usually directly to New Delhi, and the other by overland travel to Pakistan.

As refugees in Pakistan, the new middle class suffer from many of the same problems of other urban refugees. They find that they cannot live in the refugee tent villages (RTVs), and are therefore denied some of the basic refugee privileges, particularly rations of food, cooking oil, and shelter. Officially the government of Pakistan has insisted that only those who live or are registered in the camps receive rations. This decision was made especially to force the refugees into the designated camps for the explicit purpose of keeping the refugees contained and to reduce their penetration into the local Pakistani society. However, to those who cannot live in the camps it has meant no rations.   A few exceptions are refugees who came out before 1980 and were given ration cards; then there are informal ways of getting rations.   However, by and large, the urban refugees, those primarily from the Kabul middle class, are on their own and must depend on what money they bring out or must find a job in the local economy.

Despite these attempts by Pakistan's government to restrict the economic activities of the refugees, already a considerable number of the Afghan refugees have penetrated the local economy, according to two UNHCR in-house reports, both done in the Winter and Spring of 1983 (Sardie and Taskinud-din 1983).   One study indicated that the 72 percent of the males interviewed in a sample of Afghan refugees in the camps were working in the local Pakistani economy, and 87 percent of the families of the sampled camp households had at least one member employed (Sardie and Taskinud-din 1983).   Most of these workers are employed as day laborers or in transportation, since the Afghans brought out with them trucks and other commercial vehicles.   Many Afghan refugees from the new middle class have not been so fortunate.   By and large they have not found suitable work.

In the Summer of 1983 I conducted a survey among 95 middle class refugees living in Peshawar. I was obviously unable to take a random sample, given the situation in Peshawar, but I attempted to make the sample as representative as possible.

Of those interviewed, the largest group (12 percent) had been government officials in Afghanistan, and others had been university professors (8.7 percent), medical doctors (9.8 percent), and high school teachers (9.8 percent).   Sixty percent had come from Kabul, 76 percent were married and 62 percent had some college, with 55.5 percent having received a bachelor's or higher degree.   The average age in the survey group was 34. When asked why they left, 27 percent indicated that they feared conscription into the military for either themselves or their children, 69 percent feared that they would soon be jailed, 32.6 feared that they would soon be killed and 18.5 percent reported that there was no work. On an average they brought approximately $3,000 out with them.

Most of the interviewed refugees from the new middle class came out with their families, with the exception of draft age males who are often sent out alone by their families. Most have not found suitable work in Peshawar; the most common kind of work for those who find employment is work with one of the political groups. Housing in Pakistan is expensive. Many have children and it costs money to send them to Pakistan schools. For college age students the situation is especially desperate since it is virtually impossible to get into Pakistani colleges or universities.

As a consequence most of the new middle class who can are forced eventually to leave for the U.S. or Europe. Those with U.S. or European educations are generally allowed to migrate to the country in which they studied.

Fleeing to the U.S. or Europe is not the first choice of these refugees, as many would stay if they could. They recognize that the further away they go, the less the chance that they will return, and the less they can do to help their country. They recognize that exile to Europe or the U.S. is a trap, although perhaps an enticing one. But they have no choice; they must eat, their children must go to school. They cannot live forever as a marginal people.

The members of the new middle class have another problem as refugees. It has been said that there are two Afghanistans: Kabul and the rest of the country. The members of the new middle class are largely a product of Kabul. Many have lost touch with the rest of the country, and therefore with the bulk of the refugees. While rural/urban differences have largely disappeared in the West, they remain paramount in Afghanistan. The majority of the refugees are Pushtu-speaking peasant farmers, organized for the most part around traditional kin or village structures. The members of the new middle class tend to be Dari speakers whose allegiances are to the modern sector. They have lost touch with the "folk," although many would vigorously deny this. They are from the city; many have acquired a taste for modern ways and lifestyles, styles that are now considered suspect by the more traditional Afghan majority. This lifestyle gap has increased their marginality, further removing them from the rest of their countrymen.

In several ways the new middle class has tried to overcome this growing gap between them and the bulk of their people. Some have started newspapers or news services in exile. The most notable is the Peshawar-based Afghan Information Centre of Sayd Majrooh. Educated in France and from an important Afghan religious family, Professor Majrooh has attempted to provide a monthly news bulletin with objective news about the situation in Afghanistan, especially the war. However, objective war reporting is difficult, perhaps impossible, given the nature of the war.

These problems are magnified greatly in the politically charged atmosphere of Peshawar, yet the Afghan Information Centre has managed to maintain its integrity for objective news for several years. But it has had problems that demonstrate the marginality of the new middle class as refugees. Originally the Centre was to be a place where the expatriated Afghan intellectual community in Peshawar could gather and contribute in their own way to the Afghan cause. At one time a number of professionals and intellectuals were attached to the Centre and a number of projects were proposed, including a translation service and other projects that would use the skills of the intellectuals. Most of these projects had to be abandoned because they were objectionable to the insurgent agencies who find the condition of the peasants more compelling than that of the middle class.

Another example of one part of the new middle class to participate in the refugee community is the Afghan Doctors Association (ADA). First started by Dr. Ghazi Alam, the ADA operates both in Afghanistan and among the refugees in Pakistan. They have 170 or so members of which approximately 100 are in Afghanistan and 70 in Peshawar. Their outpatient clinic in Peshawar provides refugees with dental, ENT, and gynecological treatment. In addition ADA operates a school to train medics to go into Afghanistan with the Mujahideen, the Islamic word for the insurgent guerrilla groups, and they operate six clinics in Afghanistan. Many doctors travel in and out of Afghanistan at great danger to themselves to help the sick and wounded. Dr. Ghazi Alam himself spends half of each year in Afghanistan.

But the ADA also has had problems which illustrate the difficulties for members of the new middle class in Pakistan. Although they have attempted to avoid politics, a fraction of the ADA has been politically active and has run into trouble with the conservative Mujahideen groups. As a result in mid-1980 the United Nations High Commissioner for Refugees (UNHCR) decided to withhold further support to the Afghan Doctors Association on the insistence of the Pakistani Afghan Refugee Commissioner. This withdrawal of funds resulted from pressure by the six official Mujahideen groups. One doctor was kidnapped and killed for his political views. Dr. Ghazi Alam himself has since quit the organization.

This censure again points out the difficulty of the new Afghan middle class in Peshawar. They are under the intense scrutiny from the powerful Mujahideen groups. Their Western education makes them suspect, and their political activities are unwelcome unless their politics agrees with the accepted Islamic views.

THE NEW MIDDLE CLASS AND THE MUJAHIDEEN

Many members of the new middle class fleeing to Peshawar complain that they are not welcome and are in fact persecuted by major Mujahideen groups. These allegations are not completely true, because most of the six groups have members of this class working for them. Nabi Muhammadi, a moderate insurgent leader, at times has actively recruited the intellectuals and other members of the new middle class. Rabbani, another insurgent leader, was a teacher at Kabul University and is thus from this class, as was Sayyaf. Gailani's Mujahideen group has supported many of the members of this class from time to time. Nonetheless, a tension exists between the Mujahideen and the new middle class, so that even those active within the political groups find that they have to walk a thin line. Many who were active with the Mujahideen eventually have had to quit.

The suspicion is from both sides for the Mujahideen in turn suspect the motives and loyalties of the new middle class. Because they are literate and often in touch with the international community, they pose a potential threat to the Mujahideen leaders. Even those who work within the Mujahideen groups report they are closely watched.

Such tensions should not surprise students of political movements. Members of the educated middle class were the

first sought out, jailed, and killed by the Marxist government when it came to power in Afghanistan. Many university professors as well as others were jailed, tortured, and
killed. A large percentage of the country's doctors were
killed or jailed. Most leaders of revolutions or coups see
the educated as their primary threat and move rapidly to
eradicate them. The bitter irony for the new Afghan middle
class is that they were persecuted in Afghanistan, only to
escape to Pakistan where they find they are suspected and
distrusted once again.

However, the opposite is also true. The new middle class
suspects those who are now the leaders of the powerful
Mujahideen groups. In part they see the inconsistencies
and fallacies in their positions. The new middle class had
been moving toward a kind of European secularism, and
many chafe under the puritanical codes that are now
imposed by the Mujahideen leaders, all of whom are
religious.

In addition, their views of a future Afghanistan may be
more progressive than the conservative views of the
Mujahideen leaders. Many of those trained in Europe would
favor a move toward European-styled democratic socialism
rather than an Islamic government, such as the fundamentalists propose, or a return to a feudal monarchy of
socialism of any kind which is not wise in the Afghan exile
community.

THE FUTURE OF THE AFGHAN NEW
MIDDLE CLASS IN THE WAR

It is becoming clearer each day that the guerrilla insurgent war being fought in Afghanistan against the Marxist
regime of Babrak Karmal, his successor Najibullah, and the
Soviet forces has less and less connection with the seven
official groups in Peshawar, Pakistan. Recent allegations of
large scale corruption by these groups as well as the
increasing move by commanders fighting in Afghanistan to
build independent alliances have caused considerable rethink-
ing regarding the role of the official Mujahideen groups in
Pakistan and their ultimate role in the outcome of the war.
Since the official seven groups are avowedly Islamic, religious piety and at least lip service to Islamic values and
practices have become a necessary condition for survival.

This religious aspect of the war is especially problematic for groups who may want to fight in the war against the Soviet invaders, but whose ideology, real or imagined, contains some element of "socialism," even the rather benign "Christian socialism," Western European style. To those of the far right, who control the scene in Peshawar, the difference between socialism and communism, let alone various versions of Marxism, is lost. Anybody to the left of the religious Mujahideen groups is suspect, including virtually all the secular groups.

The consequence is that the secular groups of the new middle class not only are left out of any decision-making role, but more importantly, do not receive any of the arms and money that is available for the war. And they are often in physical danger, even in Pakistan, since they are suspected as being in league with the Marxist government in Kabul. They therefore operate at best on the fringes of the powerful groups, and in many cases completely underground. Since they may well be killed if found out, the middle class groups, and especially the remaining leftist groups, survive to some degree by infiltrating the established religious groups.

Among the remnants of the new middle class still active in Peshawar and in Afghanistan are the leftists and the nationalists. Since 1973, the secular leftist groups, except for Parcham and Khalq, have been forced underground. Many, perhaps most, of the members of these groups were jailed during the period of Daoud or when the communists took over in 1978. Others no doubt joined the Khalqi Marxist groups, or more likely, given the ideological and ethnic nature, the Parcham party, thus joining the ruling parties. Many others fled.

Despite the severe decrease in their numbers through capture, death or exile, and despite the passage of time, some elements from this movement are active today, primarily in Kabul. The non-aligned leftist movement has largely reorganized into several groups. The largest of these groups is the *Sazman-i-Azadibakhsh-i-Mardum-i-Afghanistan* (SAMA), the Organization for the Freedom of the Afghan People, which is actually an alliance of several groups. Other groups include *Sazman-i-Rehai'i* (the Organization for Deliverance) and *Jeb-i-Motahed-i-Melli* (the National United Front). All of these groups have members both inside and outside Afghanistan. All claim to have some success as guerrillas in Afghanistan, although by even their own accounts it is becoming more and more difficult to operate. Their military operations are primarily, although not exclusively, in the major cities, especially Kabul. They have been active in some rural areas, especially Kohistan, Kalakan, and in the North in general.

Ideologically these groups feel that they must not repeat the mistakes of the Khalq and Parcham parties by appearing to be an ideology foreign to the common Afghan and by becoming isolated from their people. This concern is one of the reasons for reorganizing and dropping old names. They have also modified their ideological position so that it makes no mention of socialism or Marxism, and they now talk of humanistic Islamic values (*Mazmun-i-Insander-i-Islam*).

Although many members of these secular leftist groups belonged to the Marxist movement of the sixties, they are not simply reusing the same old ideologies. Their flirtation with Marxist or other shades of socialism has largely passed as they have witnessed the terrible experiment with Marxism now going on.

These groups attract members of the Afghan new middle class, as did their predecessors, and the members come from Kabul University, both students and professors, as well as high school teachers and the middle level civil servants. A great number of educated people in Kabul still wish to oppose actively the present regime and the Soviet occupiers, but are not attracted to the religiously oriented Mujahideen groups. These secular groups may tap some of this support. Because they also appeal to non-Pushtun ethnic groups who largely resent the Pushtun-dominated resistance, these secular resistance groups have done well in the non-Pushtun areas of Afghanistan, especially the north. On the other hand, these secular leftist groups will probably never have much support in the traditional tribal areas, where distrust of the modern ideologies of Kabul is strong; their support will always be limited to the urban classes.

Reports on the numbers and activities of these groups are hard to assess, given their secrecy and propensity to mislead outsiders. They do seem, however, to have success as *chariks* or urban guerrillas who excel at such things as bombings and assassinations, operations that require few men, but precise timing and planning. Their most notable achievement was the assassination of the vice-director of KHAD, the Afghan secret police, in broad daylight in front of Habibia High School in Kabul, in retaliation for the arrest and the DRA's supposed murder of Majid Kalakani, one of the popular leaders of the resistance movement. While their numbers seem to be small, they are well organized and tend to approach their selected targets with care.

They are also engaged in political activities both in and out of Afghanistan. In Afghanistan they actively distribute the *shabnamas*, or night letters, bulletins of news and bits of anti-regime information passed secretly around Kabul.

Outside Afghanistan they have attempted to bring the Afghan situation to world attention. One of the groups, *Jeb-i-Motahed-i-Melli*, attempted to block the seating of the official Afghan delegation at the meeting of non-aligned nations in Delhi in 1983, an attempt which included trying to have a document condemning the brutalities of the present regime read into the minutes of that meeting.

These groups, primarily SAMA, represent a potential force in the war. Considerable potential support for their ideology has been indicated. After all, the support for the seven official Mujahideen organizations is not particularly deep. Neither the fundamentalists nor the moderates strike deep chords of sympathy among the educated of Afghanistan. One group, the fundamentalists, espouses a radical and foreign version of Islam, and the others are led by old men of another generation. While these secular groups will never have much of a tribal or rural following, they, or other groups like them, could appeal to the educated class in Afghanistan if their ideological connection with the left is muted. This educated class is now largely ignored both as refugees and as Mujahideen.

In addition to the leftist groups there are remnants of the nationalist groups, including *Afghan Mellat* and *Masawat* (Equality). While these groups no longer have much following in Afghanistan, they still are active among the exiles in Pakistan, especially among certain professional groups. Three groups are active in Peshawar, each having split from the original *Afghan Mellat*. Each has its own newspaper, published in Peshawar, and each makes claims to a highly doubtful following of several thousand. The narrowness of their ideology, their brief but damaging collaboration with the present regime, and their past connection with socialism have rendered them ineffective in the present political situation.

There are two exceptions, however. Many of the members of *Afghan Mellat* are former high officials from the governments of Zahir Shah, the last King of Afghanistan, and have close connections with several of the moderate Mujahideen groups, primarily Sayyid Ahmad Gailani's. If the movement to bring back Zahir Shah bears fruit, many of these past officials may again have some position of prominence.

The second exception is that the group called *Mellat*, considered the most leftist of these national movements, has some following among the ADA. The ADA has some influence on the Peshawar scene, although it has tried to stay out of politics. While the *Mellat* faction of the nationalists is the smallest, it is also the most radical and well organized. Its influence with the doctors could be important.

CONCLUSION

The rise of modern education in Afghanistan since the 1950s has led to the development of new middle class. While this class is very small, it has nonetheless played an important part in the development of Afghanistan. Since the ouster of Zahir Shah in 1973, this class has been split into several antagonistic groups. As a result, the bulk of this new middle class is now left out of the struggle for their country. These people who characteristically possess education, come from urban areas, and are largely non-Pushtun, would prefer a form of government in Afghanistan free from religious dogma. While many, if not most, are forced to leave Afghanistan and Pakistan for the United States or Europe, many will continue to be active in the resistance effort. But they receive little or no arms and supplies from the sources that supply the official groups and are often attacked by the official resistance groups who find them suspect. They may amount only to a few thousand, but given their location, mostly in Kabul, and their social position as the educated elite, the participation of the new middle class could nevertheless be very important to the war to liberate Afghanistan. The new middle class is now largely left out of a war that needs their help.

NOTES

1.   The early work on the new middle class was done by Halpern (1963). See pages 51-73.

2.   This assumes an exchange rate of 50 Afs. per dollar, a rate at which the Afghani hovered in the 1970s.

3.   If we estimate that there were something like a thousand university graduates in Afghanistan each year since 1932, and 200 or so educated out of the country each year since 1950, then 1000 (1978-1932) + 200 (1978-1950) = 51,600.

4.   See Amin (1982), pages 34-35. He divides the political activities of the new middle class into four groups by adding conservatives, which basically favors the quo. See also Harrison (1984). He writes of three groups, also the liberals' "Western-oriented intellectuals."

5.   See Arnold (1983) for a good discussion of the Social class background of the leaders of the two branches of the Afghan Communist Party. Also useful is Male (1982), especially for a biography of Amin.

6.   I conducted this interview in Peshawar in 1983.

6

Rationales for the Movement
of Afghan Refugees to Peshawar

Kerry M. Connor

By blood, we are immersed in love of you.
The youth lose their heads for your sake.
I come to you and my heart finds rest.
Away from you, grief clings to my heart like a snake.
I forget the throne of Delhi
When I remember the mountaintops of my Pushtun land.
If I must choose between the world and you,
I shall not hesitate to claim your barren deserts as my
  own.

--Ahmad Shah Durrani, mid-1700s,
trans. by S. Shpoon

On January 1, 1980, the *Kabul New Times* printed the
text of a speech by Babrak Karmal, new President of the
Revolutionary Council and Prime Minister of the Democratic
Republic of Afghanistan (DRA). Karmal greeted the people
of Afghanistan "on the occasion of the total collapse of the
fascist regime of Hafizullah Amin, that bloodthirsty agent of
American imperialism and demogogue tyrannical dictator."
Kabul Radio announced that the new government had
requested and was receiving from the Soviet Union "political, moral and economic assistance, including military aid."
News items from other countries reported as many as 10,000
Soviet troops engaged in Kabul street fighting during the
overthrow of Amin. Some observers estimated that nearly
100,000 Soviet troops began moving into Afghanistan on
Christmas Day of 1979.

Since those last days of December, 1979, many versions of the actual events have been proposed. Whatever the true explanation, one incontestable result was the substantial and immediate increase in the number of Afghans who sought asylum in neighboring Pakistan. The nearly three million Afghan refugees in Pakistan, however, all did not arrive during the Winter of 1979-80. Nor have they ceased crossing the border into Pakistan. What, then, provoked these millions to leave their homeland to face an uncertain future in another country with, in many cases, little but the clothes they wore?(1)

This chapter focuses on the reasons for the movement of Afghan refugees to Pakistan between December of 1977 and December of 1984. The specific reasons for leaving Afghanistan will be discussed as well as any associations between reasons for leaving and times of departure from Afghanistan. In addition, personal attributes of these refugees, such as geographical origin in Afghanistan, ethnic affiliations, and professional background, will be considered as they relate to the decision to leave their country.

PREVIOUS LITERATURE

Refugee literature has tended either to ignore altogether motives for leaving or to paint a picture of a mass exodus that is "forced, chaotic, generally terror-stricken" (Bernard, 1976). Viewing a refugee group in this way often leads to misunderstandings of subsequent behavior and thus has a negative impact on refugee programs and resettlement plans. The individual who "left for no particular reason; [he] just did not like the government" has, for example, a different experience from the one who fled because the "village was bombed again and again and nearly all the people were killed."

Research on voluntary migrants, in contrast, long has emphasized causative factors or, as Davis (1945) put it, "the motives that migrants carry in their heads." This research demonstrates that the stimulus for migrating frequently has an impact on the success of migrants in their new home (Wolpert 1964, 1966; Graves 1966; Brown and Moore 1970; Lieber 1978).

The very basic push/pull approach to the causative factors in migration often is rejected for use in refugee analysis because the pull factor is missing altogether or is eclipsed by overwhelming push factors. Refugees, as Bernard (1976) has stated, are "thrust out of their native lands in a mad rush and forced to settle down wherever circumstances dictate." Pull factors undoubtedly do exert much less influence on refugees than do push factors. However, neglecting causation in refugee movements and viewing refugees as fleeing en masse in the face of a real or imagined threat ignores the many and varied reasons refugees leave their homelands.

That individual and small group refugee movements are precipitated by different events and perceptions of these events is evident both from the small body of research on the subject and from the personal accounts of refugees. As Hansen (1981) observed among Angolans, these people have a variety of options other than becoming refugees. A Jewish doctor who fled when the Nazis seized Holland described the varying reactions:

> People . . . did not want to go, but found all sorts of excuses. . . . With their intellect they acknowledged the need to escape, but with their innermost hearts they were tied to their homes and unconciously preferred death to leaving. (Many of them got what they wished for.) (Prins 1955)

Voluntary migrants move because they are in some way not satisfied with their current home. This discontent pushes them from one place, and the various attractions of a potential new home guide their choice of destination. Although refuges may not have the same latitude in choice as voluntary migrants, they are dissatisfied with their home, albeit a dissatisfaction of a more consequential nature. The significant issue, however, is that refugees, like voluntary migrants, review their positions because they perceive themselves as in some way pushed from their homes. The time the individual refugee takes to act on this perception and the specific reasons precipitating the action vary as they do in cases of voluntary migration.

Early studies of the push factor in migration, such as those by Farr (1976) and Ravenstein (1885; 1889), treated migration as an internally-generated phenomenon. While Farr discovered no apparent order in migratory movements,

Ravenstein postulated certain "laws" of migration. These laws, however, were observations on migratory movements rather than explanations of why people migrate. Lee (1966) restated the laws in a manner more amenable to testing procedures, but added little to the understanding of causation.

Fairchild (1925) divided migratory movements into four categories (invasion, conquest, colonization, and immigration) based on the status of the culture and the degree of nonviolence in the movement. Though criticized both for its oversimplification and its ethnocentrism, the Fairchild typology received considerable attention until the 1950s, when the massive relocations of World War II generated a new interest in migration studies.

Research from this period, however, contributed little to a theoretical framework for the study of migration, with the possible exception of Petersen's (1958) typology of migrants. By distinguishing between two general types of migrants-- "innovating" and "conservative"--Petersen made apparent the significance of motivations. Innovating migrants move in order to obtain something they believe they cannot obtain in their current situation. Conservative migrants, in contrast, move to maintain their current status. Behavior after the move is contingent on the migrant's objective. However, Petersen's assumptions regarding "forced and impelled migration" are very similar to those of Fairchild. "In forced migrations," he stated, "the state or some functionally equivalent social institution" is the activating agent. He classified this "activating agent," not the individual, as innovating or conservative, thus overlooking the existence of individual reasons for becoming a refugee.

The most complete summation of push factors is found in Bogue's *Principles of Demography* (1969). This inclusive synopsis of what the author calls "the common stimulants to movement" bears closer examination because it illustrates the potential similarities between the motives of voluntary and involuntary migrants. Bogue's push factors include the following:

1. Decline in a natural resource or prices paid for it; increased demand for a particular product or the services of a particular industry; exhaustion of mines, timber, or agricultural resources.

2. Loss of employment resulting from being discharged for incompetence, for a decline in need for a particular activity, or from mechanization or automation of tasks previously performed by people.

3. Oppressive or repressive discriminatory treatment because of political, religious, or ethnic origins or membership.

4. Alienation from a community because one no longer subscribes to prevailing beliefs, customs, or modes of behavior--either within one's family or within the community.

5. Retreat from a community because it offers few or no opportunities for personal development.

6. Retreat from a community because of catastrophe.

Research on previous refugee movements has demonstrated how these stimulants to movement are common both to voluntary and involuntary migrants. By devising several techniques for looking at refugee flight and resettlement, Kunz (1969; 1973) produced the most theoretical of the refugee literature dealing with reasons for leaving. He observed that refugees fit into two categories--"anticipatory" and "acute." Anticipatory refugees recognize early that they may be forced to leave and prepare for flight. Acute refugees react to some traumatic event, such as a natural disaster, military activity, or a change in government. The emotional and practical preparations the anticipatory refugee is able to make guarantee post-flight experiences very different from those of the acute refugee.

Not all such events, even catastrophic ones, are felt simultaneously and to the same degree by those who ultimately will be affected. Nor will all react at the same time and in the same way. As individuals (or groups) decide the situation has become intolerable, they leave in what Kunz has labeled "distinct vintages," distinct in the sense that refugees who flee at the same time may develop characteristics and perspectives discrete from those who flee at other times. The concept of vintages is of particular significance in politically-motivated refugee movements because those who leave early often are convinced that persons who stayed on collaborated with or, at least, sustained the objectionable government through their toleration. Members of late vintages, on the other hand, may accuse the others of having abdicated responsibility by not opposing the government from within. Kunz contended that refugees are predisposed by vintage membership to certain types of associative behavior causing them either to shun association with some or become cohorts with others even though they have little else in common.

Following Kunz's study, Liu, Lamanna, and Murata (1979) described as "acute refugees" the Vietnamese they studied in Camp Pendleton in September, 1975. The majority of these refugees had been evacuated from South Vietnam during the week of 25 April though 1 May 1975. Seventy-five percent of the respondents, in fact, left Vietnam on two days (April 29 and 30), with little time for preparation. Fear of reprisals from North Vietnamese troops and the general situation in Vietnam were cited by the largest percentage as their initial motives for flight. The most significant of the final reasons included anti-communism, fear of reprisals, and several smaller categories suggesting occupations or relationships that would have made them potential objects of reprisals. Because of the hasty departure and short time in the camp, behavior associated with vintages or common reasons for leaving were not discussed specifically. The authors, however, made two interesting observations on behavior in the camp. First, many refugees refused all contact outside family groups and, second, the majority rejected leadership by other Vietnamese. Refugee comments on these two issues clearly indicated a general lack of trust. Post-settlement behavior of Vietnamese refugees in the United States, however, suggests that this initially suspicious attitude decreases over time. Desbarats (1985) and Desbarats and Holland (1983) found evidence of strong communal ties among these refugees, although the deepest associations remained in the extended family.

Le-Thi-Que, Rambo, and Murfin conducted similar research with Vietnamese who left approximately one month earlier than those in the Liu study. Two differences in the responses are noteworthy. First, 37 percent in this group reported leaving because of bombing or fighting in their area. Second, twice as many in Liu's group feared reprisals. Both these distinctions reflect how internal changes affect reasons for leaving. Those who left South Vietnam in late April and early May of 1975 could expect no protection from either South Vietnamese or American troops.

An even more notable difference in Vietnamese refugees' reasons for leaving was demonstrated by a study done nearly ten years earlier. Rambo, Tinker, and Le Noir (1967) reported that their respondents cited at least two and often three or four reasons for leaving. Responses fell into three categories: military activities, fear of terrorism or coercion, and economic/social factors. The authors encouraged the respondents to mention as many reasons as they considered important. Because the responses were not rank-ordered, the weight of a response can be ascertained only through frequency of citation. However, the citing of two or more reasons may reflect an inherent difference between the earlier and later groups. Those in the earlier group, for example, did not face the hectic decision-making atmosphere created by evacuation. Their motives or, at least, their retrospective analyses of motives, were likely to be expressed with more complexity than were the experiences of those who made almost instant decisions to leave.

Intense turmoil was characteristic as well of the decision-making environment of Palestinian Arabs who left their homes during the 1967 war. Two groups of Palestinian refugees--one resettled in a refugee camp and one in the Jordanian capital of Amman--were studied by Barakat and Dodd (1969; 1972; 1973). Reasons for leaving most often indicated by camp refugees included fear of air attacks, massacre by Israeli troops, and dishonor to the family, primarily in the form of insults to women. Don Peretz (1972) described the situation in Arab villages at this time:

> With schools closed, and water, sanitation, health and other public services inaccessible; with no effective leadership present; and with widely circulated stories of Jewish atrocities prevailing . . . the atmosphere was conductive to flight.

In contrast, the Amman sample was affected more by the events of the occupation period. Reasons for leaving included arrests, threats made to male family members, economic disruption, searches of homes, and other types of general harassment. The nature of the two groups' responses prompted the authors to suggest several additional motives. For example, refugees shifted their loyalties to other persons and places, a significant finding not only because it illustrates differences between camp and urban refugees but because it has implications for resettlement behavior. Most refugees interviewed in the camp came from villages where their social relations and responsibilities were family-oriented. Having made a hurried decision to leave as a family, they had little to retard their departure. The Amman refugees, on the other hand, came from urban, middle-class backgrounds and were less tradition-bound. Their decisions were complicated by business and other social obligations. These attitudinal differences are reflected in resettlement patterns.

Cuban resettlement patterns show this attitudinal shift. In the decade between 1958 and 1968 approximately a half million Cubans emigrated to the United States. The results of a study by Fagen, Brody, and O'Leary (1968) indicated that those who left in the first four years after the fall of the Batista government did not represent, as often is claimed, a particular economic sector of Cuban society, although they did share a common characteristic. As the authors stated, they were those who were squeezed, pressured, or deprived by the Revolution not because their members wholeheartedly supported the old order, but because they stood in the way of the new.

The authors argued that these Cubans did not impose exile on themselves in order to better their economic situation or even to maintain the economic status they had enjoyed under the Batista government. They left because they felt unable to live under "the imposition of a social order that violated values," which they viewed as somehow un-Cuban.

Rogg's study (1974) of the adjustment of Cuban refugees, however, indicated they left because of personal losses of freedom and economic status. One may assume that in many cases a philosophical opposition to a form of government does not rule out pragmatic considerations. Making a clear distinction between the two motives would be very difficult with only statements of respondents as the source of information.

Pedraza-Bailey (1985) attempted to analyze Cuban refugees within Kunz's framework of vintages and types of refugees. Her work is important not only because it views a refugee group over time but also because it synthesizes the research of others, for example, Amaro and Portes (1972), Portes (1978), and Llanos (1982). Research on Cuban refugees indicated a relationship between vintages and social class, i.e., the earlier the vintages, the higher the socio-economic status. Pedraza-Bailey's conclusions support this observation but explain as well how specific events in the development of the Cuban revolution motivated particular groups of people to leave at specific times and how these varying reasons affected relations among Cubans in the United States.

Some refugee-generating episodes have more easily iden-tifiable stimuli--at least in retrospect. The millions who temporarily became refugees during the Partition of India, for example, graphically illustrate Bogue's third push factor --oppressive or discriminatory treatment because of political, religious, or ethnic origins. Keller (1975) observed that this type of refugee often is not fully aware of the danger he faces and is unprepared, both emotionally and physically, to deal with the situation that emerges. When these refugees then face sudden emotional and physical hardship, the flight assumes added strain that may affect behavior long after the refugee has settled. The deepest trauma appears to be experienced by those who leave late. Keller observed three idiosyncratic behaviors of those who left in late vintages: a feeling of guilt caused by the death or injuries of family members, a sense of invulnerability from personally having survived the ordeal, and an extreme combativeness resulting from both the sense of indestructability and the need to shift guilt. These mental states can have both a negative and positive effect on subsequent behavior. The combative-ness, for example, can lead to violent and/or criminal activities. On the other hand, as Keller observed, invulner-ability may result in an inclination toward the kind of venturesomeness necessary to restore lost status.

No analysis of the specific reasons for leaving of Afghan refugees has been published to date. Suhrke and Zolberg, in a paper delivered at the American Political Science Associa-tion meetings (1984), touched peripherally on the subject. In a discussion of the relationship between particular kinds of social conflict and refugee flows, using Afghanistan and Ethiopia as case studies, the authors implicitly recognized reasons for leaving by dividing refugees from Afghanistan in Pakistan into five categories: 1) resistance party leaders, 2) "soldiers" (Mujahideen),   3) the families of leaders and Mujahideen,   4) persons affected directly by the war, and 5) "those who fled the cumulative impact of insecurity and upheaval since 1978."   The respondents' reasons for leaving in my study to be discussed below undoubtedly would fit these broad categories.   Yet, it will become clear (see Table 1) that the Suhrke and Zolberg categorization is simplistic as well as uneven.   In fact, one of the main shortcomings of their discussion of Afghan refugees in Pakistan is an overestimation of the number of refugees actually involved in resistance party activities.(2)

Two general observations may be made from this discussion of the reasons for leaving given by various refugee groups.   First, some variation between motives does exist. These differences, however, are caused either by the characteristics of the refugee group itself or by those of the event precipitating the initial thoughts of flight.   Only one group, for example, mentioned the fear of dishonor as a reason for leaving.   To Palestinian Arabs, the potential for dishonor is a very real and sufficient provocation.   Other groups may be less anxious about dishonor or consider it a painful, but insufficient, stimulus.   The nature of the war in Vietnam is an example of the effect of the event itself. Fear of reprisal, as in the case of the later vintages of Vietnamese refugees, is understandable because so many had been involved in the former government, a government that was to be replaced by one long perceived as the enemy.

The most significant observation suggested by these examples is the overall similarity in the experiences and perceptions of these experiences among the various refugee groups.   As Kunz (1981) advised, "Although refugee situations may appear unique, the study and analysis of recurring elements offer explanations of the events actually observed and enable one to predict the course which future events may take.

AFGHAN REFUGEES IN PESHAWAR

Approximately three million refugees from Afghanistan have sought and received asylum in Pakistan.(3)   A very small number of these refugees, estimated by the Govern-

Table 1: Chi-Square results showing the relationship between reasons for leaving/dates of departure from Afghanistan and other variables discussed

1. Reasons for leaving by date of departure from Afghanistan.
    X2 (0.0001, df = 261) = 1400.33605
2. Date of departure by provincial origin.
    X2 (0.0001, df = 522) = 1480.87436
3. Date of departure by district origin.
    X2 (0.0001, df = 1711) = 3982.50527
4. Date of departure by ethnic affiliation.
    X2 (0.0001, df = 261) = 1113.61139
5. Date of departure by educational level.
    X2 (0.0001, df = 464) = 589.12473
6. Date of departure by employment in Afghanistan.
    X2 (0.0001, df = 783) = 1545.49626
7. Reason for leaving by provincial origin.
    X2 (0.0001, df = 162) = 581.09174
8. Reason for leaving by district origin.
    X2 (0.0001, df = 468) = 1296.34837
9. Reason for leaving by ethnic affiliation.
    X2 (0.0001, df = 81) = 436.79216
10. Reason for leaving by educational level.
    X2 (0.0001, df = 144) = 454.27658
11. Reason for leaving by employment in Afghanistan.
    X2 (0.0001, df = 243) = 900.89761

ment of Pakistan (GOP) at around 1500, fled Afghanistan between 1973 and 1978 as political exiles from the Daoud regime.   The vast majority, however, entered Pakistan in consequence of the coup d'etat of 27-28 April 1978, the subsequent Soviet invasion in late December of 1979, and the continued escalation of hostilities between the Soviet-controlled Kabul government and resistance fighters.

The bulk of these refugees live in official refugee camps located in the NorthWest Frontier Province (NWFP) and Baluchistan, both bordering Afghanistan (Fig. 1). Several newer camps have been opened in the Punjab. Significant

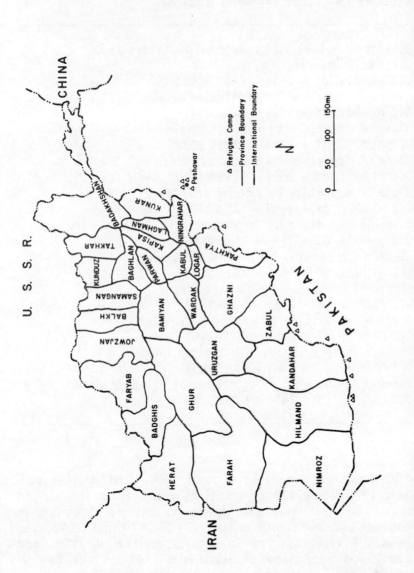

Figure 1 Map of Afghanistan provinces and some refugee camps in Pakistan. More camps have been emplaced since this figure was produced. *Source:* Adapted from data of the United Nations High Commission for Refugees.

numbers of Afghan refugees, however, live outside refugee camps, either in the villages or the cities of Pakistan. In many cases, these refugees are unregistered by the GOP.(4) The largest number of non-camp refugees are found in the city of Peshawar, located less than 40 km from the Afghan border.

Many problems hinder the study of the Peshawar refugees' reasons for leaving Afghanistan. Because many of these urban refugees are unregistered, it is difficult to estimate their numbers. The Peshawar rumor-mill (a lively, usually intriguing but often widely inaccurate source of information) claims as many as 250,000 refugees located in Peshawar. My observations coupled with those of the Commissionerate for Afghan Refugees and other knowledgeable sources offer the more conservative estimate of 60,000.(5) Although these refugees have settled throughout the city of Peshawar, eleven areas of dense and/or significant settlement exist (Fig. 2).

The sample is composed of 771 heads of refugee families interviewed during a one-year period from December of 1983 to December of 1984. Statistical random sampling techniques were not utilized because the study was initiated at a time when no hard data regarding these refugees were available. The techniques used to select informants included the following: 1) introduction to refugees in an area by the District Commissioner for Refugees, an Afghan resistance party official, or an Afghan or Pakistani acquaintance and 2) self-introduction by stopping people on the street and asking "as Afghanistanistayn?" (are you from Afghanistan?) Little resistance was encountered--only two individuals refused to be interviewed and one of these later changed his mind and consented.

Because this research was undertaken for several purposes, the interview schedule was designed to elicit data of various types. Questions concerning the informant's reason for leaving Afghanistan provide the bulk of the material for this study. Date of departure for each household was ascertained in order to evaluate vintages as well as to establish relationships between date of departure and reasons for leaving. In addition, several other categories of data were collected to determine interaction between individual attributes and reasons for leaving. These categories include 1) geographic origin, 2) ethnic and sub-ethnic

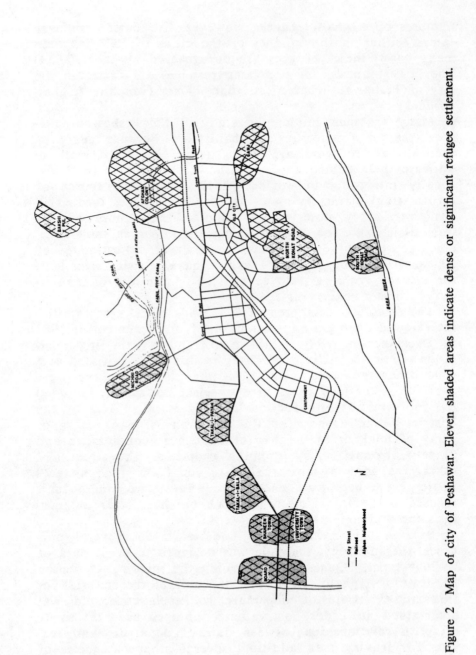

Figure 2 Map of city of Peshawar. Eleven shaded areas indicate dense or significant refugee settlement.

affiliation, 3) membership in a Peshawar-based resistance group, and 4) professional background of the head of household.

All of the questions were open-ended, although the majority were designed to produce a single answer. The respondents were encouraged to be as detailed as possible in explaining why they left Afghanistan. Nearly all, however, were quite specific about the events leading to the decision. Some social scientists express doubts about the reliability of conclusions drawn from what people say about their own motives, but as Wirth (1940) stated,

> In the study of human social life generally, while it is desirable to concentrate on overt action . . . it is not so irrelevant . . . to take account of what people say. For despite the deflections, distortions, and conceal-ment of their verbal utterances, men do betray . . . their motives and values.

In addition, any relationship between refugees' reasons for leaving and their subsequent behavior is likely to be affected by personal perceptions of why they left.

REASONS FOR LEAVING

Eleven categories of reasons for leaving Afghanistan were generated by the interview responses of the 771 heads of household (Table 2). Bombing and/or heavy fighting in an area was the reason cited by 24 percent of the refugees --the largest category--although, as the table indicates, no one reason greatly exceeds all others.

In most cases, those who left because bombing/fighting made them fear for their lives (14.53 percent) lived in areas under heavy aerial bombardment by the Soviet-directed Kabul government. In the eight years since the war in Afghanistan began, aerial bombardment has increased both in frequency and in geographic range. Intensification of the bombing of villages aims at removing bases for the resis-tance and at terrorizing villagers to prevent support and sustenance for the resistance.(6) As one respondent explained, "The planes came every day for a week. When it was over, my husband was dead and all the houses were gone. We had nowhere to live and Winter was coming on,

Table 2: Reasons for Leaving

Reason	Number	Percentage
Bombing/Fighting		
Fear for Life	112	14.53
Obstruct Livelihood	76	9.86
Avoid Military	181	23.48
Anti-Communism	93	12.06
Prison	68	8.82
Fear arrest	52	6.74
Suspect family member	29	3.76
Harassment	23	2.98
In Pakistan	7	.91
Other	14	1.82
	771	100.01

so we started on foot to Pakistan." In other cases, the terror came on foot and in tanks, "Military forces came to our village. They said they knew we were hiding Mujahideen. There were no Mujahideen, only women, children, and old people. But they killed about 240 people anyway."(7)

Heavy bombing also interrupted many economic activities. Farmers, for example, reported being unable to get seed because trucks could not get through, or planting seed but not being able to harvest because of the bombing or fighting. In addition, large numbers of several groups, whose semi-nomadic trading and laboring activities require travel throughout Afghanistan, felt forced to leave because they no longer could pursue their means of livelihood.

In very close competition with bombing/fighting is leaving to avoid service in the Afghan military. Even when individuals are not opposed actively to the government, few are willing to fight against their own countrymen. This reason may account for a larger number of refugees than is reflected by the percentage cited here (23.48 percent). Because of the interdependency of the Afghan family, a man

of conscription age often leaves accompanied by his whole
extended family. In one village in Ningrahar province, for
example, nearly two-thirds of the population left for this
reason. One former resident explained,

> I already had done my national service before the
> coup [of April 1978]. But they kept changing the
> regulations because they cannot get anyone to join
> willingly. So we all decided to go to Pakistan
> rather than to try to hide until we were too old to
> be conscripted.

Desertion and mutiny, in some cases with whole regiments going over to the resistance, are not uncommon
events. Although deserters and mutineers often remain
inside Afghanistan to fight with the resistance, many do go
to Pakistan as refugees and most now send their families
there.

Fifteen percent of the respondents reported going to
Pakistan because they were active in the resistance. The
majority of active Mujahideen (holy warriors) appear to
remain inside Afghanistan, receiving orders and supplies
from commanders who make periodic visits to headquarters
in Pakistan. Most, however, have found it increasingly
difficult to keep their families in their villages and thus
move them to Pakistan. Those who think they can find
work often settle in Peshawar. Able-bodied males (and some
who no longer are so able-bodied) spend winters in Pakistan
and return to Afghanistan to fight in the Spring.

One of the less able-bodied is referred to by his
Peshawar neighbors as "Mr. Mujahideen." He said he
remembers well the reign of Habibullah Khan (1901-1919), so
he is by no means a young man. He has two wives, who
have given him four sons and two daughters, all under the
age of twelve. He had many other children who would be
much older had they lived. He gave the following account:

> Six months after the coup the people of my village
> began to fight against the government. I lived in
> the mountains and fought for about a year. But my
> knee was injured badly and I could not fight any-
> more so I got what was left of my family and
> brought them to Pakistan. I did not go to the

camps because I still can work and I plan to fight again when my knee gets better.

Sometimes motives for joining the resistance eventually result in refugees living in Pakistan. One former city-dweller said he and many like him had joined the resistance very early because they were against the government but also because they had no real jobs and were very poor. Perhaps because of a lack of commitment, these people began spending more and more time in Pakistan and less time inside Afghanistan fighting. Their economic marginality, however, is not improved in Pakistan. "I am poorer now," he added, "and I am ready to go back to Pakistan as a normal and non-political person."

Not surprisingly, anti-communism is cited by a relatively large percentage of the respondents as their sole reason for leaving Afghanistan. In general, all the Afghan refugees regard communism as inherently incompatable with Islam. But this group considers their departure from the homeland as a protest against "the selling out of our country to those infidels." As one man explained, "No one bothered me because I am a cripple. But I am also a *malang* (hereditary beggar) and God has always taken care of me. While others may, I could not stay under that Godless government."

Imprisonment or fear of arrest accounts for 16 percent of the reasons given. Forty-one of the heads of household had been jailed, sometimes repeatedly, and twenty-seven had close family members imprisoned (many remain in prison, some have died from torture and/or disease, others have been executed), and fifty-two of the respondents feared they would be arrested if they remained in Afghanistan.

The motives and procedures of the Kabul governments since the coup d'etat of 1978 are worthy of a separate study and are beyond the scope of this chapter. However, one noteworthy fact is that not only "likely" individuals (e.g., former government officials, avowed anti-communists, religious leaders) have been arrested, but also a large number of seemingly ordinary, non-political persons. Often these arrests stem from an old enmity between the arrested and someone in the government. In other cases, individuals have been alerted to potential arrest by the incarceration of others. As one former merchant reported,

I was not involved in any political group. I stayed out of everybody's way because I wanted to continue my business.   I was in Germany when I received a telegram telling me not to return to Kabul because all the other shop owners on my street had been arrested.

The fear of arrest was, in most cases, a realistic one.

Like the bombing of the villages, many arrests are designed to provoke fear, as illustrated in the following reports:

I was arrested twice under Taraki, and once under Amin.(8)   Each time I was tortured and then released.   Some others were tortured and kept, some were executed, and some also were released. No explanations were given, no charges were made.

I was imprisoned twice.   I was not charged with any crime and they released me the first time after three months and the second time after two months. I guess it was because I was a landowner and they wanted to frighten me because of that.

An additional reason for the frequent releases without explanation may lie in inadequate space afforded by the prisons and jails, even though, as several respondents stated in the cities, homes and government buildings are used as temporary jails.   This interpretation provides some hint of the number of people who have been arrested, as little attention is paid to even minimal comfort and the space needs of the prisoners. A former Peace Corps employee (an Afghan) described his experience in prison,

I was tortured with electric charges, my nails were pulled out and long needles were pushed into my fingers.   When I confessed to nothing, they made me watch others being tortured.   This was the worst part.   They, for example, would tie a man's penis with a nylon thread, force him to drink much water and also give him a pill to produce urine. They did this until his bladder exploded.   I think they finally released me because the prison was so

crowded--there was only one hole to use as a toilet
for about 1500 people. Also they had so few people
to control the prisoners.

Others have been imprisoned for more specific reasons.
But even for these individuals, the decision to execute, try
and sentence, or release appears to be either totally capri-
cious, designed to set an example or, probably, a combination of both. In the Spring of 1982, for example, several
members of the Afghan intelligentsia were arrested for their
alleged anti-government activities. One, a former Kabul
professor, related his experience,

> There were five of us arrested. I was interrogated
> for forty days but then released. I went back to
> my job but I could not tolerate the strain because
> some of the others were to be tried and I did not
> know what would happen to them or to myself
> because I was under constant surveillance.(9)

Those who left Afghanistan because they were members
of "suspect families" number only twenty-nine of the
Peshawar sample. Although many are members of families
leading resistance parties, they are significant as a separate
group because they have been forced to leave Afghanistan
even had they not been involved in the resistance. One of
these, the Mujaddidi family, were known as the Hazrat of
Shor Bazaar (a part of Kabul where they lived), Hazrat
being an honorific reserved for religious leaders. This
family is associated with the Naqshbandi order of a type of
Islamic mystic devotionalism known as Sufism. Many family
members perished during the first purges after the 1978
coup. Sibghatullah Mujaddidi, who had been jailed in the
1950s for opposition to the Daoud government, was in
Denmark as director of an Islamic center. He went to
Pakistan in the Fall of 1978 to set up the Afghan National
Liberation Front and was joined there by members of his
family who were able to escape Afghanistan or who also had
been out of Afghanistan.

A second automatically suspect family is that of the
Gailani, also associated with Sufism, although of the
Qadiriya order. The present leader of this family, Sayed
Ahmed Gailani, served as advisor to the Taraki government

for two months after the coup. Realizing that he had been misled by promises of reform, he left Afghanistan and started his own National Liberation Front (NIFA) with headquarters in Peshawar. The complicated subject of the role of religion in jihad (holy war) is discussed elsewhere.(10)

Suffice to say here, these two families and others like them were forced to flee Afghanistan because of the potential following they command. The strength of this following is illustrated by some aspects of the settlement pattern of Afghan refugees living in Peshawar. Of the 106 respondents in very close proximity to the home office of Sayed Ahmed Gailani, 72 percent are members of the resistance party he leads.

Those who cited harassment, usually in the form of pressure to join the communist-controlled organization,(11) tended to have been in positions of some authority or employed in professions allowing them to exert influence over others. The following experience of a married couple, both medical doctors and lecturers, is a good example:

> My husband was not allowed to teach at all because
> he refused to join the party. I was also told to
> teach communist subjects or be fired. Even if I
> had wanted to do this, which I did not, what kind
> of communist subjects would I teach in a medical
> school?

In another case, an American-trained English instructor was told she would not be permitted to teach unless she joined the party. When she refused, she lost her job, her house was searched, and her father was arrested. Reasons for leaving cited by several other Kabul University lecturers included harassment to join the party, uncomfortable relationships with party members, being spied on by party members, and failure to be promoted or receive salary increases.

Government efforts to indoctrinate children and youths are another type of reported harassment. An increasing number of young children are being sent to the Soviet Union for education. Teenagers are urged to join various government-sponsored youth groups. Respondents stated that these clubs really are communist indoctrination centers where "loose" behavior (e.g., liquor being served, sexual relations encouraged) is promoted in order to destroy the influence of religion.   Parents generally are reluctant to send their children to schools where, they fear, the children will be influenced by promises or rewards.

Seven of the informants were in Pakistan at the time of the 1978 coup.   Five were followers of Gulbuddin Hekmatyar, currently leader of Hizb-i-Islami, one of the major resistance parties.   Hekmatyar, a former engineering student at Kabul University, fled Afghanistan in 1974 as the result of involvement in several groups opposing Daoud's reformist policies as well as the growing leftist orientation in internal affairs.   These followers of Hekmatyar are all active in the resistance effort.   The remaining two respondents went to Pakistan to find work as day laborers.   They also are active Mujahid.

The final category includes fourteen refugees whose reasons for leaving did not fit easily into any other category.   In most cases, motives in this group were personal. One, for example, suffers from a serious kidney ailment and believed he could get better medical treatment in Pakistan. Two others are dentists who went to Pakistan to help refugees.   Two persons insisted they had no reason for leaving; they simply wanted to emigrate.   The claim has been made that some economically-marginal families have used the political situation as an excuse to go to Pakistan where they believe they could find jobs or, at least, take advantage of relief facilities. Numerous refugees claim they know of many poor Afghans who went to Pakistan in the early stages of the conflict because they had heard they would get free lodging, clothing, food, and good medical care.   As word reached home that conditions in Pakistan were not quite so bright and few jobs were available to the unskilled, this movement appears to have waned.

REASONS BY DATES OF DEPARTURE AND RELATED ATTRIBUTES

Four periods of intensified refugee outflow from Afghanistan to Peshawar occurred (Fig. 3). Those who left Afghanistan during these periods account for 69 percent of the sample population. In addition, a substantial drop in

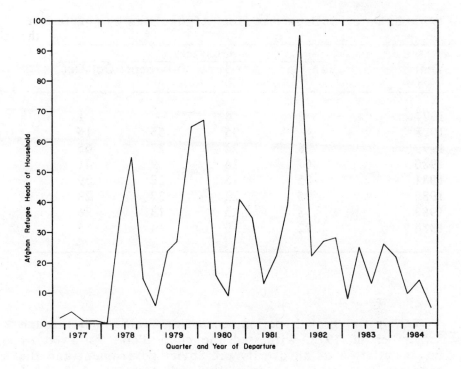

Figure 3   Refugee outflow from Afghanistan to Peshawar.

the number of refugees occurred just before each peak period (Table 3).

   That there is an association between reasons for leaving and dates of departure is indicated by a chi-square probability level of 0.0001 (Table 3). Nonetheless, explanations for these periods of increased refugee outflow are suggested by events in Afghanistan. Moreover, these data indicate that these events disparately affected respondents, i.e., chi-square analysis demonstrates significant associations between dates of departure/reasons for leaving and other variables including origin, ethnicity, and employment in Afghanistan (Table 1).

Table 3: Dates of Departure from Afghanistan by quarters

| | Quarters | | | |
Year	Jan-Mar	Apr-June	July-Sept	Oct-Dec
1977	2	4	--	1
1978	--	35	55	15
1979	6	24	27	65
1980	67	16	9	41
1981	35	13	22	39
1982	95	22	27	28
1983	8	25	13	26
1984	22	10	14	5

The initial growth period, occurring from April through September of 1978, witnessed the coup d'etat followed by the installation of an overtly pro-Soviet government and the concommitant arrests, executions, and generalized fear of arrests. As Fullerton (1983) stated, "'enemies' of the April Revolution were rounded up by the thousands--monarchists, conservatives, theologians, Social Democrats and Nationalists." Moreover, during the Summer of 1978, resistance to the new government began to organize, most notably in the rural areas of eastern Afghanistan.

During the second peak period, two major upheavals occurred. In September, 1979, Nur Muhammad Taraki was killed. He was replaced by Hafizullah Amin, who had been Foreign and Prime Minister and who undoubtedly was responsible for Taraki's death, although the details remain obscure. In late December, Amin himself was murdered, if not by the Soviets directly, at least on their orders. Soviet troops then secured control over all the major cities of Afghanistan and replaced Amin with Babrak Karmal, former Ambassador to Czechoslovakia and leader of the Parcham faction of the Afghan communist party. Since it quickly became obvious that the Karmal government could not stand on its own, Soviet advisors, supported by thousands of Soviet troops, virtually have controlled the Kabul government since late December of 1979.

The increase in the number of refugees to Peshawar
between October of 1980 and April of 1981 is attributed less
easily to specific events. This situation is true especially in
the light of the substantial downward trend between April
and October of 1980--a period of large-scale anti-government demonstrations in urban areas resulting in the arrests
of thousands (mainly students) and a series of mutinies and
desertions of Afghan soldiers. Three plausible explanations,
however, many be proposed.

First, the economic and social climate of Afghanistan
appears to have deteriorated considerably by this time.
Deprivations were felt most by urban-dwellers. Prices rose
sharply while incomes declined, food and firewood had
become scarce, utilities such as water and electricity frequently were cut off, and educational facilities outside of
major cities effectively ceased to exist.

Second, new military conscription techniques, including
press gangs who literally took young men off the streets,
caused many to flee. Both Bradsher (1983) and Hyman
(1982; 1984) reported that the attendance of males at Kabul
University dropped drastically after mid-1980.

Finally, the various resistance groups, while continuing
to suffer from disunity among their leaders, became more
organized inside Afghanistan and field commanders were able
to mobilize large segments of the population.

The continued failure of the Afghan military to attract
and retain personnel resulted in a series of new conscription
regulations enacted during late Summer in 1981 and 1982,
coinciding with the fourth period of increased refugee
outflow. In August, 1981, the Kabul government announced
that all males under 35, who had completed national service
prior to October 22, 1978, must serve an additional year. In
August, 1982, national service was extended from two to
three years, deferrals for university students were withdrawn (although one suspects that the children of high
officials were not included), and those under 35 who had
served before 1977 were called back for one year.   In
addition, the government's inability to defeat resistance
forces, who had extended their control over large areas of
rural Afghanistan, led to a sizable expansion in the government's military offensive. The number of internal refugees
(i.e., people from rural areas who fled to the cities to avoid
the bombing) reportedly increased dramatically during this
period.

The changing conditions and events occurring inside Afghanistan at this time would appear to be good potential explanations for the increase in refugee outflow observed in the Peshawar sample group. But do the responses of the refugees themselves support these suppositions or do they suggest other explanations?

Period 1 - April through September 1979

Of the 90 respondents who fled Afghanistan during the four months following the coup, 86 percent cited one of four reasons: bombing/fighting, suspect family member, imprisonment, and active participation with Mujahideen. Bombing/fighting accounted for by far the largest group (51 percent), all of whom came from Ningrahar province, one of the areas of early resistance. Ten percent left because they were members of suspect families, and 13 percent were among those imprisoned immediately after the change in government. The remaining 11 percent left to join the resistance groups forming in Pakistan.

Geographical origin of the respondents also is significant--92 percent came either from Kabul and its environs or from Ningrahar province (Fig. 1). Of the refugees from Ningrahar, 68 percent cited bombing/fighting as their reason for leaving. Slightly over half of these were farmers or landowners whose work was interrupted by the fighting.

In addition to farmers, who constitute 38 percent of the whole group, 23 percent were employed in those professions most likely to be affected quickly by a change to a pro-Soviet government; e.g., government employees, professionals, religious leaders, large merchants, and large landowners. Fifteen percent were university students. While it is impossible to state with certainty, their early departure may indicate they had been involved in one of the Islamist movements popular at Kabul University. The reasons for leaving suggest that the majority who left Afghanistan from the end of April through September of 1978 were those most sensitive to the change in government and the resistance it produced.

Period 2 - September 1979 through March 1980

The reasons for leaving cited by the 132 respondents who left during this period do imply a response to the disorder in the new Kabul government(s). Anti-communism (23 percent), for example, became the second most cited motive for leaving--predictable in the light of the Soviet invasion. The number of those who left because they had been imprisoned (8 percent) remained relatively high, while fear of arrest grew in significance to nearly 12 percent of the sample. Harassment to join the party, not cited at all by the first group, provoked the departure of 5 percent during this second period.

Bombing/fighting was a major stimulus for flight in this period as it was for all the refugees in the Peshawar sample. Differences in geographic origin of the respondents in this group, however, indicate the broadened scope of resistance activities and government attempts to suppress them. In the first period of increased refugee outflow, all those citing bombing/fighting were from one province. Four provinces are represented by this second group--Ningrahar (remaining high at 72 percent), Kunar (5.12 percent), Logar (5.12 percent), and Laghman (17.95 percent). These provinces are all located in the Kabul neighborhood where resistance efforts were escalating. In fact, all the respondents in this group were from provinces in the general Kabul area.

Examination of the reasons by geographic origin reveals a perceptible distinction between urban and rural dwellers. Of those who lived in urban areas, 74 percent left because they either had been imprisoned or feared they would be arrested. In the rural areas, in contrast, only 14 percent fled because of arrest or fear of arrest. Their major stimuli to flight were anti-communism and bombing/fighting.

Profession appears to have had some impact on decisions to leave Afghanistan. A government controlled directly by Moscow, for example, had a more notable effect on certain professions than was demonstrated in the first period. Thirty-seven percent were employed in such professions and 19 percent had remained in government positions after the coup of April, 1978. Farmers, who as a group suffered greatly from bombing/fighting, constituted 17 percent of the sample. Students, young men of draft age as well as those often involved in anti-government activities, made up 15 percent. Skilled and semi-skilled workers were the only other sizable professional group. In most cases, these individuals lived or worked in Kabul city or one of the provincial capitals.

Period 3 - October 1980 through March 1981

Escalated conscription, mobilization of new resistance fighters, and economic deterioration were suggested earlier as possible explanations for this rise in the number of refugees. The reasons cited by the 76 respondents support increases in both avoiding the military (29 percent) and becoming actively involved in the resistance movement (17 percent). That those who left because of bombing/fighting were fewer may be associated with profession, e.g., only five respondents were farmers.

The reasons themselves provide no direct information on the effects of the economic situation. Only one respondent in the entire Peshawar sample, in fact, stated he left for specific economic reasons. Profession and geographic origin, however, suggest that many who left during this period may have suffered economically. For example, 49 percent were employed in low paying jobs (e.g., unskilled laborers, street vendors, very low level government jobs), and the majority lived in the urban areas most seriously affected by socio-economic deprivations.

Period 4 - July 1981 through December 1982

Nearly one-third of all the refugees in Peshawar sample left Afghanistan during this last interval. Four categories of reasons for leaving account for 85 percent of their responses--avoid military service (37.34 percent), bombing/fighting (19.31 percent), active Mujahideen involvement (14.59 percent), and anti-communist beliefs (13.30 percent). The large number who left to avoid serving in the military supports the contention that changes in conscription regulations influenced refugee outflow. Of the refugees in this group, 41 percent fled between January and March of 1982. Fifty-three percent of these left to avoid military service. Geographic origin is significant as well. Forty-nine percent of those who fled between July of 1981 and December of 1982 were from Kabul, where the new regulations were initiated.

The frequency of bombing/fighting and active participation in the resistance as specified reasons for leaving suggests an association with the acceleration in both the government's military offensive and resistance efforts.

Geographic origins also imply that the war had extended to more areas of the country. Thirteen provinces, as compared to a maximum in earlier periods of only seven, are represented. Those provinces not mentioned by earlier vintages include Balkh, Jowzjan, Takhar, Ghur, Uruzghan, and Herat (Fig. 1).

Professional background shows some association with the primary reasons for leaving. Farmers and several groups of semi-nomadic traders and agricultural workers made up 40 percent of the sample. Withdrawal of deferrals for students may have influenced the thirty university students who left- -30 percent of all the students in the Peshawar sample. Among the remainder of the population (semi-skilled laborers, shopkeepers, and street vendors), one would expect to find many who had not done their national service or who were under 35 and thus forced to serve another year.

Statistics from the GOP indicate that the number of refugees entering Pakistan decreased consistently throughout 1983 and 1984. Reasons for leaving cited by those who went to Pakistan during these two years continued to be dominated by avoiding military service, while becoming active in the resistance gained in importance.

REASONS BY ETHNICITY

The association between ethnic affiliation and reasons for leaving is difficult to assess because of the predominance of one major ethnic group (Pushtun) among all the refugees in the NWFP. An unpublished report from the office of the District Commissioner for Refugees indicates that approximately 89 percent of the refugees living in camps in the NWFP are of Pushtun descent. The Peshawar sample is somewhat more ethnically diverse--ten groups are represented, including Pushtun, Tajik, Hazara, Aimaq, Uzbek, Turkman, Gujar, Sadat, and Baluch.

Pushtuns, who all consider themselves descendants of one eponymous ancestor (Qais, called Abd ur-Rashid or "slave of the director" by the Prophet Muhammad), numbered between 6.5 and 7 million in Afghanistan.[12] They are most densely settled in the eastern provinces of Afghanistan (with perhaps an equal number in the western provinces of Pakistan), although many Pushtuns have migrated over the years to the city of Kabul as well as to other parts of the country.

The majority of the approximately 3.5 million Persian-speaking Tajiks are found in the northeastern provinces of Afghanistan. Nearly all of the Tajiks in the Peshawar sample, however, were from the city of Kabul or the eastern provinces. Little research has been done on Tajiks living south of the Hindu Kush, and thus their specific origin has not been established. The third largest group of respondents referred to themselves as "Arab." At least two separate groups in Afghanistan claim Arab descent--one living in the northeast and another living around the Jalalabad area (Ningrahar province) and in Kabul.(13)   Most of the Peshawar sample were from south of the Hindu Kush. Another group, who sometimes are confused with the Arabs, are those who call themselves Sadat (plural of Sayyid and the term used by those in the sample). These individuals claim direct descendancy from the Prophet Muhammad through his daughter Fatima. Unlike the Arabs in Afghanistan, however, these Sadat come from a variety of ethno-linguistic groups.

Turkomans and Uzbeks live primarily in the north of Afghanistan as well as across the border in Soviet Central Asia. Hyman (1982; 1984) gave their numbers in Afghanistan as 300,000 and 1.3 million, respectively.   The very small number of Uzbek respondents, however, had been living in the city of Kabul as had the two Baluch interviewed. The homeland of the approximately 100,000 Baluch in Afghanistan is in the southwestern part of the country.

Approximately 1 million Hazaras, who are Shi'i Muslim as opposed to the majority in Afghanistan who are of the Sunni sect, live in the central highlands, also the home of about 800,000 Aimaqs. The Hazara are distinguished physically by mongoloid features giving rise to the often heard but probably mythical story that they are descendants of Ghenghis Khan's soldiers. Many Hazara have migrated to the city of Kabul to find work, usually as unskilled laborers. Both the Hazara and the Aimaqs in this study, however, were from the central highlands.

Gujar or Jat are two of the terms assigned to a collection of semi-nomadic bands. Some travel the roads of Afghanistan, stopping near villages to sell various articles, tell fortunes, show dancing monkeys, and so on, much like the gypsies of Eastern Europe. The refugees in Peshawar of this type referred to themselves as "banglewals" because, they said, they sold bangles and other such trinkets. Others practice particular trades, for example, traveling around during the harvest season to thresh wheat and rice. In Peshawar, these people called themselves "chajalbafs"-- perhaps in reference to the winnowing tray (*chaj*) they make for threshing. A third group of traveling traders is known as the Sheikh Mohammedi (or Mohmandi). Nearly all persons from these three groups formerly spent at least part of the year in or around the city of Kabul. It is interesting to note that they all claimed to be of Pushtun descent.(14)

Only five ethnic groups were represented among those who left during the first period: Pushtun (71 percent), Tajik (22.22 percent), Arab (3.33 percent), Sadat (1.11 percent), and Uzbek (2.22 percent). The two major motives cited by Pushtuns were bombing/fighting and suspect family member. Those who left because of bombing/fighting lived in Ningrahar province, while the suspect family members were from the Kabul area. Since Kabul governments had been controlled by Pushtuns since at least 1747,(15) not surprisingly, a relatively large number of suspect family members left immediately after the coup.

Among Tajiks, 45 percent had been imprisoned and 20 percent left to avoid military service. Other reasons were scattered. Fifty-five percent lived in eastern provinces, 40 percent in Kabul, and 5 percent were from the northeast of Afghanistan.

The Arabs, all from eastern provinces, left because they became involved in the early resistance movement. Two Uzbeks, from the northeast, cited anti-communism. The one Sadat, from Kabul, had been arrested during the coup.

During the second period, 60.61 percent were Pushtun, 26.52 percent Tajiks, 8.33 percent Sadat, 3.78 percent Arab, and .76 percent Hazara. The Pushtuns' reasons for leaving were more diverse than in the first period--32.5 percent left because of bombing/fighting, 17.5 percent because of anti-communism, 13.75 percent because of fear of arrest, and 11.25 percent because of actual arrest. The majority of Pushtuns were from the eastern provinces, with 12.5 percent from Kabul and 1.25 percent from provinces in the southeast. Again, the involvement of Pushtuns in former governments undoubtedly is associated with the relatively large number of those imprisoned or who feared arrest.

Avoiding military service, bombing/fighting, and anti-communism each accounted for 28.57 percent of the Tajiks' reasons for leaving. The vast majority of Tajiks in this period came from provinces in the east. The eleven Sadat, from Kabul and the east, stated a variety of reasons including prison (1 respondent), fear of arrest (1 respondent), active participation in the resistance (2 respondents), harassment (2 respondents), and military avoidance (3 respondents). The one Hazara, from Kabul, left because he feared arrest, while the four Arabs, from the eastern provinces, left because of bombing/fighting in their areas.

As opposed to the other three intervals, Tajiks dominated Period 3 at 51.32 percent of the total. Pushtuns accounted for 36.84 percent, Arabs 6.58 percent, and Sadat 5.26 percent. The large number of Tajiks, mainly from Kabul and provincial centers of the eastern provinces, may result from their susceptibility to draft--nearly 50 percent cited avoiding the military as their reason for leaving. The five Arabs and four Sadat cited avoiding military service, anti-communism, and prison as their reasons for leaving. Origins were divided equally between Kabul and the eastern provinces.

Pushtuns gave very mixed reasons during this period; for example, bombing/fighting, active participation in the resistance, and "other" each were cited by 17.84 percent. Fourteen percent left to avoid military service, while prison and anti-communism each provoked the flight of 10.71 percent. Moreover, their geographic origins were varied: 35.71 percent were from eastern provinces, 28.57 percent from Kabul, 28.57 percent from provinces in the northeast, and 7.14 percent from the southeast. The number of those active in the resistance coupled with this expansion of geographic origin may be related to the general escalation of resistance activities.

The fourth period of refugee outflow is characterized by an increase in the number of ethnic groups represented as well as more diversity in geographic origin. This change is consistent with the overall reasons for leaving discussed earlier and may result from the new conscription regulations as well as the enlargement of the government's offensive against the resistance.

The Pushtuns' reasons from leaving included avoiding the military and anti-communism (24.1 percent each), prison and fear of arrest (16.87 percent), and bombing/fighting (12.05

percent). These refugees came from six areas of Afghanistan: Kabul (55.42 percent), the eastern provinces (32.53 percent), northeastern provinces (3.61 percent), northern provinces (2.41 percent), and western provinces (2.41 percent).

The percentage of those who left to avoid the military and arrest/arrest fear are similarly high for the Tajiks in this group. Moreover, these Tajiks also came mainly from urban areas where the conscription laws were initiated and arrests more frequent.

The seven Arabs, from Kabul and the east, cited harassment, anti-communism, and involvement in the resistance as their reasons for leaving Afghanistan. Avoiding service in the military, being a suspect family member, and fearing communism were the reasons given by the five Sadat, also from Kabul and the east. The five Hazaras, from the central highlands, left to become active Mujahid, as did the three Turkomans from the north. One Aimaq, from the northeast, escaped military service. Three individuals, two Baluch and one Uzbek, left for personal reasons.

Finally, two groups of semi-nomadic traders and agricultural workers also left Afghanistan during this period. They left, in some cases, because they no longer were able to move freely as a result of the bombing and fighting and, in other cases, because the new government had rescinded the deferral from military service they had enjoyed under former governments.

DISCUSSION

The causative factors in the movement of Afghan refugees to Peshawar, Pakistan, as cited by 771 heads of refugee households have been examined. An attempt has been made to enhance the explicit information provided by the reasons given with implicit support from such data as the respondent's dates of departure from Afghanistan, geographic origins, professions, and ethnic affiliations.

The discussion of reasons for leaving demonstrates that these refugees made their decisions to leave based on specific events or perceptions of events they believed made their remaining in their homeland intolerable. They did not flee en masse as refugee movements often are depicted. That many Afghans did not reach this conclusion and remained in Afghanistan further supports the individual quality of a refugee's decision to leave. The results of these individual decisions, however, are not unique, as is evidenced by the relatively limited number of categories generated by the reasons given. The majority left because they suffered from the effects of bombing and/or fighting in their home areas, they refused to fight against their countrymen, they became active in the resistance against the new government and no longer could protect their families inside Afghanistan, they were unwilling to suggest tacit acceptance of a communist government by staying in the country, or they had been imprisoned or feared they would be imprisoned. Smaller numbers fled because they were members of particular families made suspect by their role in Afghan society or were those under constant harassment to pledge loyalty to the government.

Other refugee studies have found similar categories of causative factors. Vietnamese refugees, for example, also cited bombing/fighting, fear of communism, economic factors, and fear of reprisals as major provocations for flight. The imprisonment, fear of arrest, suspect family member, and other related categories, as stated by Afghan refugees, certainly can be considered forms of reprisal or fear of reprisal. Economic factors influenced those farmers and traders whose livelihood activities were obstructed by the war, as well as all those who lost jobs because of associations with past governments or failure to join a government party.

The distinction between urban and rural Palestinian Arab refugees holds for Afghan refugees as well. Rural Palestinian Arabs fled primarily because of airplanes and the fear of massacre by Israeli troops. Rural Afghans also cited fear of airplanes (bombing) and instances of massacres by government soldiers as major causes for leaving. Both urban Palestinian Arabs and urban Afghans were more affected by arrest, fear of arrest, economic disruptions, and general harassment.

The large number of Afghans who left because of anti-communism or refusal to live under a communist-controlled government is reminiscent of the philosophical motivations expressed by exiles from Cuba. Unlike the Cuban situation, these data provide no clear correlation between the dates of departure of Afghan refugees and socioeconomic status, because the majority of Afghan refugees from the elite classes are not in Pakistan.

Finally, the many Hindus who fled from Pakistan during Partition did so because they were members of a particular religious and/or ethnic group. While one hesitates to draw too close an analogy between this group and any other, it is true that many Afghan refugees as well as those from other areas of the world have been forced to flee simply because of their membership in a certain group.

A brief survey of Bogue's summary of push factors for voluntary migrants demonstrates how easily it can be adapted to describe the primary causative factors for forced migrants:

1. A large proportion of the refugees in this and other refugee movements have fled because their economic opportunities were, in a sense, "exhausted." Heavy bombing and fighting, for example, have made it difficult or impossible for many to continue their livelihood activities and forced them to leave their homes.

2. Economic factors also form the basis for Bogue's second category headed by "loss of employment resulting from being discharged for incompetence." "Incompetence" is a relative term, one defined by the individual or group in charge. In the case of a change in government, many of those employed by or sympathetic to the former government at least will be judged as unsuitable and therefore incompetent to do the job. Moreover, those who are harassed to display active support for a new government, or lose their jobs when they refuse, also fit this category.

3. Those who suffer imprisonment, fear arrest, are members of suspect families, or fear reprisals are victims of "oppressive or repressive discriminatory treatment because of religious, political or ethnic origins or membership."

4. "Alienation . . . because one no longer subscribes to prevailing beliefs, actions, or modes of behavior" applies in general to those who left because they are opposed to communism and the beliefs/behaviors they associate with communism, and, in a less direct way, to those who refused to aid the government in suppressing resistance. Prevailing beliefs, actions, and behaviors are not neces-

sarily those of the majority, but rather of those in control, especially when that control in exercised by punishing those who are in opposition. The alienation, then, takes the form of flight.

5. Leaving because one no longer enjoys opportunities for personal development or employment is relevant to anyone perceived as being opposed to the new government.

6. Retreat because of disaster is, for both voluntary and involuntary migrants, an inclusive category. Bogue chose to define disaster as flood, fire, drought, or any other "natural" disaster. For those on the losing side of a battle, however, their defeat is very much a disaster and thus has the same results. For most Afghans, the Soviet invasion of their country and subsequent control of the government as well as the ongoing war certainly are disasters.

The intent of this discussion is not to suggest that Bogue's summary of push factors should be adapted for use in refugee analysis but rather to demonstrate that the causes of refugee movements are no more unique than are those of voluntary migrants. As Kunz so clearly pointed out, it will continue to be difficult to build a theoretical framework for the analysis (and thus the understanding) of refugee movements until conceptualization of the repetitive characteristics of such movements occurs. Constructing typologies of refugee causalities is one positive step toward a more theoretical approach to the study of refugees. Yet many elements of a functional theoretical approach need to be developed. For example, although vintages undoubtedly exist among Afghan refugees, a detailed analysis of the kinds of behaviors associated is yet to be done.(16) Second, typologies and other categorizations, such as Kunz's "acute" versus "anticipatory" refugee types, are not as easy to apply as one first assumes. When a refugee states that his family fled during the middle of the night and went on foot through the mountains to the safety of the border, one immediately labels this family as acute refugees. One may learn later, however, that his description of the flight obscured elements of the whole decision-making proces, i.e., of the days and weeks the family had feared they might be forced to leave and quietly made some practical and/or physical preparations.

Truly valid longitudinal studies focus on the same individuals as those studied earlier. Such research is scarce. In order to develop a theoretical framework that will produce data useful in the resettlement of refugees, more longitudinal studies as well as a more complete understanding of refugee types will be necessary.

NOTES

1. The majority of those who have fled Afghanistan have been granted asylum in Pakistan. Large numbers of Afghan refugees, however, are living in other countries. The United States Department of State, U.S. Bureau for Refugee Programs estimates the presence of 780,000 Afghans listed as refugees in Iran and 7,500 in India. In addition, smaller numbers of Afghan refugees have emigrated to the United States, Canada, Australia, and the Middle East. For more information on Afghan refugees in Iran, see "Islamic Republic of Iran: Unnoticed Asylum Country" by Annick Billard in the November 1985 issue of *Refugees* magazine (United Nations High Commissioner for Refugees).

2. I am in the process of completing an analysis of the residential choices of self-settled Afghan refugees living in Peshawar. Resistance party membership as well as degree and type of involvement in the resistance parties is one of the variables investigated. The data collected from 976 heads of refugee households indicates that, while the majority do hold a membership card in one of the parties, 59.8 percent of the respondents are not involved in party activities.

3. Estimates of Afghan refugees in Pakistan vary. In January, 1985, the U.S. Committee for Refugees reported on the results of a census undertaken by the Government of Pakistan during 1984 (see Allen K. Jones, *Afghan Refugees: Five Years Later*, January, 1985). The number of registered refugees was reported as 2.4 million, a rather lower figure than the 2.9 or 3 million often claimed by the GOP (see, for example, *Humanitarian Assistance Programme for Refugees in Pakistan*, August, 1983, or any of the dozens of news releases issued by the GOP). This comment is made, however, only for the sake of accuracy and is not intended to accuse the GOP of consciously padding the numbers of refugees. Counting refugees who are not forced to remain

in one place is a difficult business at best.

4.   In 1982 the Pakistani government decided to restrict registration to those refugees who settled in camps. This attempt to discourage refugees from seeking accommodations in urban areas has not been very successful and thus the GOP has initiated several recent programs to move refugees out of the cities.

5.   During the Summer of 1984, the Government of Pakistan accelerated its plans to remove all Afghan refugee "bachelors" and offices of Resistance parties from Peshawar following a bomb blast outside of one of the resistance headquarters in which four persons died.   Many rumors circulated that all refugees would be removed from Peshawar.   At the time of publication, however, Afghan refugees remain in Peshawar.

6.   Discussants at a Rand Corporation-sponsored international conference on international terrorism and sub-national conflict have suggested that "dumping" refugees on another country is becoming a new factor in international conflict. They were, of course, referring specifically to the Mariel flotilla episode.   Some observers of the Afghan situation (including this author) have speculated that the Soviet-controlled Kabul government intentionally provokes people to leave Afghanistan in order to do the following: 1) rid the country of potential opposition, and 2) cause problems for the Government of Pakistan.   Pedraza-Bailey (1985) makes a similar argument concerning Cuban and U.S. government cooperation in getting exiles out of Cuba prior to the Mariel refugees.

7.   The behavior of some Mujahideen is reported as responsible on occasion for the flight of Afghans. None of the refugees in this study claimed to have been harassed by resistance fighters or commanders, but reliable sources do state that there have been instances where Mujahideen have acted like "kings" in a village, demanding food, clothing, and exorbitant taxes.   Villagers who refused allegedly were punished and, in a few cases, even executed.

8.   Nur Muhammad Taraki took over as President of the new Kabul government shortly after the coup d'etat of April, 1978. He died under very questionable circumstances in September of 1979 and was replaced by Hafizullah Amin, former Foreign and Prime Minister of the DRA.

9.   I arrived in Kabul on the first flight from Europe

after the 1978 "Saur" Revolution.   As a Fulbright Fellow I was to work with Hasan Kakar, a well-known historian at Kabul University.   Professor Kakar was courageous enough to help me even though he knew he was under surveillance. He was one of the five arrested and currently is serving an eight-year term in prison.

10. For an example specific to the Afghan situation, see David Busby Edwards, "Redefining Islam: Ideology and Conflict in the Afghan Jehad," paper presented to the 13th Annual Conference on South Asia, University of Wisconsin, November, 1984.

11. The number and variety of "parties" available has become something of a joke among the refugees.   It is not necessary to join an overtly political organization.   One may, for example, become a member of a chess group as long as it is sanctioned by the government.

12. Ethnicity in Afghanistan has been the subject of much study as well as debate.   Because this study is not concerned with the origins of ethnic groups, but rather with how these people categorize themselves ethnically, only a brief discussion of those ethnic groups represented in the Peshawar sample is included.   In addition, all the respondents referred to themselves by their major ethnic category (e.g., Tajik, Uzbek), with the exception of Pushtuns who most often referred to themselves by their "sub-tribe," clan, or some other category of common patrilineal descent or geographic origin.   These are included as well as major Pushtun sub-divisions, such as Durrani or Ghilzai, down to small groups who identify themselves by their area of origin or common descent.   The data do not indicate any strong correlation between subgroups and reasons for leaving and, in the few cases where a modest association existed, geographic location was more relevant.

13. For additional information on Arabs living north of the Hindu Kush, see Barfield (1981); for short discussions on those south of the Hindu Kush, see Elphinstone (reprint ed., 1969); Ferdinand (1969, 130); Jenkins (1879, 5).

14. For a discussion of Pushtun descent claims among these groups, see Olesen (1982); Dupree (1973).   Ferdinand, in the chapter he wrote for Humlum (1959), stated that they were of Indian origin.   Their physical characteristics as well as certain behaviors do tend to suggest an Indian origin.

15. A loose confederation of peoples and areas that make

up most of modern Afghanistan usually are attributed to the acceptance as leader of Ahmad Shah Durrani in 1747.

16. No associative behavior among the refugees in Peshawar is as yet apparent, although there are suggestions that such inclusive and exclusive behaviors may be emerging based, at least in part, on dates of departure (e.g., harassment of others; threats made to those who left Afghanistan recently; and expressions of envy toward those who came early, have been able to get jobs, and accumulate some goods).   This author is in the process of analyzing the settlement patterns of the refugees in Peshawar, which will provide a more conclusive view of the role of vintages. In addition, a longitudinal study of a smaller group of these refugees is planned.

7

Humanitarian Response
to an Inhuman Strategy

Ralph H. Magnus

BACKGROUND

To understand the problems associated with the provision
of humanitarian aid to the Mujahideen and civilian population remaining inside Afghanistan, one must first understand
that many of the problems to be faced predate the current
Soviet-Afghan conflict. Indeed, they are closely related to
some of the fundamental features of Afghan culture, society,
history, and politics. Obviously the current conflict enor-
mously compounds these problems, raising them to crisis
levels, for it is truly said that the Soviet military strategy
is based upon the destruction or "rubbleization" of the 85
percent of Afghanistan that is rural, since the Soviets have
little hope of winning Afghan allegiance to a communist
regime, nor are they willing to commit the troops necessary
to control Afghanistan by force.(1)

Afghanistan is a land marked by multiple divisions and
diversity: geographic from burning sands to perpetual ice;
ethnic from more than twenty distinct groups; tribal from
many dozens of confederations, sub-tribes, clans, lineages,
etc.; and cultural from Western-oriented and educated elites
to Islamic scholars and illiterate nomads. One of the most
fundamental of these divisions, both traditionally and growing ever deeper in the twentieth century, has been between
the 10 to 15 percent of urban Afghanistan and the 90 to 85
percent of rural Afghanistan. Although the two are not, as
has sometimes been alleged, in a state of perpetual war,
they are in many respects two different worlds culturally,
socially, and politically.

To be sure, the urban-based government officials did penetrate the countryside for the traditional purpose of extracting taxes and conscripts and, at least in recent years, for the more popular purpose of providing services and benefits. It is also true that the rural sector of Afghan society, to an extent almost unique in the Third World, succeeded in penetrating the urban world of modern economic development and government. As the provision of government benefits gradually became more of a normal feature of state-rural relations in the mid-twentieth century, something of the old barriers against the state in the rural areas began to break down. Increasingly, the people wanted and demanded their fair share of the roads, hospitals, schools, seeds, and tractors which the Kabul government was beginning to be able to supply from its own resources and from extensive foreign aid programs. One of the major failings of the old regime, a failing which made its passing in 1973 a matter of indifference to much of the country, was in its failure to provide fairly, honestly, and efficiently the goods and services it had promised to the Afghan people.(2) Complaints on this score were clearly voiced in the vote of confidence debates, broadcast live by Radio Kabul, of the governments appointed under the liberal constitution of 1964. One member of the *Wolesi Jirgah* (the lower house of the parliament) from the Shinwari tribe complained that previous governments had given only unfulfilled promises to the rural people: there were no hospitals in his district and only one elementary school, which the local people had tried unsuccessfully to have raised to secondary school status. Another member complained that the Third Development Plan made no provisions for balanced national development, but instead gave all the advantages to Kabul and a few other places (American Embassy 1967). The new newspaper *Khalq*, the short-lived organ of the People's Democratic Party of Afghanistan (PDPA or Khalq Party), praised the questioning given to the government by the *Wolesi Jirgah* members on such vital issues as the concentration of development activities and services in Kabul ("Balanced Education" 1966).

Severe drought conditions in the Winters of 1970-71 and 1971-72 brought about particularly hard times for rural Afghans, and in the isolated central province of Ghowr there was actual famine. Here, the failings and alleged corruption of the government's relief efforts had a powerful effect in further discrediting the monarchy and its experiment with "new democracy."(3)   Of course the Marxist elements of the urban elite, particularly the Parcham faction of the PDPA in alliance with former Prime Minister, Sardar Muhammad Daoud Khan (the King's cousin), were better organized than were the supporters of the 1964 Constitution. They had as well the support of the U.S.S.R. which took advantage of popular discontent with this, and other, failings of the regime.   The 42-old reign of Muhammad Zahir Shah and the two hundred 26-old Durrani monarchy were overthrown by a military coup on July 17, 1973.

It should not be assumed, however, that there was no progress under the monarchy or in the brief republic of President Muhammad Daoud (1973-78).   The first faculty of what was to become Kabul University was the medical faculty, opened by King Muhammed Nadir in 1932.   Yet, twenty-five years later, at the start of the systematic plans initiated by Muhammad Daoud as Prime Minister, there were but 149 medical doctors (and 1,380 hospital beds) in the country.   By 1971 these had increased to 757 doctors and 3,322 beds (Brandt 1974).   In 1963 a second medical faculty of what was to become the University of Ningrahar in Jelalabad was opened. In contrast to Kabul University, where the language of instruction was Dari, and which had had European and Turkish instructors since its inception (and which had an advisory agreement with the University of Lyon), the Ningrahar faculty had an American advisory team provided by USAID and taught in Pushtu.   The Swedish Committee of Afghanistan, which is trying to aid medical care (primarily) inside Afghanistan today, estimates that there were probably 1,000 Afghan MDs in the country at the time of the Khalqi coup of April 1978 (Fange 1985).   Other medical training facilities included those for pharmacists, nurses (male and female), and midwives. Medical education, as all higher education in Afghanistan, was free, with the proviso that graduates serve a term of government-assigned service upon graduation.   In practice, virtually all trained medical personnel were government employees of one sort or another, though many had private clinics as well.

Despite genuine progress in opening rural health clinics in the 1970s, modern health facilities remained heavily concentrated in the capital.(4)   There both bilateral and international agencies supported a number of foreign aid projects. These included the American CARE-MEDICO team, American Peace Corps, the Czech-built Wazir Akhbar Khan Hospital, the WHO and UNICEF. Certainly, a major achievement in the health field was the elimination of smallpox by 1973 and the virtual eradication of malaria by 1978. Nevertheless, by most commonly accepted standards (even given the unreliability of statistics) the health care situation of Afghanistan was abysmally poor. For instance, life expectancy was only 33.4 years in 1960 and 37.4 in 1978. Infant mortality was 204.8 per thousand in 1981--all rankings that put Afghanistan in the company of such states as Chad, Mali, East Timor, and Yemen (World Bank 1983).

In food supplies, however, Afghanistan was not normally in too bad a position. In 1961-65 the caloric intake figure was estimated at 124 per cent of minimum requirements, with protein intake at 95.9 per cent. By 1977 these figures had dropped to 106.9 percent and 80.5 percent, respectively (World Bank 1983).

Education was the area of major social achievement by the old regime, however. Primary school enrollments rose from 9 percent in 1960 to 16 percent in 1965 and 28 percent in 1970. High school enrollments and higher education experienced ever higher growth rates. In the end, these burgeoning enrollments brought nothing but grief for the monarchy. Too many secondary graduates were produced to be absorbed by the university and higher education systems and, once graduated, a sufficient number of good government jobs in the capital or large cities was no longer available for those who felt this was their right by virtue of their diploma. Thus, they were unemployed, underemployed, or employed in undesirable locations in the provinces, these same provinces that they had sought to escape by coming to the capital for a modern education. Disgruntled students and young graduates became the basis of the PDPA and other Marxist parties, as well as a major component of the newly organized "Islamist" parties.(5)

THE PROBLEM

The task of providing humanitarian assistance to the victims of the conflict in Afghanistan is a complex amalgam consisting of the inherent natural factors of conditions in

Afghanistan in general, the more or less "normal" disruptions that would be found in any wartime situation, and multiplied many-fold by the deliberate terrorist strategy and tactics of the Soviet forces. The Soviet terrorist tactics may have originally resulted from lack of discipline, inexperience and frustrations in dealing with a hostile population and an active guerrilla movement, as well as the common response of a modern high-technology military force to use firepower in lavish quantities at the first signs of resistance. That these terror tactics were a major, if not *the* major, facet of Soviet operations soon became clear. This decision was indeed a logical solution in a situation in which the Soviets, for whatever reasons, have limited their forces to considerably less than would be necessary to achieve victory in a guerrilla war by military means.

Initially, the Soviets had hoped to have a relatively efficient Afghan puppet army to serve as useful auxiliaries, but this hope has been continually frustrated. They soon shifted to the tactic of countering the Mujahideen indirectly by attacking the entire civilian population of rural areas, thus reversing the dictum of Mao Zedong that guerrillas were the fish that swam in the sea of people by emptying the fish-bowl of its water.(6) In order to survive, the people will either be forced to flee to the cities, where they will be more easily controlled, or to the neighboring countries of Iran and Pakistan. There they will contribute to the further destabilization of these nations with consequences to be exploited by the Soviet Union at a later date.

These efforts have brought about tremendous suffering to the ordinary Afghan and have achieved some successes, but they have been met with determined resistance as well. The Afghan farmer is a very tough individual and not easily driven from his ancestral land. If necessary, he will leave the main valley and go up to a side valley. He will farm at night. He will send most of the population to safety in refugee camps and keep a small contingent to continue farming in the home village. Instead of threshing on outside floors, he will thresh inside ruined buildings. Refugees in Pakistan will even "commute" across the border to plant and tend fields. More recently, the active Mujahideen, who, like most soldiers, spend only a fraction of their time actually fighting, have taken to planting crops themselves in abandoned areas. In general, given the slightest hope of survival, the Afghan peasant will continue to farm in his own village.(7)

In some cases, however, the Soviet de-population tactics have been successful, making the Mujahideen more dependent upon supply routes which present tempting targets for the enemy. Undoubtedly, the Soviets would be much more successful if they combined "carrot" tactics of promising exemption from attack to a particular area in return for forming a government-sponsored militia and keeping Mujahideen from operating in that area. These tactics, largely carried out by the KGB-trained and commanded Afghan KHAD (*Khedamat-e Ettelahat-e-Dawlati*, or Government Information Service, the Kabul regime's secret police) have met with some temporary success. However, these agents and the Soviets do not have sufficient forces to protect these neutralized areas from Mujahideen retaliation, nor do they have an ideology to compete with that of the Islamic jihad and the popular hatred of the foreign, Godless Communists. In the Afghan tribal system, particularly with the Pushtuns, the tribal khan does not have the authority to commit the tribe (or his division of it on such matters; he can and has been overruled by the tribal *jirgah*).(8)

The provision of medical care has been, in practice, a major area of focus for humanitarian relief efforts, both those of the Afghan Mujahideen themselves and of international donors. In carrying out this task Afghan medical personnel have a difficult position, even disregarding for the moment (as one cannot disregard in practice) the fact of direct military action aimed at frustrating such efforts by the Soviets and Karmal forces. First, there are the "normal" problems of operating a medical clinic in rural Afghanistan: the securing of supplies and medicines, the payment of personnel (including the doctors themselves), the securing of transportation and a suitable building, and the lack of access to advanced medical facilities in the cities for severe cases. Even more fundamental is the immense cultural gap between the urban-scientifically educated Afghan medical personnel and the rural Mujahideen and their supporters. This fundamental division of Afghan society has been reinforced by the fact that, for the average Mujahid, the urbanized doctors are just the kind of elitist representatives of the old regime who, in their eyes, through their neglect or self-interest sold out Afghanistan in the first place to the foreigners.

Even if the doctor's credentials as a "good Mujahid" are eventually accepted, he must face the fact that he is an outsider operating in what is often a closed and alien society--a society that might not even speak the same language.   To be sure, such things happened in peace-time Afghanistan, but then the doctor was supported by the authority and resources of the government.   As a fellow Mujahid, the Mujahideen doctor has a common bond with all Mujahideen of whatever social class or ethnic group.   He is also the provider of a highly desirable commodity that can even be life-saving.   These ideological and practical ties to operate in practice smooth over the differences in culture and outlook between the modernized doctor and the traditional villager.   Yet, the distressing reality in some cases, as in other areas of coordinating the jihad, is that both traditional divisions and the modern divisions among various Mujahidden parties and factions hamper the common effort.

Thus, Pushtun doctors want to practice in Pushtun areas, Ghilzai in Ghilzai areas, Hazara in the Hazarajat, etc.   This is only natural; each ethnic group would prefer to have doctors from among its own numbers, but it is not always possible.   Pushtun doctors, in particular, are not likely to be popular in non-Pushtun areas, where they might be identified as representatives of the previous regime which oppressed other ethnic groups.(9)   The obvious solution, in fact practiced in most cases, is for a doctor to go to his home area, or at least to the home of some relatives if he happens to be from a major city.   Yet, here the reverse problem arises: the doctor can be *too* close to the local ties of tribe, clan, and family and become inadvertently involved in local disputes having nothing to do with his duties or with the jihad.   Thus, there have been cases where doctors have been driven out or even murdered in such conflicts.(10)

From the formal political dimension of the rival Mujahideen parties, as least until the achievements of the all-party unity between the so-called fundamentalist alliance and the moderate alliance of May 1985, two major rival doctors' organizations, one associated with each alliance, emerged.   For the moderates, the Society of Afghan Doctors and Medical Personnel Outside Afghanistan (SAD), which the doctors working in the Pakistani refugee camps had formed, worked in their own hospital to care for wounded and ill party members and supporters (and, of course, their families). In 1982 the SAD decided to support the establishment of clinics inside Afghanistan. But even this small group had internal splits. Some of its leaders were related to the Mujaddidi family (and to the Afghan royal family as well), the hereditary leaders of the *Naqshbandiyya* order of Sufis in Afghanistan and of the Mujahideen political party *Jebhey-e Nejad-e Melli*, or National Liberation Front. A number of its members also belonged to the strongly nationalist Pushtun secular party, the *Afghan Mellat* (Afghan Nation). When the *Afghan Mellat* affiliation split the group in late 1983, the majority of the doctors formed a new organization, the *Union of Afghan Mujahideen Doctors*, blaming "external intervention" and "political differences" prevailing in the SAD for deflecting them from their proper target: "to serve the ailing masses and humanity, especially inside Afghanistan in liberated parts."(11)

The Islamic "fundamentalist" party alliance, for its part, had a much looser organizational structure. Their medical director, Dr. Barakzai, had been a professor at the Ningrahar medical faculty, and had a strong contingent of his former students working in the Alliance's hospital in Peshawar and rotating to serve inside Afghanistan. He stressed that medical personnel had the same duty as all Mujahideen to serve in the jihad as best they could, just like ordinary soldiers. Hence, they neither asked for nor received a salary for their work, although the doctors working at the hospital received a small living allowance. They had no system of organized clinics inside Afghanistan; if individual doctors wanted to work inside they would simply take leave for a few months and join a group as their doctor. He himself kept up a regular practice across the Durand Line, visiting his patients on a regular basis (and traveling mostly by car).(12)

Although obviously divided by their political allegiances, doctors from each organization spoke well of the others. They stressed that all medical personnel had a common duty, dictated both by their Islamic duty and their medical oath, to help all in need, regardless of their political affiliations.

Almost simultaneously with the establishment of the Society of Afghan Doctors' first clinics inside Afghanistan in late 1982, the Swedish Committee for Afghanistan (SCA), an organization founded immediately after the Soviet invasion in 1979, began its aid operations in Peshawar. This organization, which will be discussed in greater detail later, adopted a philosophy that the best way to get medical care inside Afghanistan was through trained Afghan medical personnel. Thus, they undertook to support and expand the operations of the SAD's clinics by providing them with medicines and medical supplies, as well as offering a modest salary (the same as medical personnel would be getting working in the health care system set up for the Afghan refugees in Pakistan). This small salary would enable them to continue to support their families privately, without relying on the charity of the refugee aid system. This final provision proved to be crucial, since as scientifically educated, urban Afghans, they felt uncomfortable in the refugee camp structure. They believed this structure was too much under the influence of their traditional tribal leaders or the Islamic revolutionary parties.(13)

The Swedish Committee soon realized that even the Union of Afghan Mujahideen Doctors, despite their efforts to act in a non-partisan manner, was too internally divided to work with as a group. They thus shifted their emphasis to working with and supporting doctors and medical personnel on an individual basis, providing they wished to serve the health needs of the people inside Afghanistan.

To work with the Swedish Committee, doctors must secure the pledges of all commanders in a region, promising to protect the clinic and not to use it as a political football. They also pledge to arrange for the transportation of supplies. The doctors and medical personnel agree to serve all who are in need and to account for their medical supplies received from the Swedish Committee. Word quickly spread among both the Mujahideen inside Afghanistan and among the medical personnel in Pakistan of the aid extended by the SCA. Actual clinics were established by a dual process: in some cases the initiative came from the medical personnel and in other cases from a request by the commanders in a particular region. In still other cases doctors and groups had already been working on their own and requested aid in the form of supplies.

In one of these latter cases the representatives of Isma'il Khan, the regional Mujahideen commander recognized by all parties in the Herat area and neighboring regions, came to Peshawar to describe their plight. They said that they had several graduate doctors and other trained medical personnel and operated a regular hospital located in a village only a few kilometers from Herat city. However, they had very little medicine and even less equipment (one stethoscope for the entire hospital, for instance). When asked about their current sources of medicines, they replied that they could go to Iran and buy what was available in local drugstores, but they received no aid from the Iranian authorities, which is why they were coming as far as Peshawar.(14)

In this manner, the Swedish Committee for Afghanistan gradually built up a network of clinics to which they offered support. Beginning with six clinics in the Winter of 1982-83 (each with a graduate MD and one or more other trained medical aides), they distributed ten tons of medicines and medical supplies in 1983. By 1984 they had aided some 44 doctors, 67 trained medical personnel (including medical students, pharmacists, and nurses), and 383 trained paramedics, distributing 32 tons of supplies. In attempting to extend their network of medical aid in 1984, the SCA began to send out shipments of supplies to medical personnel who had been reliably reported to be working inside, even if they had not contacted the Committee on their own, offering further regular deliveries if they wished and agreed to account for their usage. It was predicted that they would distribute 50 tons of supplies in 1985 (Fange 1985).

However, the Committee gradually came to the conclusion, which was shared by other private organizations providing humanitarian aid to the Afghans, that the basic lack of sufficient numbers of trained Afghan medical personnel means that these efforts will soon reach their limits. From two and a half years of extensive interviews and cross-checking, Anders Fange of the Swedish Committee has concluded that in 1985 only 200 Afghan MDs are working inside Afghanistan, and only 50 of these work in rural areas controlled by the Mujahideen. Thus, the major expansion of medical care cannot come until expanded medical training facilities are provided in Pakistan for medical and paramedical personnel. There is a need as well to upgrade the professional training of Afghan doctors and paramedics to make them more effective (1985).

Certainly another major problem for the population remaining inside Afghanistan is that of food, one of the more controversial topics discussed by humanitarian aid groups and governments. A major part of the problem is the lack of hard data needed to grasp the true dimensions, and hence to devise necessary aid programs. By 1985 a consensus began to emerge that the food situation in the interior of Afghanistan had not, as yet, reached a critical level, except for a few isolated instances, but it was becoming more serious daily. Not only have the Soviets aimed a major portion of their effort at the destruction of food supplies, and even at irrigation systems, but they have made preemptive efforts to purchase what food is produced at good prices to ensure that it comes under their control instead of that of the Mujahideen. It is also clear that food production has dropped drastically in general. However, the exodus of the refugees has meant that there are fewer mouths to feed. In some cases, those of internal refugees who have fled the destruction of the countryside to Afghan cities, the food situation creates problems for the Soviets and the Karmal regime, and supplies have to be imported from the U.S.S.R.

A number of humanitarian aid groups, particularly the French AFRANE, have concentrated their relief efforts on the food situation. Some of these have agreed, following the Oxford Conference in May 1985 on humanitarian aid to Afghans, that probably the most feasible way to provide relief would be through funds for local purchases inside Afghanistan. Except in a few favored locations close to the Pakistan or Iranian borders, or where very favorable transportation facilities are available, the logistics of transporting sufficient food supplies to make an impact are virtually impossible. On the other hand, Afghanistan is large and the Afghans are ingenious and enterprising. However much they might try, the Soviets and their supporters will find it impossible to stop the movement of food between Mujahideen-controlled areas and the Soviet/Kabul-controlled cities and large towns. One reason for this is that some products of the countryside, including firewood, are desperately needed in the cities. Politically, as the DRA regime desperately seeks to build up its legitimacy through extending its control over the countryside, there will have to be areas in which it will have to encourage food production.

INTERNATIONAL RESPONSE

With few exceptions, the international, humanitarian aid effort for the people inside Afghanistan, in contrast to the major and effective aid program for the Afghan refugees in

Pakistan, was late in starting.   Aid to the refugees, of
course, was a moral as well as a political necessity in order
to relieve the human suffering and the special burdens this
placed on Pakistan.   It was clearly easier to work with a
cooperative government and established international agencies such as the United Nations High Commissioner for
Refugees (UNHCR) and the International Committee of Red
Cross.   Thus, by early 1983 seventeen registered private
voluntary organizations (PVOs) were cooperating in the
refugee relief effort coordinated by the UNHCR and the
Pakistani Chief Commissioner for Afghan Refugees, Brigadier
(Retd) Sa'id Azhar.(15)

Inside Afghanistan, however, foreign humanitarian aid
remained almost exclusively the province of the three
French medical aid organizations: Medicins Sans Frontieres
(MSF), Aide Medicale Internationale (AMI), and Medicins du
Monde (MM).   MSF, the largest and oldest of these, was
founded in 1971 by doctors who had provided aid in the
Biafran/Nigerian civil war.   Its philosophy, and those of its
sister organizations as well, was to provide immediate aid in
conflict situations.   This aid was provided with the cooperation of governments, if possible, but if governments
attempted to obstruct this assistance, they would go ahead
in a clandestine manner (Malhuret 1983/84).

MSF began its operations in Afghanistan in May 1980.
In 1981 four of the French hospitals were bombed by the
Soviets.   Doctors at one of them, hoping in vain for recognition of their humanitarian status, had unwisely identified
the hospital with a large red cross on the roof.   In January
1983 Dr. Phillipe Augoyard of AMI was captured by the
Soviets and exhibited at a show trial in Kabul.   He was
sentenced to a long prison term, but the political outcome
was far from favorable for the Soviets.   Protests were
mounted in Europe to which even the French Communist
Party felt obliged to join.   Finally, after a delegation from
all the medical groups had been received by the French
foreign ministry, France warned that it would withdraw its
charge d'affaires from Kabul.   All NATO countries had
withdrawn their ambassadors from Kabul after the Soviet
invasion.   Dr. Augoyard was promptly "pardoned" for his
crime of trying to bring medical care to the Afghan people
and released.(16)

The number of personnel employed in Afghanistan by the

French medical groups varies from time to time. They will be called French groups since they are headquartered in France, even though many of their personnel are of other nationalities. MSF is the largest, with roughly twenty at any one time, and AMI and MM between them have perhaps half this number. Their aim is to establish permanent clinics, usually with two people, and rotate personnel every four to six months. Special survey teams are also sent to scout locations for future clinics in case they are forced to move or if they have additional personnel to send. Because of the sensitivity of the Pakistani authorities, they maintain a discreet silence over how they have gotten into Afghanistan. Once, to their amazement, one of their returning teams was personally welcomed by President Zia-ul-Haq, with pictures in the newspaper and on television.(17) On the other hand, on occasion they have been turned back while attempting to pass through their tribal territory in Pakistan on their way to the border. In general, it seems as if the Pakistani authorities are aware of their operations, but as they work swiftly and discreetly, and have no permanent headquarters or base in Pakistan, they are officially ignored. The groups operate separately but share information, and their logistics are coordinated for the Afghanistan operation.

A number of other European groups, including the Afghan French Solidarity Organization (AFRANE) and the Bureau Internationale de l'Afghanistan (BIA), are active in the relief effort inside Afghanistan. In particular, AFRANE has actively publicized the food situation and provided food aid. British, Dutch, West German, Danish, Swedish, and Norwegian groups are active as well. Most of the European groups are multi-functional: they raise and provide funds for humanitarian relief, they obtain and disseminate to the public and to their governments information about conditions inside Afghanistan, they hold demonstrations and conferences and produce specialized studies. Most of them also operate as political pressure groups on their respective governments.

In 1982 the Swedish Committee for Afghanistan underwent a dramatic transformation.(18) Operating on small voluntary contributions (and containing many veterans of the anti-Vietnam war movement), it had operated mainly as an informational pressure group. Through coincidence, however, Sixten Heppling and Karl Shoenmeyer had served together in Afghanistan in the 1960s with the United Nations and UNICEF, and were now officials (Heppling was the director) of the Swedish International Development Authority (SIDA).

Heppling's and Shoenmeyer's personal involvement secured a modest grant to the Swedish Committee for Afghanistan for humanitarian relief, which was part of the general mandate of SIDA as Sweden's aid program for the developing nations. The Soviet embassy officially protested this action, but were rebuffed by the government. After a preliminary survey, an office of the Swedish Committee was opened in Peshawar, Pakistan, in November of 1982 and was headed by a young journalist, Anders Fange, who had already reported from inside Afghanistan on Swedish radio and written in leading newspapers. Although working in a supposedly temporary arrangement, Mr. Fange has remained associated with the Swedish Committee.

SCA decided to concentrate on providing humanitarian aid through Afghan doctors rather than trying to send in Swedish or other foreign personnel. As this was the time that the Society of Afghan Doctors was attempting to begin their operations inside Afghanistan, they supported the initial six clinics the SAD set up. As their operations became more successful, they received more funding from the Swedish government, as well as aid from Afghanistan support organizations, including the British Afghanistan Support Committee and the Americares Foundation. Their medical programs increased many-fold until they were supporting 51 clinics inside Afghanistan at the end of 1985. More modest programs have begun distributing food and clothing. In 1984 they began the funding of the Afghanistan Educational Committee for the foundation and support of schools in Mujahideen-controlled areas of Afghanistan. In the Fall of 1984 some 43 schools with 3,327 pupils were in operation, and applications had been received by the Spring of 1985 for the establishment of 200 more (Afghanistan Education Committee 1985).

American groups have followed the general process described for the European humanitarian aid groups. However, the Americans faced special problems. Both the United States and the Pakistani governments were cautious concerning the involvement of American groups, as these would inevitably draw Soviet charges of being CIA fronts. The consistent policy line of the United States, both under the Carter and Reagan administrations, was not to have the Afghanistan conflict seen as a Soviet-American confrontation but rather as an issue for the international community and especially the Islamic nations to assert their own valid concerns regarding the Soviet actions against the Afghan people. Although the United States was the major supporter of the Afghan refugee relief effort, this aid was channeled through the United Nations. Therefore, only one of the seventeen private voluntary organizations aiding the Afghan refugee relief effort in Pakistan, the International Rescue Committee, was American.

Many American groups were established to aid the cause of the Afghan people. These groups fell into two broad categories: the "establishment" groups, raising funds to be transferred to official refugee aid projects through the State Department or the United Nations channels and other "maverick" groups interested in more direct and overt political action. Many aimed at publicizing the Soviet actions in Afghanistan, a necessary element, but not particularly humanitarian aid. Others were primarily interested in influencing actions of the U.S. government, either through Congress or through the bureaucracy. A few, no doubt, did wish to send arms to the Afghan Mujahideen.

Of course, the United States' tax codes and the IRS play a crucial role in determining the status of charitable organizations. Organizations which are intended to be political lobbying groups, much less weapons smuggling conduits, were of course not granted charitable tax-exempt status. Unfortunately, organizations which attempted to state openly that they wished to send humanitarian aid to people inside Afghanistan, as opposed to the refugees, were also denied this status. Seemingly through an oversight, however, one small American group, American Aid for Afghans of Portland, Oregon (AAA), was granted a charitable status in 1980. Although effective, its efforts to date have been limited and relatively small in scale. One of the most effective of these has been a program which has contributed many thousands of pairs of boots. In the words of AAA founder Don Weidenweber, "the transportation and distribution problem takes care of itself on the feet of the recipients."(19)

In late 1982, the Americares Foundation of New Canaan, Connecticut, decided to explore the possibility of aiding the Afghan people inside Afghanistan. Americares' President, Robert C. Macauley, had founded Americares in 1979, but had been involved in charitable work during the Vietnam war and was a major supporter of Father Bruce Ritter's Covenant House, a shelter for runaway children in New York City. In March 1982 Americares carried out its first international humanitarian relief effort by airlifting a chartered jet of donated medical supplies to Poland. In the wake of the Russian-inspired crackdown on Solidarity, the West had imposed economic sanctions on Poland, but in any case Poland had no foreign exchange with which to purchase medicines.

Macauley's audience with Pope John Paul II and contacts with the Polish Embassy in Washington resulted in agreement that the Polish church would supervise the distribution of these supplies. A second airlift was carried out in December 1982, with further shipments being made on a regular basis (with transport donated on the national Polish shipping line). In the wake of Israeli invasion of Lebanon in 1982 and the siege of Beirut that summer, Americans carried out another medical supply airlift to Beirut in late August.(20)

Following preliminary contacts with Medicins Sans Frontieres in Paris and the State Department and Pakistani Embassy in Washington, Americares decided to explore the feasibility of getting medical supplies to the people inside Afghanistan through a preliminary survey in Pakistan in April 1983. When this survey yielded positive results, an advisory committee headed by Dr. Zbigniew Brezezinski, the former National Security Advisor who had already become interested in Americares through its work in Polish relief, was formed for "Americares for Afghans." A public campaign for contributions opened in June with a Washington press conference featuring Dr. Brezezinski. Medicines were largely donated by pharmaceutical companies, but some individuals and small groups (including some from Afghans in the United States) also contributed. In August 1983 a chartered Pakistan International Airways Cargo 707 arrived in Islamabad with 40 tons of medicines and medical supplies, all of which had been determined to be needed inside Afghanistan in the course of the earlier survey. A large overflow was shipped by sea on transport donated by the Pakistani government on their national shipping line.

The Soviets, through their Washington TASS correspondent (who had attended the Americares press conference) immediately denounced this effort as "only a cover for the delivery of additional armaments and military aid to the enemies of the Afghan revolution" ("U.S. Medicines" 1983).(21)   No doubt, he was persuaded of this by the endorsements obtained for the Americares effort from former Presidents Carter, Ford, and Nixon, as well as from President Reagan (Archibald 1983).(22)   Americares has continued its medical shipments, mostly by sea, although it did manage to obtain free transportation for one shipment on board a USAF C-141 which accompanied the visit of Vice President Bush to Pakistan in May 1984.   Also in 1984 Americares organized the medical evacuation of two groups of wounded and sick Afghans, for whom proper care was not available in Pakistan, at facilities in the United States.   The first group was treated at Walter Reed Army Hospital in Washington, D.C., and the second at Henrico Doctor's Hospital in Richmond, Virginia (Engel 1984).

Finally, by August 1984 the political climate concerning American humanitarian aid inside Afghanistan had turned almost a full circle in Washington.   Americares received some of the first government funds for a humanitarian purpose, funds left over from the State Department's regular appropriation for civilian disaster relief.   Although one might well question the designation of the consequences of the Soviet invasion of Afghanistan as a "disaster" of the type of earthquake and hurricane relief usually funded under this program, the funds were certainly put to good use. Several more sums were forthcoming, and in the USAID budget submission for fiscal year 1986, funds were specifically designated for humanitarian aid inside Afghanistan. By November 1985 these funds had been increased to $15 million by Congressional action and were included in the 1986 fiscal year budget.(23) This shift is a far cry, indeed, from the Spring of 1983 when the best endorsement Americares could elicit from the State Department for its efforts to raise the contributions was, "Maybe we could say that it is not inconsistent with American policy objectives." Now, an office of USAID has already opened in Islamabad to supervise the distribution of relief funds and, of course, the

Government of Pakistan is now busy organizing its own "private" humanitarian aid group to work with the USAID office.

THE FUTURE

Of course, with government money come government controls. Thus the International Medical Corps group, founded by Dr. Robert Simon, which sent several American medical teams inside Afghanistan for a time in 1984 and 1985 (and which had received supplies from Americares), reversed its strongly held position of supporting American medical personnel inside Afghanistan. It instead worked to obtain a grant from USAID to support the medical training of Afghans in Pakistan. This group will not send American medical personnel inside Afghanistan, but might send other nationalities. In 1985 American Aid for Afghans, however, did send in two American medical teams (to Panjshir and to Kandahar) though they have since left with the onset of winter. One member of the press, *Arizona Republic* (Phoenix) reporter Charles Thornton, who accompanied the medical team near Kandahar, was killed in action on September 25, 1985.(24) The Kabul regime promptly claimed that he had been an American spy responsible for the shooting down (by a missile) of an Ariana Afghan Airlines civilian plane near Kandahar. Such incidents could only serve to reinforce American policy of discouraging the participation of American citizens in humanitarian aid projects inside Afghanistan.

The overwhelming problem for Afghanistan is the war being conducted there by the Soviet Union, and humanitarian aid, it must be admitted, has thus far had only limited impact in alleviating the suffering there. Yet, in a modern guerrilla war the dimension of the support of the civilian population cannot be neglected. In purely military terms, the people are the water in which the guerrilla swims. More importantly, the Afghan people are the moral objective of the entire war. To maintain a living, free population, able to rule themselves and to worship God as they wish, is the objective of the entire resistance movement, and it should be the objective as well of the international support for that movement. As the world has seen in the recent case of famine relief in Africa, moral objectives can be used to mobilize world opinion and provide genuinely effective relief. And in the case of the Holocaust of World War II, ignored moral objectives return to haunt those who ignore them as well as those who perpetrate atrocities. This situation is true, whether these horrors take place at Auschwitz or Pul-i-Charki, at the Katyn Forest or Kerala.

The new and open program of humanitarian aid now being developed by the United States should be only the beginning of a much broader effort to raise the world's level of knowledge and understanding as to the significance of the ongoing events in Afghanistan as well as to the need for effective aid to Afghan victims. However, the undoubted advantages of funds, organization, and official sponsorship for relief inside Afghanistan must not obscure the fundamental moral imperative of providing help to individuals in need, and to do this by any means possible in a desperate and ever-shifting environment. Both the United States and Pakistan, now accepting official responsibility for a humanitarian aid program to the victims of the war inside Afghanistan, must resist the temptation to manipulate these programs for the reasons of political expediency.

NOTES

1. Louis Dupree coined the term "rubbleization" (and the term "migratory genocide" as well) to describe Soviet tactics in Afghanistan. See his articles "Afghanistan in 1982" and "Afghanistan in 1983." For a broader discussion of the conflict, including constraints on Soviet actions, see Ralph H. Magnus (1985), especially in the contributions by Dupree, Brigadier Noor A. Husain, Jiri Valenta, and Claude Malhuret.

2. Article 36 of the Afghan Constitution of 1964 stated: "It is the duty of the State to provide, within the limits of its means, balanced facilities for the prevention and treatment of diseases for all Afghans. The aim of the State in this respect is to reach a stage where suitable medical facilities will be available to all Afghans." (See Royal Government of Afghanistan, 1964.) The regime was well aware of the people's desires. "We know that across the Amu Darya and Ab-i-Panja, only 40 meters wide in many places, we can see the results of Soviet development in Tajikistan SSR and Uzbekistan SSR. Our Afghan Uzbeks

and Tajiks will not wait forever. We must begin to improve their lot--and the lot of all our countrymen--now, not next year, but now," were the words King Muhammad Zahir used to Louis Dupree in 1963, at the time a committee of experts was busy drafting the new democratic constitution. See Dupree, "An Informal Talk with King Muhammad Zahir of Afghanistan."

3.   See Kakar (1978), p. 213. Professor Kakar is currently (1985) a political prisoner of the Karmal regime for his attempts to organize independent political activities at Kabul University.

4.   See Harvey Smith (1973). The Royal Government's programs of providing health care to rural areas are described in Rahel (1970), pp. 383-387. A detailed study of the rural care system as it existed on the eve of the Soviet invasion is given by O'Connor (1980).

5.   See Yousefzai (1974), pp. 180-181. The educational backgrounds of the current leaders of the Islamist Mujahideen parties are discussed by Naby (1985), pp. 59-81.

6.   See Malhuret (1983/84). Dr. Malhuret was the director of Medicins Sans Frontieres, and was appointed a Minister of State for humanitarian issues in the cabinet of Prime Minister Jacques Chirac in 1986.

7.   This was the assessment of Katarina Engberg of the Swedish Committee for Afghanistan following her visit to the area in Kunar province served by one of the SCA-aided clincis. See Magnus (1985), pp. 119-122.

8.   An instance of this type of action is described by Dr. Sayd Bahauddin Majrooh, the Director of the Afghan Information Centre, Peshawar (Magnus 1985, 88). Numerous other examples have been given, along with invaluable information on the conditions faced by the Afghan Mujahideen and civilian population, in his Centre's *Monthly Bulletin*.

9.   This distrust is particularly true of the Hazara people of central Afghanistan, and was conveyed to the author in several interviews by Hajji M. Ibrahim, the Director of Aid Committee for Afghans, an organization of Hazaras which has operated clinics in the Hazarajat (Peshawar, April 1983).

10.   Other instances were mentioned in interviews with other Afghan Mujahideen doctors in 1983.

11.   This information comes from personal communication

from Dr. Abdullah Osman, President of the Union of Afghan Mujahideen Doctors (and former President of the Society of Afghan Doctors and Medical Personnel Outside Afghanistan), December 3, 1983.

12. This information is from an interview with Dr. Barakzai in Peshawar, April 1983.

13. This is the assessment of Anders Fange, the resident director of the Swedish Committee for Afghanistan.

14. An interview with representatives of Commander Isma'il Khan in Peshawar, April 1983, provided this information.

15. This information comes from an interview with Brigadier (Retd.) Sa'id Azhar in Islamabad, April 1983. These voluntary organizations had increased to 20 by July 1985. See U.S. Department of State (1985).

16. This interview with Dr. Malhuret took place in Monterey, California, in November 1983.

17. The interview with a French diplomat occurred in Islamabad in April 1983.

18. Information about the origins of the Swedish Committee for Afghanistan and its operations are given in Fange (1985), and have been supplemented by numerous conversations with SCA members in Pakistan and the United States. The decision to set up an office in Pakistan seems to have been made in May 1982.

19. The telephone interview with Don Weidenweber took place in October 1985. Mr. Weidenweber presented his group's aims at the meeting of the Afghanistan Studies Association in Washington, D.C., in November 1980.

20. Since March 1983 I have served as Project Director of Americares for Afghans. See Americares Foundation (1983).

21. This article (p. D-3) quotes a Moscow TASS report in English 2020 GMT June 1983.

22. President Reagan's letter to Robert C. Macauley, dated The White House, June 20, 1983, reads in full: "The humanitarian endeavor which you are promoting, AMERICARES for Afghans, is a heartwarming effort to support Afghanistan's war victims. The medical supplies you provide will surely help alleviate the suffering of these unfortunate people.

"Please convey my appreciation to the other generous citizens connected with this project; it is an effort which I am pleased to endorse."

23. The State Department announced in May 1985 that it was seeking Congressional approval for reprogramming $4 million from the current fiscal year and to request $5 million for the 1986 fiscal year, the first time the administration had called for open aid for Afghan groups inside Afghanistan. See *The New York Times* and *The Washington Post* for May 9, 1985. This amount was raised to $15 million by Congressional action (P.L. 99-83, August 8, 1985), following hearings by the Congressional Task Force Task Force on Afghanistan.

24. This telephone interview with Don Weidenweber occurred in October 1985. See also *Afghan Update* (Washington, D.C.), No. 20, October 7, 1985, pp. 1-2. This publication of the American Afghan Education Fund is one of the best sources of information on American governmental and non-governmental actions on the Afghanistan issue.

Bibliography

Adamec, Ludwig W. 1974. *Afghanistan's foreign affairs to the mid-twentieth century: Relations with the USSR, Germany, and Britain.* Tucson, AZ: University of Arizona Press.

Adams, James. December 16, 1984. Afghans get new missiles. *The Times* (London).

Afghan Update. September 30, 1985. Issue XIX.

Afghanistan, Democratic Republic of, Ministry of Foreign Affairs. Information and Publication Department. n.d. *Revolutionary Afghanistan: Through honest eyes.*

Afghanistan asks return of 2 "lost" copters, crews. July 15, 1985. *The Blade* (Toledo, Ohio).

Afghanistan Education Committee. April 1985. *A generation of illiterates? Information from and about the Afghanistan Education Committee.* Peshawar: Afghanistan Education Committee.

Afghanistan Forum. July 1985. XIII (4).

Ahmed, Akbar L. 1976. *Millennium and charisma among Pathans: A critical essay in social anthropology.* London: Routledge and Kegan Paul.

Ahmed, Akbar S. 1980. *Pukhtun economy and society.* London: Routledge and Kegan Paul.

Ahmed, Akbar S., and David M. Hart, eds. 1984. *Islam in tribal societies: From the Atlas to the Indus.* London: Routledge and Kegan Paul.

Aliboni, Roberto. 1985. *The Red Sea region.* Syracuse, NY: Syracuse UP.

Allan, Pierre, and Albert A. Stahel. December 1983. Tribal guerrilla warfare against a colonial power. *Journal of Conflict Resolution* 27(4):590-617.

Amaro, N. V., and A. Portes. 1972. Una sociologia del exilo: Situacion de los grupos cubanos en los Estados Unidos. *Aportes* 23:6-24.

American Embassy, Kabul. November 11-13, 1967. *Vote of confidence debate, Etemadi government*, Tape #8.

Americares Foundation. May 1983. *Americares Foundation.* New Canaan, CT: Americares Foundation.

Amin, A. Rasul. 1984. A general reflection of the stealthy Sovietisation of Afghanistan. *Central Asian Survey* 3(1):47- 61.

Amin, Tahir. 1982. *Afghanistan crisis: Implications and options for the Muslim world, Iran and Pakistan.* Islamabad, Pakistan: Institute of Policy Studies.

Amin, Tahir. April, 1984. Afghan resistance: Past, present and future. *Asian Survey* 24(4):377-379.

Anderson, J. W. 1979. *Doing Pakhtu.*

Archibald, George. June 21, 1983. Medical drive to begin for Afghan refugees. *Washington Times* 4A.

Area handbook for Afghanistan. 1973. 4th ed. DA Pam 550-65. Washington, DC: USGPO.

ARIN [Afghan Refugee Information Network]. March/April 1985. 17:4.

ARIN. June/July, 1984. Newsletter 14.

ARIN. January, 1985. Newsletter 16.

ARIN. March/April, 1985. Newsletter 17.

Arnold, Anthony. 1981. *Afghanistan: The Soviet invasion in perspective.* Stanford, CA: Hoover Institution Press, Stanford University.

Arnold, Anthony. 1983. *Afghanistan's two-party communism: Parcham and Khalq.* Stanford, CA: Hoover Institution Press.

Azhar, Brig. (Ret'd) Said. The Afghan refugee problem analyzed. *Defense Journal* (Karachi, Pakistan: Ma'aref) 9(11):9.

Aziz, Sultan A. 1984. Pushtun political tribal structure. M.A. thesis, Bowling Green State University, Bowling Green, OH.

Bailleau-Lajoinie, Simone. 1980. *Condition des femmes en Afghanistan.* Paris: Editions sociales.

Balanced education. May 2, 1966. *Khalq* (Kabul) 4. (American Embassy translation).

Barakat, Halim, and Peter Dodd. 1972. Palestinian refugees: Two surveys of uprootedness. In *Political dynamics in the*

Middle East, eds. *Paul Y. Hammond and Sidney S. Alexander. New York: Elsevier Publishing Co.*

Barfield, Thomas. 1981. *The Central Asian Arabs of Afghanistan: Pastoral Nomadism in Transition.* Austin, TX: University of Texas Press.

Barth, Fredrik. 1969. *Ethnic groups and boundaries: The social organization of culture difference.* Boston: Little, Brown, and Company.

Barth, Fredrik. 1981. Selected essays of Fredrik Barth. In *Volume 1: Process and form in social life,* ed. Adam Kuper. Boston: Routledge and Kegan Paul.

Barth, Fredrik. 1985. *Political leadership among Swat Pathans.* Reprint ed. London: University of London Athlone Press.

Beloff, Samuel. 1985. The Soviet air forces: A study in military and political constraints. Unpublished M. A. thesis, Bowling Green State University, Bowling Green, OH.

Benningsen, Alexandre. *The Soviet Union and Muslim guerrilla wars, 1920-1981: Lessons for Afghanistan.* Santa Monica, CA: The Rand Corporation.

Bennigsen, Alexandre, and Marie Broxup. 1983. *Islamic threat to the Soviet state.* New York: St. Martin's Press.

Bennigsen, Alexandre, and Chantel Lemercier-Quelquejay. 1965. *Islam in the Soviet Union.* London: Cambridge University Press.

Bernard, William S. 1976. Immigrants and refugees: Their similarities, differences, and needs. *International Migration Review* 14:267-278.

Bernstein, Carl. July 18, 1981. Arms for Afghanistan. *The New Republic* 8-10.

Bernstein, Richard. March 24, 1985. Remaking Afghanistan in the Soviet image. *New York Times Magazine* 30-33+.

Bill, James, and Carl Leiden. 1983. *Politics in the Middle East.* Boston: Little, Brown.

Billard, Annick. November 1985. Islamic Republic of Iran: Unnoticed asylum country. *Refugees* 19-22.

The Blade. Toledo, Ohio. July 15, 1985.

Blechman, Barry M., and Edward N. Luttwak, eds. 1985. *International security yearbook 1984/85.* Boulder, CO: Westview Publishing Co.

Bodansky, Yossef. Winter 1982/83. The bear on the Chessboraf: Soviet military gains in Afghanistan. *World Affairs*

145(3):273-298.

Bodansky, Yossef. May 28, 1984. Soviets use Afghanistan to test 'liquid fire.' *Jane's Defence Weekly.*

Boesen, Inger. 1983. *Conflicts of solidarity in Pukhtun women's lives, women in Islamic societies: Social attitudes and historical perspective.* Copenhagen: Scandanavian Institute of Asian Studies.

Bogue, Donald J. 1969. *Principles of demography.* New York: Wiley.

Bonner, Arthur. October 31, 1985. An Odyssey with Afghan rebels transporting vital flow of arms. *New York Times.*

Bonner, Arthur. November 1, 1985. 5 defectors, turned Afghan, fight 'holy war.' *New York Times.*

Bonosky, Philip. 1984. *Afghanistan unveiled.* New York: International Publishers.

Bonosky, Philip. 1985. *Washington's secret war against Afghanistan.* New York: International Publishers.

Bowen, John Charles Edward. 1982. *Plain tales of the Afghan border.* Windlesham, Surrey, UK: Springwood Books Ltd.

Bradsher, Henry S. 1985. *Afghanistan and the Soviet Union.* Durham, NC: Duke Press Policy Series.

Bradsher, Henry S. Fall 1986. Stagnation and change in Afghanistan. *Journal of South Asian and Middle Eastern Studies.* 10(1):3-35.

Brandt, Marvin. 1974. Recent economic development. In *Afghanistan in the 1970s,* ed. Louis Dupree and Linette Albert. New York: Praeger Special Studies in International Development and Economics.

Broder, Jonathan. August 26, 1984. Afghan political feud burdens Soviets. *Chicago Tribune,* Section 1:12.

Broder, Jonathan. September 9, 1984. Heat of battle molds rival Afghan rebels into an army. *Chicago Tribune,* Section 1:4.

Caravans on moonless nights: How the CIA supports and supplies the anti-Soviet guerrillas. June 11, 1984. *Time* 38-40.

Caroe, Sir Olaf. 1983. *The pathans, 550 B.C.-A.D. 1957.* Reprint ed. Karachi: Oxford University Press.

Centlivres, Pierre, and Micheline Centlivres, et. al. 1984. *Afghanistan: la colonisation impossible.* Paris: Les Editions du Cerf.

Chaffetz, David. 1980. Afghanistan in Turmoil. *International Affairs* 56(1).

Chaffetz, David. 1980. Afghanistan in Turmoil. *International Affairs* 56(1).

Chaffetz, David. 1981. *A journey through Afghanistan: A memorial.* Chicago: Regnery Gateway, Inc.

Chaliand, Gerand. 1982. *Report from Afghanistan.* Trans. by Tamar Jacoby. New York: Viking Press and Penguin Books.

Chirot, Daniel. 1977. *Social change in the twentieth century.* New York: Harcourt, Brace, Jovanovich.

Christensen, Hanne. 1984. *Afghan refugees in Pakistan: From emergency towards self-reliance.* Geneva: United Nations Institute for Social Development.

Cloughley, B. W. December 1984/January 1985. Deep and dangerous divisions. *Pacific Defense Review.*

Cockburn, Andrew. 1984. *The threat: Inside the Soviet military machine.* New York: Vintage Books.

Collins, Joseph J. 1982. Afghanistan: The empire strikes out. *Parameters, Journal of the U.S. Army War College* 12(1):32-41.

Collins, Joseph J. 1985. *The Soviet invasion of Afghanistan: A study of the use of force in Soviet foreign policy.* Lexington, MA: Lexington Books.

Coughlin, William J. November 30-December 6, 1986. Soviets consolidate grip on Afghan's Wakhan corridor: annexation of strategic zone nearly complete. *Middle East Times* (Cairo).

Cordesman, Anthony H. August 1983. The Soviet arms trade: Patterns for the 1980s. Part II. *Armed Forces Journal International* 34-44+.

Cordesman, Anthony H. 1984. *The gulf and the search for strategic stability.* Boulder, CO: Westview Press.

Crisis and conflict analysis team. June 1984. *Report on Afghanistan, No. 3.* Islamabad, Pakistan: Institute of Strategic Studies.

Crisis and conflict analysis team. July 1984. *Report on Afghanistan, No. 4.* Islamabad, Pakistan: Institute of Strategic Studies.

Crisis and conflict analysis team. August 1984. *Afghanistan Report, No. 5.* Islamabad, Pakistan: Institute of Strategic Studies.

Crisis and conflict analysis team. September 1984. *Afghanistan Report, No. 6.* Islamabad, Pakistan: Institute of Strategic Studies.

Journal International 78-105.

Cynkin, Thomas M. Summer 1982. Aftermath of the Saur coup. *Fletcher Forum* 6(2):269-298.

Dameyer, Christina. April 29, 1985. Afghan intellectuals in Pakistan wage a holy war 'by the pen.' *Christian Science Monitor* 31.

Dastarac, Alexander, and M. Levant. July-August 1980. What went wrong in Afghanistan? *MERIP Reports* 10(6).

Davis, Anthony. November 12, 1984. Afghan rebel has enhanced reputation. *The Washington Post* National Weekly Edition.

Davis, Anthony. April 1, 1985. Afghanistan: Standoff at Barikot. *Washington Post Weekly Edition* 2(22):17.

Davis, V. C. 1945. Development of a scale to rate attitudes of community satisfaction. *Rural Sociology* 10:246-255.

Delloye, Isabelle. 1980. *Des femmes d'Afghanistan.* Paris: Editions des Femmes.

Delparech, Bernard. Septembre 1984. Un gouvernement toujours sous tutelle: La longue lutte de l'Afghanistan. *Le Monde Diplomatique* 22-23.

Delury, George E., ed. 1983. *World encyclopedia of political systems and parties.* Facts on File.

Denker, Debra. June, 1985. Along Afghanistan's war torn frontier. *National Geographic* 167(5):772-797.

Desbarats, Jacqueline, and Linda Holland. 1983. Indochinese settlement patterns in Orange County. *Amerasia Journal* 10(1):23-46.

Desbarats, Jacqueline. 1985. Indochinese resettlement in the United States. *Annals of the Association of American Geographers* 75(4):522-538.

Deutsch, Karl W. 1980. *Politics and government: How people decide their fate.* 3rd ed. Boston: Houghton Mifflin Co.

Dodd, Peter, and Halim Barakat. 1969. *River without bridges: A study of the exodus of the 1970 Palestinian Arab Refugees.* Beirut: The Institute for Palestine Studies.

Dowell, William. Autumn 1982. With Massoud's rebels. *Washington Quarterly* 209-216.

Dupree, Louis. 1973. *Afghanistan.* Princeton, NJ: Princeton University Press.

Dupree, Louis. February 1983. Afghanistan in 1982: Still no solution. *Asian Survey* 13:2.

Dupree, Louis. February 1984. Afghanistan in 1983: And still no solution. *Asian Survey* 14:2.

ton University Press.

Dupree, Louis. February 1983. Afghanistan in 1982: Still no solution. *Asian Survey* 13:2.

Dupree, Louis. February 1984. Afghanistan in 1983: And still no solution. *Asian Survey* 14:2.

Dupree, Louis. July-August 1979. Afghanistan under the Khalq. *Problems of Communism* 28.

Dupree, Louis. 1979. The Democratic Republic of Afghanistan: 1979. *AUFS Reports* (Asia) no. 44.

Dupree, Louis. An informal talk with King Mohammad Zahir of Afghanistan. *American University Field Staff Reports, South Asia Series* 7(9) Afghanistan, Report LD-9-63.

Dupree, Louis. 1979. Red flag over the Hindu Kush, part II: The accidental coup, or Taraki in Blunderland. *AUFS Reports* (Asia) no. 45.

Dupree, Louis. 1980. *Afghanistan*. Princeton, NJ: Princeton University Press.

Dupree, Louis. 1980. Red flag over the Hindu Kush, part III: Rhetoric and reform, or promises! promises! *AUFS Reports* (Asia) no. 23.

Dupree, Louis. 1980. Red flag over the Hindu Kush, part V: Repression, or security through terror, purges I-IV. *AUFS Reports* (Asia) no. 28.

Dupree, Louis. 1980. Red flag over the Hindu Kush, part VI: Repression, or security through terror, purges IV-VI. *AUFS Reports* (Asia) no. 29.

Dupree, Louis. 1980. Red flags over the Hindu Kush. *American University Field Staff* nos. 28-29.

Dupree, Louis, and Linette Albert, eds. 1974. *Afghanistan in the 1970s*. New York: Praeger Publishers.

Dupree, Nancy Hatch. 1984. Revolutionary rhetoric and Afghan women. In *Revolutions and rebellions in Afghanistan: Anthropological perspectives*, ed. M. N. Shahrani and R. L. Canfield, 312-321.

Dupree, Nancy Hatch. March, 1984. *Afghanistan Forum* 12(2):17. Dupree, Nancy. April 21, 1986. The Afghan refugee family abroad: A focus on Pakistan. Conference on War in Afghanistan and the Plight of the Afghan Family, Center for Strategic and International Studies, Georgetown University, Washington, DC.

Dupree, Nancy Hatch. The women's dimension among Afghan refugees in Pakistan. Overseas Education Fund.

Edwards, David Busby. November 1984. Redefining Islam:

El-Sayad, Mohammad. 1984. Egypt. In *Arms production in developing countries*, James Everett Katz, ed. Lexington, MA: Lexington Books.

Elphinstone, Mountstuart. 1969. *An Account of the Kingdom of Caubal and its dependencies in Persia, Tartary, and India*. Reprint. Graz, Austria: Akademische Druck-u. Verlagsanstalt.

Emadi, Hafizullah. 1986. Afghanistan's struggle for national liberation. In *The rise and fall of democracies in third world societies* (Publication No. 27). Williamsburg, VA: College of William and Mary, Studies in Third World Societies.

Engle, Margaret. October 10, 1984. Seven Afghans are mending in the district. *The Washington Post* B1, B4.

Erulkar, Matthew D. November 26, 1984. Letter to the editor. *The New York Times*.

Etienne, Gilbert. 1985. *Rural development in Asia: Meetings with peasants*. Rev. Ed. Trans. by Arati Sharma. New Delhi: Sage Publications.

Evans, Richard. September 12, 1985. The battle for Paktia. *Far Eastern Economic Review* 48-49.

Ezell, Edward Clinton. 1985. *The AK47 story: Evolution in the Kalashnikov weapons*. Harrisburg, PA: Stackpole Books.

Fager, Richard R., Richard A. Brody, and Thomas J. O'Leary. 1968. *Cubans in exile: Disaffection and the revolution*. Stanford, CA: Stanford University Press.

Fairchild, H. P. 1925. *Immigration: A world movement and its American significance*. New York: Putnam.

Fange, Anders. 1985. Information, standpoints, statistics. Unpublished typescript. Peshawar, Pakistan: Swedish Committee for Afghanistan.

Far Eastern Economic Review. September 12, 1985, p. 13.

Farr, W. 1976. Birth places of the people and the laws of migration. *Geographical Magazine* 3:35-37.

FBIS, v. 8 January 1980, Egypt, D1, MENA NC07135 Cairo MENA in Arabic 1240 GMT 7 Jan 80 NC.

Ferdinand, Klaus. 1969. Nomadism in Afghanistan. *Viehwirthschaft und Hirtenkultur*, Budapest.

Ferdinand, Klaus. 1959. Nomadism in Afghanistan. In *La Geographie de l'Afghanistan Etude d'un Pays Aride*. Copenhagen: Gyldendal.

Ferri, Mauro. Ott./Dic. 1984. Arm: sovietiche in Afghanistan:

l'aereo dal nome gentile. In *Afghanistan Passato e Presente.* Anno 2(4-5):19.

Foucher, Michel. Septembre 1984. Les espaces de la guerre et de la resistance: La geopolitique des deux camps. *Le Monde Diplomatique* 22-23.

Franceschi, Patrice. 1981. *Ils ont choisi la liberte. La guerre d'Afghanistan.* Paris: Les Editions Arthaud.

Franceschi, Patrice. 1984. *Guerre en Afghanistan, 27 avril 1978-31 mai 1984.* Paris: La Table Ronde.

Franck, Peter G. 1960. *Afghanistan between East and West: The economics of competitive co-existence.* Washington, DC: National Planning Assoc.

Fraser-Tytler, W. K. 1953. *Afghanistan: A study of political developments in central and southern Asia.* London: Oxford University Press.

Fullerton, John. 1984. *The Soviet invasion of Afghanistan.* Hong Kong: Far Eastern Economic Review, Ltd.

Furlong, R. D. M., and Theodor Winkler. 1980. The Soviet invasion of Afghanistan. *International Defense Review* (Geneva) 13(2):168-170.

Gall, Sandy. 1983. *Behind Russian lines: An Afghan journal.* London: Sidgwick and Jackson.

de Gaury, Gerald, and H. V. F. Winstone, eds. 1982. *The road to Kabul: An anthology.* New York: Macmillan Publishing Co., Inc.

Gawecki, Marek. 1983. *Wies srodkowego i polnocnego Afghanistanu.* Warsaw: Polskie Towarzystwo Ludoznowcze.

Gearing, Julian. Summer 1985. Brits in Afghanistan. *Free Afghanistan* (London), no. 2, 18.

Girardet, Edward. September 26, 1984. Report from Afghanistan: The conflict--and civilian toll--worse than ever. *Christian Science Monitor* 1, 32.

Girardet, Edward. October 2, 1984. Afghan guerrilla leader holds his own against Soviet offensive. *Christian Science Monitor* 1, 36.

Girardet, Edward. October 10, 1984. People under attack. *Christian Science Monitor* 20-21.

Girardet, Edward. October 23, 1984. Soviets step up war against reporters in Afghanistan. *Christian Science Monitor* 9.

Girardet, Edward. November 5, 1984. Soviets launch pre-winter Afghan offensive to block supply lines. *Christian Science Monitor* 16.

Girardet, Edward. November 20, 1984. Arming Afghan guerrillas: Perils, secrecy. *Christian Science Monitor* 15-16.

Girardet, Edward. 1985. *Afghanistan: The Soviet war.* New York: St. Martin's Press.

Glad, James. July 4. *Far Eastern Economic Review* 22-25.

Gluckhoded, V. 1981. Economy of independent Afghanistan. In *Afghanistan: Past and present,* ed. Editorial Board of *Social Sciences Today,* 236, 240. Moscow: USSR Academy of Sciences.

Goodwin, Jan. February 1985. War torn! The story of two women. *Ladies Home Journal* 90.

Gopalakrishnan, R. 1982. *The geography and politics of Afghanistan.* New Delhi: Concept Publishing Co.

Government of Pakistan, Commissionerate for Afghan Refugees. August 1983. *Humanitarian assistance program for Afghan refugees in Pakistan.*

Gregorian, Vartan. 1969. *The emergence of modern Afghanistan: Politics of reform and modernization, 1880-1946.* Stanford, CA: Stanford University Press.

Griffiths, John C. 1981. *Afghanistan: Key to a continent.* Boulder, CO: Westview Press.

Grinter, Lawrence E. 1982. The Soviet invasion of Afghanistan: Its inevitability and its consequences. *Parameters, Journal of the US Army War College* 12(4).

Gulick, John. 1976. *The Middle East: An anthropological perspective.* Pacific Palisades, CA: Goodyear.

Gunston, John. October 29, 1984. Soviets using Su-25s in attacks on rebel units. *Aviation Week & Space Technology* 38-44.

Gupta, Bhabani Sen. 1982. *The Afghan syndrome: How to live with Soviet power.* New Delhi: Vikas Publishing House Pvt. Ltd.

Gupta, Bhabani Sen. 1986. *Afghanistan.* Boulder, CO: Lynne Rienner Publishers, Inc.

Habibi, Abdul Hakim. n.d. *Afghanistan: A nation in love with freedom.* Cedar Rapids, IA: Igram Press.

Hall, Lt. Col. Johnnie H. May-June 1982. To save the pilot's life--Soviet air rescue service. *Air University Review* 48-57.

Halliday, Fred. November-December 1978. Revolution in Afghanistan. *New Left Review* 112.

Halliday, Fred. January-February 1980. War and revolution in Afghanistan. *New Left Review* 119:21.

Halliday, Fred. 1982. *Threat from the East? Soviet policy from Afghanistan and Iran to the Horn of Africa.*

Halpern, Manfred. 1963. *The politics of social change in the Middle East and North Africa.* Princeton, NJ: Princeton University Press.

Hammond, Thomas T. 1984. *Red flag over Afghanistan: The communist coup, the Soviet invasion, and the consequences.* Boulder, CO: Westview Press.

Hansen, Art. 1981. Refugee dynamics: Angolans in Zambia, 1966 to 1972. *International Migration Review* 15: 175-194.

Hansen, James H. January 1984. Afghanistan: The Soviet experience. *Jane's Defence Review.*

Haqqani, Hussain. February 14, 1985. The Chinese connection. *Far Eastern Economic Review* 24-25.

Haqqani, Hussain. February 14, 1985. Deadly winter games. *Far Eastern Economic Review* 24-25.

Harkavy, Robert E., and Stephanie G. Neuman, eds. 1985. *The lessons of recent wars in the third world.* Lexington, MA: Lexington Books.

Harrison, P. G., E. J. Everett-Heath, G. M. Moss, and A. W. Mowatt. 1985. *Military helicopters, Brassey's Battlefield Weapons Systems and Technology Systems*, Volume XI. London: Brassey's Defence Publishers Pergamon.

Harrison, Selig S. Winter 1980-81. Dateline Afghanistan: Exit through Finland? *Foreign Policy* 41.

Harrison, Selig S. 1981. *In Afghanistan's shadow: Baluch nationalism and Soviet temptations.* New York: Carnegie Endowment for International Peace.

Harrison, Selig S. Summer 1983. A breakthrough in Afghanistan? *Foreign Policy* 51:3-26.

Harrison, Selig. Winter 1984. Afghanistan: "Self-determination" and a Soviet force. *Parameters* 14(4):34.

Hart, David M. 1985. *Guardians of the Khyber Pass: The social organisation and history of the Afridis of Pakistan.* Lahore, Pakistan: Vanguard Books.

Hauner, Milan. November 1982. Afghanistan between the great powers, 1938-1945. *International Journal of Middle East Studies* 14(4):481-499.

Hearing and markup before the Committee on Foreign Affairs, House of Representatives, 97th Congress, 2nd Session. 1982. Washington, DC: Government Printing Office.

Hearing before the Committee on Foreign Relations, United States Senate, 97th Congress, 2nd Session. 1982. Washington, DC: Government Printing Office.

Hearing before the Subcommittee on Human Rights and International Organizations of the Committee on Foreign Affairs, House of Representatives, and the Commission on Security and Cooperation in Europe, 97th Congress, 1st Session. 1981. Washington, DC: Government Printing Office.

Hearings before the Subcommittees on Europe and the Middle East and on Asian and Pacific Affairs of the Committee on Foreign Affairs, House of Representatives, 97th Congress, 1st Session. 1983. Washington DC: Government Printing office.

Hellicopter protection from IR missiles. October 5, 1985. *Jane's Defence Weekly* 743.

Hewett, Ed A. 1984. *Energy, economics, and foreign policy in the Soviet Union.* Washington, DC: Brookings.

Hough, Jerry F. 1985. *The struggle for the third world: Soviet debate and American options.* Washington, DC: Brookings.

Howell, Evelyn. 1979. *Mizh: A monograph on government's relations with the Mahsud tribe.* Karachi, Pakistan: Oxford University Press.

Hunte, Pamela Anne. 1984. *The sociocultural context of perinatality in Afghanistan.* Ann Arbor, MI: University Microforms International.

Hunte, Pamela. April 21, 1986. The physical and mental health status of Afghans with special emphasis on women and children. Conference on War in the Afghan Family, Center For Strategic and International Studies, Georgetown University, Washington, DC.

Hyman, Anthony. 1982. *Afghanistan under Soviet domination, 1964-81.* New York: St. Martin's Press.

Hyman, Anthony. July 1984. The struggle for Afghanistan. *The World Today* 40(7):276-284.

Hyman, Anthony. July 1985. Afghanistan: The battle of the classrooms. *The Middle East* 129:50-51.

Ilyinsky, Mikhail. 1982. *Afghanistan: Onward march of the revolution.* New Delhi: Sterling Publishers.

International Labour Office, UN High Commissioner for Refugees. 1983. *Tradition and dynamism among Afghan refugees, a report on income-generating activities for*

Afghan refugees in Pakistan. Geneva: International Labour Office and UN High Commissioner for Refugees.

Isby, David C. Afghanistan, 1982: The war continues. *International Defense Review* (Geneva) 15(11):1523-1528.

Isby, David C. 1983. Soviet tactics in the war in Afghanistan. *Jane's Defence Review* 4(7).

Isby, David C. September 1984. Harassing the bear: New Afghan tactics stall Soviet victory. *Soldier of Fortune* 38-41+.

Isby, David. 1986. *Russia's War in Afghanistan.* London: Osprey Publishing Ltd.

Jeffries, Ron. December 1985. Freedom fighters' medcap: Journal of an American EMT. *Soldier of Fortune* 30-35, 86-92.

Jenkins, William. 1879. *Reports on the District of Jelalabad, chiefly in regard to revenue.* Calcutta: Government of India.

Jones, Allen K. 1985. *Afghan refugees: Five years later.* U.S. Committee for Refugees.

Jones, Ellen. 1985. *The red army and society: A sociology of the Soviet military.* Winchester, MA: Allen & Unwin.

Kakar, Hasan. 1978. The fall of the Afghan monarchy in 1973. *International Journal of Middle East Studies* 9:213.

Kakar, Hasan Kawun. 1979. *Government and society in Afghanistan: The reign of 'Abd at Rahman Khan.* Austin, TX: University of Texas Press.

Kamrany, Nake M. October 1986. The continuing war in Afghanistan. *Current History* 333-336.

Karp, Craig M. Summer 1986. The war in Afghanistan. *Foreign Affairs* 64(5): 1026-1047.

Katz, James Everett, ed. 1984. *Arms production in developing countries: An analysis of decision-making.* Lexington, MA: D. C. Heath.

Kauppi, Mark V., and R. Craig Nations, eds. 1983. *The Soviet Union and the Middle East in the 1980s: Opportunities, constraints, and dilemmas.* Lexington, MA: Lexington Books.

Keegan, John. November 1985. The ordeal of Afghanistan. *Atlantic Monthly* 94-105.

Keller, Stephen L. 1975. *Uprooting and social change: The role of refugees in development.* Delhi: Manchar Book Service.

Kempe, Frederick. December 18, 1984. Afghan guerrillas now

fight social problems imperiling resistance. *Wall Street Journal.*

Kempe, Frederick. December 26, 1984. Afghan refugees are a daunting challenge for Pakistani hosts. *Wall Street Journal.*

Keshavan, Narayan. December 7-13, 1986. Afghan rebels seek to oust Kabul mission from U.N. *Middle East Times* (Cairo).

Khalilzad, Zalmay. 1984. Afghanistan and international security. In *Asian perspectives on international security.* Donald High McMillen, ed. New York: St. Martin's Press.

Khalilzad, Zalmay. 1984. *The security of Southwest Asia.* London: International Institute for Strategic Studies.

Khalilzad, Zalmay. October 1985. The Soviet dilemma in Afghanistan. *Current History* 334-337.

Klare, Michael T. 1985. *American arms supermarket.* Austin, TX: University of Texas Press.

Kline, David. Spring 1983. The conceding of Afghanistan. *Washington Quarterly* 6(2):130-139.

Knabe, Erika. 1977. Women in the social stratification of Afghanistan. In *Commoners, climbers, and notables*, 331. Leiden: E. J. Brill.

Kunz, Egon F. 1969. *Blood and gold: Hungarians in Australia.* Melbourne: Cheshire.

Kunz, Egon F. 1973. The refugee in flight: Kinetic models and forms of displacement. *International Migration Review* 7:125-147.

Lajoinie, Simone Bailleau. 1980. *Conditions de femmes en Afghanistan.* Paris: Editions Sociales.

Latham, Richard J. 1984. People's Republic of China: The restructuring of defense-industrial policies. In *Arms production in developing countries.* James Everett Katz, ed. Lexington, MA: Lexington Books.

Lee, E. S. 1966. A theory of migration. *Demography* 3:47-57.

Le-Thi-Que, A. Terry Rambo, and Gary D. Murfin. 1975. Why they fled: Refugee movement during the Spring 1975 communist offensive in South Vietnam. *Asian Studies* (Quezon City: Philippine Center for Advanced Studies) 16:855-867.

Lindhom, Charles. 1982. *Generosity and jealousy: The Swat Pukhtun of Northern Pakistan.* New York: Columbia University Press.

Liu, William T., Maryanne Lamanna, and Alice Murata. 1979.

Transition to nowhere: Vietnamese refugees in America.
Nashville: Charter House.

Llanos, Jose. 1982. *Cuban Americans: Masters of survival.*
Cambridge, MA: ABT.

Lunz, Egon F. 1981. Exile and resettlement: Refugee theory.
International Migration Review 15:42-52.

Magnus, Ralph H. Winter 1975. Muhammad Zahir Khan,
former king of Afghanistan. *Middle East Journal* 29(1):77-
80.

Magnus, Ralph H. 1983. Tribal Marxism: The Soviet
encounter with Afghanistan. *Conflict* 4:339-368.

Magnus, Ralph H. 1984. Afghanistan and gulf security: A
continuing relationship. In *Gulf security into the 1980s*,
Ralph H. Magnus, Robert G. Darius, and John W. Amos II,
eds. Stanford, CA: Hoover Institution Press.

Magnus, Ralph. 1985. *Afghan alternatives: Issues, options and
policies.* New Brunswick, NJ: Transaction Books.

Magnus, Ralph H. 1985. The Afghan stalemate. *Parameters,
Journal of the US Army War College* 15(2):80-81.

Magnus, Ralph H. 1985. *Afghanistan: Marx, mullah and
mujahid.* Boulder, CO: Westview Press.

Magnus, Ralph H. 1985. Soviet strategy in Afghanistan:
Military and political tactics. In *Crisis and issues in the
Middle East*, Charles G. Macdonald, ed. Westport, CT:
Greenwood Press.

Magnus, Ralph H. 1985. The Karmal regime in Kabul: A
Soviet model for the future of the Middle East. In *Ideol-
ogy and power in the Middle East, studies in honor of
George Lenczowski*, Peter Chelkowski and Robert J.
Pranger, eds. Durham, NC: Duke University Press.

Magnus, Ralph H. 1985. The military and politics in
Afghanistan: Before and after the revolution. In *The role
of the military in contemporary Asia*, Edward A. Olsen
and Stephen Jurika, eds. Boulder, CO: Westview Press.

Magnus, Ralph H. 1986. The military and politics in
Afghanistan: Before and after the revolution. In *The
armed forces in contemporary Asian societies*, Edward A.
Olsen and Stephen Jurika, Jr., eds. Boulder, CO: Westview
Press.

Male, Beverley. 1982. *Revolutionary Afghanistan.* New York:
St. Martin's.

Malhuret, Claude. Winter 1983/84. Report from Afghanistan.
Foreign Affairs 62(2):427.

Maprayil, Cyriac. 1982. *The Soviets and Afghanistan.* London: Cosmic Press.

Martin, Mike. 1984. *Afghanistan: Inside a rebel stronghold.* Poole, Dorset, UK: Blandford Press.

Massell, Gregory. 1974. *The surrogate proletariat: Moslem women and revolutionary strategies in Soviet Central Asia 1919-1929.* Princeton: Princeton University Press.

Merriam, John G. 1979. U.S. wheat to Egypt: The use of an agricultural commodity as a foreign policy tool. In *The role of U.S. agriculture in foreign policy*, Richard M. Fraenkel,Don F. Hadwiger, and William P. Brown, eds. New York: Praeger Publishers.

Merriam, John G. January 1982. Egypt after Sadat. *Current History* 5-8, 38-39.

Metge, Pierre. Avril 1984. La resistance afghane affaiblie par ses divisions, *Le Monde Diplomatique* 18-19.

Middleton, Drew. December 21, 1984. U.S. arms doing Afghan rebels little good. *Cleveland Plain Dealer.*

Misra, K. P., ed. 1981. *Afghanistan in crisis.* New Delhi: Vikas Publishing House Pvt. Ltd.

Missen, Francois. 1983. *La nuit Afghane.* Le Pre aux Cierce.

Monks, Alfred L. 1981. *The Soviet intervention in Afghanistan.* Washington, DC. American Enterprise Institute for Public Policy.

Moorcraft, Paul L. April 1985. Bloody standoff in Afghanistan: A report from Mujahideen country. *Army* 26-36.

Moorhouse, Geoffrey. 1984. *To the frontier.* New York: Holt, Rinehart and Winston.

Morgan, Robin, ed. 1984. *Sisterhood is global: The international women's movement anthology.* Garden City, NY: Anchor Press/Doubleday.

MacMunn, George. 1977. *Afghanistan: From Darius to Amanullah.* Quetta, Pakistan: Gosha-E-Adab.

McGhee, George. 1983. *Envoy to the middle world.* New York: Harper and Row.

McLachlan, K. S., and W. Whittaken. 1983. *A bibliography of Afghanistan.* Boulder, CO: Westview Press.

McMillen, Donald Hugh, ed. 1984. *Asian perspectives on international security.* New York: St. Martin's Press.

Naby, Eden. 1985. The Afghan resistance movement. In *Afghan alternatives: Issues, options and policies*, ed. Ralph H. Magnus. New Brunswick, NJ: Transaction Books.

Nayar, Kuldip. 1981. *Report on Afghanistan.* New Delhi:

Allied Publishers Pvt. Ltd.

Newell, Nancy Peabody, and Richard S. Newell. 1981. *The struggle for Afghanistan.* Ithaca, NY: Cornell University Press.

Newell, Richard S. 1972. *The politics of Afghanistan.* Ithaca, NY: Cornell University Press.

Niesewand, Peter. 1984. *Scimitar.* London: Panther Books-Granada Publishing Ltd.

Nogee, Joseph L., and Robert H. Donaldson. 1984. *Soviet foreign policy since World War II.* 2nd ed. Elmsford, NY: Pergamon Press, Inc.

Noorzoy, M. S. 1985. Long term economic relations between Afghanistan and the Soviet Union: An interpretive study. *International Journal of Middle East Studies* 17(2):151-173.

O'Connor, Robert W., ed. 1980. *Managing health systems in developing areas: Experiences from Afghanistan.* Lexington, MA: Lexington Books.

Olsen, Edward A., and Stephen Jurika, Jr., eds. 1985. *The armed forces in contemporary Asian societies.* Boulder, CO: Westview Publishing Co.

Ottaway, David B. February 10, 1986. Is our Afghan aid a pool of money in search of a policy? *The Washington Post National Weekly Edition* 15.

Pakistan affairs. June 1, 1986. Vol. XXXIX, No. 11, Ramadan 24. Washington, DC: Embassy of Pakistan, Information Division.

Pedraza-Bailey, Sylvia. 1985. Cuba's exiles: Portrait of a refugee migration. *International Migration Review* 19(1): 4-34.

Perera, Judith. February 1984. But does it have military muscle? *The Middle East* 14-16.

Peretz, Don. 1972. The Palestinian Arab refugee problem. In *Political dynamics in the Middle East,* eds. Paul Y. Hammond and Sidney S. Alexander. New York: American Elsevier Publishing Co.

Petkov, Boris. 1983. *Afghanistan today: Impressions of a journalist.* New Delhi: Sterling Publishers.

Petersen, W. 1958. A general typology of migration. *American Sociological Review* 23:256-266.

de Ponfilly, Christophe. 1985. *Le clandestin dans la guerre des resistants.* Paris: Editions Robert Leffont.

Portes, A. 1977. *Structural causes of immigration.* Duke

University, Department of Sociology.

Pottinger, George. 1983. *The Afghan connection: The extraordinary adventures of Major Eldred Pottinger.* Edinburgh: Scottish Academic Press, Ltd.

Poullada, Leon B. 1973. *Reform and rebellion in Afghanistan, 1919-1929.* Ithaca, NY: Cornell University Press.

Poullada, Leon B. Winter 1981. Afghanistan and the United States: The crucial years. *Middle East Journal* 1978-190.

Prins, S. A. 1955. The individual in flight. In *Flight and resettlement*, ed. H. B. M. Murphy. UNESCO, Population and Culture Series II.

'Proximity' talks come nowhere. October 1984/Muharram 1405. *Arabia* 6-11.

Rahel, Shafie, ed. 1970. *The Kabul Times annual, 1970.* Kabul: Kabul Times Publishing Co., Information and Culture Ministry.

Rahman, Rath-ur-, and Bashir A. Qureshi. 1981. *Afghans meet Soviet challenge.* Peshawar, Pakistani Institute of Regional Studies.

Rambo, A. Terry, Jerry M. Tinker, and John D. LeNoir. 1967. *The refugee situation in Phu-Yen Province, Viet Nam.* McLean, VA: Human Sciences Research.

Ravenstein, E. G. 1885. The laws of migration. *Journal of the Royal Statistical Society* 48:167-235.

Ravenstein, E. G. 1889. The laws of migration. *Journal of the Royal Statistical Society* 52:241-305.

Reeves, Richard. October 1, 1984. A reporter at large: Journey to Pakistan. *The New Yorker* 39.

Reeves, Richard. 1984. *Pakistan: Between the Hindu Kush and the Arabian Sea.* New York: Simon and Schuster.

Reports on refugee aid, reports of staff study missions to the Committee on Foreign Affairs, U.S. House of Representatives. March, 1981. Washington, DC: U.S. Government Printing Office.

Reshtia, Sayed Qassem. 1984. *The Price of liberty, the tragedy of Afghanistan.* Rome: Bardi Editore.

Richter, Linda Clark. Winter 1983. The impact of women of regime change in Afghanistan. *Journal of South Asian and Middle Eastern Studies* 7(2):58-68.

Ridgeway, R. T. I. 1983. *Pathans.* Peshawar, Pakistan: Saeed Book Bank.

Rieser, Eugen. January 1983. On guerrilla paths in Afghanistan. *Swiss Review of World Affairs* 22(10):12-19.

Ritch, John B., III. 1984. U.S. Congress, Senate. A staff report prepared for the Committee on Foreign Relations. Hidden war: The struggle for Afghanistan. 98th Congress, 2nd Session. Washington, DC: Government Printing Office.

Rogg, Eleanor Meyer. 1974. *The assimilation of Cuban exiles: The role of community and class.* New York: Aberdeen Press.

Ro'i, Yaacov, ed. 1984. *The USSR and the Muslim world.* Winchester, MA: Allen and Unwin.

Rosenfeld, Stephen S. September 19, 1986. Afghan resistance: At the mercy of a superpower. *Washington Post.*

Roy, Olivier. Avril, 1984; 27 Mars, 1985; 3 Avril 1985. L'essor du Khomeynisme parmi la minorite chiite. *Le Monde Diplomatique* (Paris) C5-6.

Roy, Olivier. 1985. *Afghanistan: Islam and political modernity.* Washington: Foreign Broadcast Information Service.

Roy, Olivier. 1985. A five year assessment, 1979-1984. In *Afghanistan--A spirit of resistance,* 4. London: Afghanistan Support Committee.

Roy, Olivier. 1986. *Islam and resistance in Afghanistan.* Cambridge, UK: Cambridge University Press.

Roy, Olivier. 1985. *L'Afghanistan: Islam et modernite politique.* Trans. by First Edition. Paris: Editions du Seuil.

Roy, Olivier, Robin Ade (Shah Jehan), and Agency Afghan Press. May 1984/Sha'ban 1404. The lonely jihad continues. *Arabia* 66-75.

Rubinstein, A. Z. 1982. *Soviet policy towards Turkey, Iran, and Afghanistan.* New York: Praeger Publishers.

Rubinstein, Alvin Z., ed. 1983. *The great game: Rivalry in the Persian Gulf and South Asia.* New York: Praeger.

Rupert, James. February 3, 1986. The struggle for Afghanistan's soul. *Washington Post National Weekly Edition* 6-9.

Rupert, James. May 26, 1986. Portrait of the Afghan as a young man. *The Washington Post National Weekly Edition* 16-17.

Ryan, Nigel. 1983. *A hitch or two in Afghanistan: A journey behind Russian lines.* London: Weidenfeld and Nicolson.

Sabatier, R. C. May 1985. Russia's scorched earth policy. *The Middle East* 51.

Saikal, Amin. March 1984. The Pakistan unrest and the Afghanistan problem. *World Today* 40(3):102-106.

Sardar, Riffat. Winter 1985. The Afghan crisis: Seven years later. *Journal of South Asian and Middle Eastern Studies* 9(2):67-81.

Sardie, Marie, and Mamoona Taskinud-din. September 1983. *Nutrition, status, socio-economic factors.* Peshawar, Pakistan: UNHCR.

Schneiter, Vincent. 1980. La guerre de liberation au nouristan (Juillet 1978-Mars 1979). *Les Temps Modernes* 237-244.

Schultheis, Robert. September 10, 1984. Reviving the songs of old: A village struggles back. *Time* 26-27.

Sciolino, Elaine. June 26, 1986. Accord appears distant in talks on Afghanistan. *The New York Times* 9.

Seymour, Gerald. 1984. *In honour bound.* New York: W. W. Norton and Co.

Shah, Idries. 1986. *Kara Kush.* New York: Stein and Day.

Shahrani, M. Nazif. 1984. Introduction: Marxist "revolution" and Islamic resistance in Afghanistan. In *Revolutions and rebellions in Afghanistan: Anthropological perspectives,* ed. M. N. Shahrani and R. L. Canfield, 3-57.

Sick, Gary. 1985. *All fall down: America's tragic encounter with Iran.* New York: Random House.

Smith, Harvey H. ed. 1973. *Area handbook for Afghanistan.* Washington, DC: U.S. Government Printing Office.

Solomon, Richard H., and Masataka Kosaka, eds. 1986. *The Soviet Far East military buildup: Nuclear dilemmas and Asian security.* Dover, MA: Auburn House Publishing Co.

Soviet air force in Afghanistan. July 7, 1984. *Jane's Defence Weekly* 1104-1005.

Soviet military power is industrial priority. September 21, 1985. *Jane's Defence Weekly.*

Soviet occupation of Afghanistan and certain human rights matters, hearing and markup before the Committee on Foreign Affairs, the 97th Congress, 2nd Session. 1982. Washington, DC: Government Printing Office.

Sovietiques pris au piege Afghan, les. 13 Novembre 1985. *Jeune Afrique* 1297:25.

Spain, James W. 1962. *The way of the Pathans.* Karachi: Oxford University Press.

Stahel, Albert A., and Paul Bucherer. *Afghanistan-5 jahre und Kleinkrieg.* Frauenfeld, Switzerland: Huber and Co., AG.

Staudt, Kathleen A. February, 1980. *Women's organizations*

in rural development. Washington, DC: Office of Women in Development, Agency for International Development, International Development Cooperation Agency.

Steele, Jonathan. July-August 1986. Moscow's Kabul campaign. *MERIP* 16(4):4-11.

Stepanov, V. May 1984. Afghanistan on the path of revolutionary change. *International Affairs* 5:25-33.

Stevenson, Matthew. February 1984. Traveling the Afghan archipelago. *American Spectator* 11-15.

Stewart, Rhea Talley. 1973. *Fire in Afghanistan, 1914-1929.* Garden City, NY: Doubleday and Co.

Stork, Joe. July-August 1986. The CIA in Afghanistan. *MERIP* 16(4):4-11.

Suhrke, Astri, and Aristide R. Zolberg. 1984. Social conflict and refugees in the Third World: The cases of Ethiopia and Afghanistan. Paper presented at the American Political Science Association, Washington, DC.

Tabibi, Dr. Abdul Hakim. 1985. *Afghanistan: A nation in love with freedom.* Cedar Rapids, IA: Igram Press.

Tapper, Richard, ed. 1983. *The conflict of tribe and state in Iran and Afghanistan.* London: Croom Helm.

Tavakolian, Bahram. Summer, 1984. Women and socio-economic change among Sheikhanzai nomads of Western Afghanistan. *Middle East Journal* 452.

"Tears, blood and cries," human rights in Afghanistan since the invasion, 197-1984. December 1984. New York: The U.S. Helsinki Watch Committee.

Thank you, my sister. March 21, 1983. *The Afghanistan Jehad.*

Thomas, Craig. 1985. *Lion's run.* New York: Bantam Books.

Trousdale, William, ed. *War in Afghanistan, 1879-80.* Detroit, MI: Wayne State University Press.

Urban, Mark. January 12, 1985. The limited contingent of Soviet forces in Afghanistan. *Jane's Defence Weekly* 71-73.

U.S. Committee on Refugees. 1983. *Afghan refugees in Pakistan: Will they go home again?* New York: U.S. Committee on Refugees.

U.S. Committee for Refugees. 1985. *Afghan refugees: Five years later.* American Council for Nationalities.

U.S. Department of State, Bureau of Public Affairs. February 1981. *Afghanistan: A year of occupation,* Special report no. 79.

U.S. Department of State, Bureau of public Affairs. August 1981. *Afghanistan: 18 months of occupation*, Special report no. 86.

U.S. Department of State, Bureau of Public Affairs. November 24, 1982. *Call for Soviet withdrawal from Afghanistan*, Current policy no. 441.

U.S. Department of State, Bureau of Public Affairs. November 1982. *Chemical warfare in Southeast Asia and Afghanistan: An update*, Report from Secretary of State George P. Shultz, Special report no. 104.

U.S. Department of State, Bureau of Public Affairs. December 1983. *Afghanistan: Four years of occupation*, Special report no. 112.

U.S. Department of State, Bureau of Public Affairs. February 21, 1984. *Chemical weapons use in Southweat Asia and Afghanistan*, Current policy no. 553.

U.S. Department of State, Bureau of Public Affairs. July 1985. *Gist* (Afghan Refugees in Pakistan).

U.S. medicines "cover" for arms to Afghan rebels. June 23, 1983. *Foreign Broadcast Information Service, USSR International Affairs, South Asia*.

Van Dyk, Jere. 1983. *In Afghanistan, an American odyssey*. New York: Coward-McCann, Inc.

Van Praag, Nicholas. October 1985. Afghans in the USA. *Refugees* 22:15-16.

Victor, Jean-Christophe. 1983. *La cite des murmures*. Paris: J-C Lattes.

Victor, Paul-Emile. 1985. *Afghanistan: La solidarite oubliee*. Paris: Fondation de France.

Weaver, Mary Anne. Arming Afghans: A tortuous task. *Christian Science Monitor* 1, 48.

Weber, Max. 1947. *The theory of social and economic organization*. Trans. by A.M. Henderson and Talcott Parsons. New York: Oxford University Press.

Weck, Herve de. Mars 1985. Un conflit trop oublie en Afghanistan. *Revue Militaire Suisse* 3:123-132.

Weston, Christine. 1962. *Afghanistan*. New York: Charles Scribner's Sons.

Wheeler, Jack. September 1984. Fighting the Soviet imperialists: The mujaheddin in Afghanistan. *Reason* 22-30.

Wilber, Donald N., et al. 1962. *Afghanistan: Its people, its society, its culture*. New Haven, CT: Hoaf Press.

Wimbush, S. Enders, and Alex Alexiev. 1981. *Soviet Central*

Asian soldiers in Afghanistan. Santa Monica, CA: Rand Corporation N-1634/1.

Winchester, Mike. September 1984. Night raiders on Russia's border. *Soldier of Fortune* 54-61+

Wirth, Louis. 1940. Ideological aspects of social disorganization. *American Sociological Review* V.

Wiser, Charlotte Viall, and William H. Wiser. 1951. *Behind mud walls.* New York: Agricultural Missions, Inc.

World Bank. 1983. *World tables.* Baltimore and London: World Bank and Johns Hopkins.

Wrase, Michael. August 1985. Afghan refugees seek jobs. *Refugees* 20:18.

Yared, Marc. Septembre 1985. L'enjeu de la bataille de Khost. *Jeune Afrique* 1290:38.

York, Susan. 1980. *Afghan refugees in Pakistan.* London: International Disaster Institute.

Yousefzai, Baqui. 1974. Kabul university students: A potential political force. In *Afghanistan in the 1970s*, ed. Louis Dupree and Linette Albert. New York: Praeger Special Studies in International Development and Economics.

Yodfat, Aryeh Y. 1983. *The Soviet Union and the Arabian Peninsula.* New York: St. Martin's Press.

Zermatten, E. M. G. Mars 1985. La dissuasion, Raymond Aron, l'Afghanistan et nous..." *Revue Militaire Suisse* 3:110-122.

Ziring, L. 1981. *Iran, Turkey and Afghanistan.*

Newspapers

Kabul Times.   May 13, 1978.
May 20, 1978.
June 13, 1978.
October 18, 1978.
December 2, 1978.
February 8, 1979.
February 13, 1979.
April 2, 1979.
May 16, 1979.

Afghan Resistance